ONLINE INFORMATION RETRIEVAL

An introductory manual to principles and practice

Third Edition

John Convey *Senior Librarian, Lancashire Library*

CLIVE BINGLEY  LONDON

Published by
Library Association Publishing Ltd
7 Ridgmount Street
London WC1E 7AE

First published 1977
Second edition 1984
This third, revised edition 1989

British Library Cataloguing in Publication Data

Convey, John
Online information retrieval: an introductory manual to principles and practice. — 3rd ed.
1. On-line bibliographic information retrieval systems
I. Title II. Houghton, Bernard, *1935–1985*. Online information retrieval systems
025'.04

ISBN 0-85157-438-6

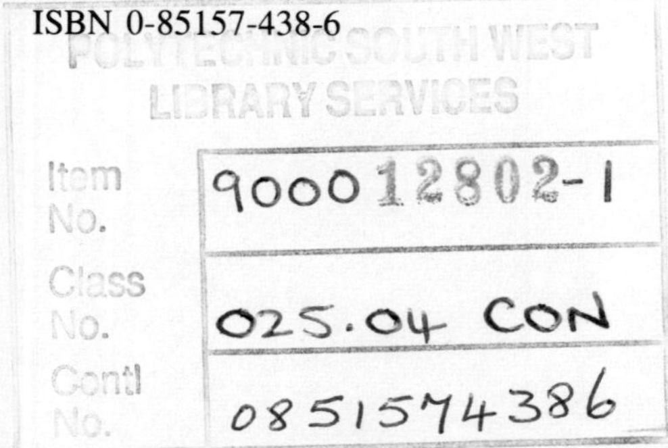

Typeset in 10/12pt Times by Library Association Publishing Ltd
Printed and made in Great Britain by Bookcraft Ltd, Midsomer Norton, Avon.

This book
is dedicated to
the memory of
Bernard Houghton

ONLINE INFORMATION RETRIEVAL

An introductory manual to principles and practice

Third Edition

Contents

Introduction

This work is written for those who require an introduction to online information retrieval – students of librarianship and information science, practising librarians, information scientists and information workers, and the increasing number of 'end-users' who are using online information retrieval systems to help solve their information problems.

Bernard Houghton, the co-author of the previous editions of this book, sadly died in 1985; this third edition, written by John Convey, updates, considerably enlarges and rearranges the text published in 1984. The title of the previous editions, i.e. *Online information retrieval systems*, has been modified by the omission of the word 'systems'; we believe the new, more general, title reflects more truly the scope of the book as outlined below.

Part One covers the early development of online information retrieval; databases; the online industry, including details of database producers, online hosts, telecommunications, online users and an overview of the online industry as a whole; hardware and software; principles of online searching; an in-depth study of the searching process from initial enquiry to document delivery; costs; CD-ROM and its relationship to online and printed publications; overview of advantages of online information retrieval; and the future of online information retrieval.

Part Two features seven online hosts: DIALOG Information Services Inc., European Space Agency Information Retrieval Service (ESA-IRS), BLAISE-LINE, National Library of Medicine (BLAISE-LINK), ORBIT, Pergamon Financial Data Services, and Data-Star. The aim of this Part is twofold: to show practical applications of the principles outlined in Part One, and to form part of a training programme for searchers new to online information retrieval. There are three consecutive Units for each online host, each Unit introducing features and commands for that particular online host. Each online operation is given the same paragraph number for each of the seven online hosts (e.g. truncation is included in paragraph 2.2). There is an extensive list of references to aid further research. The Appendices include useful contacts, sources of information, and the databases offered by the seven online hosts featured in Part Two – these databases are arranged by subject for easier use.

Southport, April 1989

PART ONE

Introduction to online information retrieval

Chapter 1

The development of online information retrieval

What is online information retrieval? 'Information retrieval' using a computer is the searching for, and the retrieving of, selected information from the data held on a computer; the data is normally held in the form of 'databases'. A database is a collection of related items of information held in a form intelligible to the computer (i.e. machine-readable); these items may be references to journal papers, they may be the latest balance sheets for companies, they may be the full text of journal papers; the term 'record' will be used in this book to describe an item held on a database. Records on a database may cover references to the literature in a narrow subject field (e.g. AIDS), or a much more general subject area (e.g. applied science and technology); they may cover a particular type of publication (e.g. World Patent Index covers patents). Normally the computers used in online information retrieval have several, and sometimes hundreds, of databases available for searching.

When you are 'online', you are connected directly to the central processing unit (CPU) of a computer using a terminal; the word 'terminal' will be used to describe this device throughout this book – for different types of 'terminal', see Chapter 4. The terminal enables the searcher to interact with the computer, i.e the searcher interrogates the computer and receives an immediate response – this is sometimes termed 'conversational mode', as it is like having a conversation with the computer; and in the context of online information retrieval, the terminal is normally remote from the computer it is interrogating – the connection is made by using telephone lines and telecommunications networks; even though a terminal is in Liverpool and the computer in Palo Alto, California, it is still possible to interrogate the computer in 'conversational mode'. The term 'searcher' will be used in this book to describe the person who actually conducts the online search.

The general availability of online information retrieval systems is the inevitable technological consequence of applying computers to the processing of bibliographic and other types of information. In the field of library and information work the computer revolution has proceeded, and continues to proceed, rapidly and the following is a brief introduction to the stages of its development.

Initially, computers were employed to produce printed abstracting and indexing services more efficiently. Indexing services, such as *Index medicus* in the field of medicine, listed bibliographic details of the latest published information, which was mainly in the form of journal papers; the bibliographic details included author, title, journal reference and language, arranged under subject headings. Abstracting services, such as *Chemical abstracts* in the field of chemistry, gave bibliographic details plus a summary or 'abstract' of the paper. These services are sometimes referred to as 'secondary services', as they make reference to the 'primary literature', i.e. the journal articles, conference proceedings etc. themselves.

The tremendous growth in the amount of literature, particularly in the scientific and technical fields, has been well documented.[1,2] De Solla Price writes about the 'exponential growth' in scientists, scientific periodicals and scientific papers from about 1665, with a doubling every 15 years or so. This growth had been going on for a long time before the advent of the computer. It was estimated that the total number of scientific journal titles which had ever been published was 36,000 in 1930, but had risen to 60,000 by 1960; and the number of scientific papers being published in 1964 was estimated to be at least 600,000.[1] A cumulated total of all the papers indexed in the four publications *Chemical abstracts*, *Engineering index*, *Index medicus* and *Physics abstracts* gives a figure of just under 200,000 in 1950, which had risen to about 300,000 by 1960, and to over 800,000 by 1976; in 1988 this figure was nearly one million.[3] The power of the computer was harnessed to help with this marked growth in the literature. From the early 1960s the data for the production of the printed indexes and abstracting services was stored on magnetic tape in machine-readable form, but in the early stages of development the printed version of the secondary services was the sole product. Soon, however, it became apparent that, as a by-product of the generation of data in machine-readable form necessary for the production of these secondary services, the data could be used to produce selective listings, for example current-awareness and retrospective literature searches. The United Kingdom Chemical Information Service (UKCIS) introduced the Chemical-Biological Activities (CBAC) service in 1966. These searches were not conducted 'online' at this early stage, but at an information centre which had the appropriate tapes available on its own computer. Users would send their requests for information to the information centre, where the searches were conducted in batch mode – i.e. a number of searches or user-profiles were run at one time on the computer, which produced listings of records tailor-made to a client's subject interest.

The final stage of development began in the mid 1960s and continues strongly today – 'online' access to this data held in machine-readable form, where terminals physically remote from the computer storing the databases are used both by intermediaries (e.g. librarians, information scientists, information officers) acting on behalf of their users and, increasingly, by end-users themselves (i.e. those who ultimately use the information from the search) to search in a conversational manner the machine-readable data stored in the computer. This was made possible by technological developments throughout the 1960s and early 1970s – telephone lines capable of carrying data without corrupting it; a new generation of computers operating at higher speeds and capable of sharing their central processing unit (CPU) time with a number of searchers at once in a conversational mode; drums, discs and other direct access devices with increased storage capacity; and improvements in cable and microwave communications.[4] The online information retrieval industry has expanded rapidly over more than 20 years (see Chapter 3). Many 'online' databases with no corresponding printed version now exist; and some databases are now appearing in other forms, such as floppy disc, and more recently on Compact Disc – Read Only Memory (CD-ROM) discs; in these cases 'online' searching ceases to be 'remote', for the database is connected directly to the terminal. It is still too early to say what effect the CD-ROM medium of providing information will have on either remote online searching or printed publications. CD-ROM is dealt with in some detail in Chapter 8.

The computer was first publicly applied to the processing of bibliographic information in 1961, when the Chemical Abstracts Service (CAS) produced Chemical Titles (CT), a machine-generated alphabetical subject index to the 600 most influential journals covered by the parent journal *Chemical abstracts*. The keyword-in-context (KWIC) format devised for CT manipulated actual keywords taken from the titles of the papers published in the journals, so dispensing with the intellectual processes involved in indexing the papers. The KWIC indexing principle thus represents a crude form of the natural language and full-text searching facility now available in some measure in all online information retrieval systems (see Chapter 5). The KWIC index could be produced quickly and cheaply, and was readily adopted by other secondary services to alleviate the problems imposed by the phenomenal growth of the literature.

By the end of the 1960s a whole range of new CAS publications had been produced from the machine-readable database. In this system the abstracting and indexing information was culled from the source journals in a single process of intellectual analysis before it was entered into the database. Computerization was steadily adopted by other services and by 1970 the first phase of the computer revolution was completed. The new processing methods gave the secondary services the increased flexibility necessary to adapt to the changing patterns of research. They were now able to produce not only a single abstracting publication but also to repackage the records held in the database to meet the varying needs of groups and individual users.

The result of this first phase of the revolution was greatly improved secondary publications; they were more up to date, more comprehensive in their coverage of the literature, and they were equipped with better indexes which cumulated more frequently. In addition, users were offered the facility, by the computer centres, of having their specific subject requests searched on the database to give both current and retrospective information in their spheres of interest.

These current-awareness and retrospective searches were run in 'batch mode' in information centres, most of which dealt with a specific discipline or subject field, e.g. the UK MEDLARS service based at the British Library Lending Division at Boston Spa, the United Kingdom Chemical Information Service (UKCIS) at Nottingham University, the service on the UCLA campus in Los Angeles, used by students and staff.[4] These information centres acquired the machine-readable tapes from the database producers, loaded them into their own computers and produced the necessary software to enable the batch processing of current-awareness and retrospective searches. Batch processing of searches was economical in terms of machine time but it had two serious disadvantages. Firstly, it necessitated the user experiencing delays of maybe three weeks before receiving the search product from the information centre, as it was necessary to accumulate a sufficient number of searches to make batch processing economical; secondly, the user was forced to search 'blind', i.e. was unable to sample the relevance of the records retrieved by the search strategy formulated by a search analyst at the information centre.

Online information retrieval systems, which enabled the user to communicate directly in a conversational mode with a remote computer, were being developed by the System Development Corporation (SDC) as long ago as 1965. The following year, the Lockheed Missile and Space Corporation, now DIALOG Information Services Inc., introduced its DIALOG system, an upgraded version of which became operational in 1969. After a developmental period which extended into the early 1970s, the use of online information retrieval systems became widespread in the United States and later in Europe. Batch processing of searches is now virtually obsolete, and even these searches can be entered online. Fuller details of these later developments are given in the next two chapters. Meadow has given an online database 'timeline', a chronological listing of developments in the online industry.[5,6]

Chapter 2

Databases

As mentioned in the previous chapter, a database is a collection of related items of information; in the context of online information retrieval, databases are collections of records in machine-readable form that are made available for searching from remote computer terminals. The records in the database are normally related by their subject content (e.g. chemistry), or by the type of publication referred to (e.g. patents, newspapers). The word 'file' is often used to describe a database on online systems.

Databases may be classified as either 'reference' or 'source' databases.[1] 'Reference' databases include bibliographic and referral databases; the latter refer to the name and/or address of a person or organization; the former give the main bibliographic details to uniquely identify the paper, book etc. referred to, and will normally give additional subject information – keywords, classification numbers and in many cases an abstract or summary; this subject information both increases the number of terms under which a record may be found during an online search and gives the end-user more detailed information about the record, thus helping the end-user to decide whether or not to order a copy of the actual book, paper etc. Online bibliographic databases are in most cases the machine-readable versions of the printed abstracting and indexing services, although there are a number of databases available in machine-readable online format only.

What the end-user receives from an online search of a bibliographic database is a bibliography or list of references on the subject of the search; from this list the end-user selects the most relevant and orders copies of the original books, papers etc.

A typical example of a record to be found on an online indexing and abstracting service is given below; the main fields are displayed here – many more fields are often available for displaying. The record is taken from the Rapra database on the ORBIT service:

Accession No.	344561
Title	Fire rules mean more business for foam and fabric makers
Author	Rawsthorn A
Source	Financial Times No. 30437, 14th Jan. 1988, p.7.
Location	UK
Index Terms	COMBUSTION MODIFICATION; FLAMMABILITY; COMMERCIAL INFORMATION; COMPANY; COMPANIES; FABRIC; FLAME RETARDANT; FURNITURE; MARKET; PLASTIC; REGULATION; RESILIENCE; SALES; TECHNICAL; THERMOPLASTIC; UPHOLSTERY
Abstract	The announcement of the revised fire regulations which cover the fire resistance of upholstered furniture has created opportunities for the British foam and fabric industries. For the foam industry these rules offer a chance to increase sales of the combustion-modified high resilience foams developed over the last few years. Similarly, fabric manufacturers should be able to take advantage of demand for flame retardant fabrics. These opportunities are discussed in detail.

The bibliographic databases may cover a wide subject area (e.g. science), or a more specific subject such as chemistry, or specific areas within that subject (e.g. chemical hazards). A hierarchical display of databases relating to agriculture may look something like that shown in Fig. 1 (this shows a selection of databases only).[2]

In the Aslib United Kingdom information technology survey of 1987 respondents were asked to list the databases accessed frequently; the most popular were scientific, technical and biomedical bibliographic databases, some of the most used being Chemical Abstracts (30%), MEDLINE (22%), INSPEC (20%), BIOSIS (18%) and COMPENDEX (15%).[3] Databases such as Predicasts, ICC, Abi/Inform, Polis and Textline had more than 5% of users, which shows the increase in interest in business databases in line with their availability online. The survey also showed an increase in 'fact retrieval' as a reason for online searching – 64% compared with only 38% in the 1982 survey.[4] A list of databases from several online host systems, arranged by subject, is given in Appendix 2.

'Source', 'non-bibliographic' or 'factual' databases include numeric, textual-numeric, properties, and full-text databases. These databases are sometimes called 'databanks'. 'Source' databases are offered by a wider range of producers than bibliographic databases and are particularly important in the fields of business, economics, trade and commerce.

Science (general)
GENERAL SCIENCE INDEX
PASCAL
SCISEARCH
SRIS CATALOGUE
  Agriculture
  AGRIBUSINESS USA
  AGRICOLA
  AGRIS
  AGROCHEMICALS HANDBOOK
  BIOLOGICAL AND AGRICULTURAL INDEX
  CAB ABSTRACTS
  CAB ECONOMICS, DEVELOPMENT AND EDUCATION
  CURRENT CONTENTS – AGRICULTURE
  DICIS
  EUROPEAN DIRECTORY OF AGROCHEMICAL PRODUCTS
  USDA/CRIS
    Forestry
    FOREST
    Food Science and Technology
    CAB HUMAN NUTRITION
    FOOD SCIENCE AND TECHNOLOGY ABSTRACTS
    FOODS ADLIBRA
      Coffee
      COFFEELINE
    Agriculture, tropical
    TROPAG
  Life sciences
  AFEE
  BIOSIS etc.

Fig. 1 Hierarchical display of databases in agriculture

The records in these databases do not 'refer' the user to books, papers etc. but give the full information immediately.

'Numeric' databases consist of information expressed primarily as numbers presented in the form of tables or 'time-series'. They usually comprise a measurement (population or quantity), a time-series (statistics collected over a period of time) and a variable (production, imports, exports etc. of a specific commodity). O'Leary states that most leading numeric databanks have a common 'core' of key economic and financial statistics – business indicators; national and personal income; prices, employment and earnings; industry sales, profits, orders and shipments; population and labour force; data on major sectors like agriculture, energy, construction, manufacturing and transportation.[5] In addition they often contain directory information and full-text information for current business news. They can usually be related to a particular country. They are usually far more expensive to access than bibliographic databases, a major cost element being a heavy 'up-front', or subscription, charge before access is allowed, in addition to online costs. On this subject of cost, O'Leary states that the costs are comparable to those for searching the business databases on hosts such as DIALOG Information Services Inc. and Pergamon Financial Data Services, but the costs are more complicated.

Numeric databases often possess some computational features whereby the retrieved data can be analysed and manipulated using, for instance, regression techniques or seasonality analysis to adjust time-series and to generate forecasts. In most cases these databases will be accessed by the end-user who is not employed solely as an information worker but is more likely to be an economist or financial analyst producing a report for decision-makers in planning and management. The typical users of these databases are the multinational and national corporations but their use is now spreading to medium-sized and smaller companies. In an attempt to promote their use the British Library Research and Development Department published a workbook designed to introduce members of the library and information professions to the conventions of online access to non-bibliographic databases.[6] This same organization also published a state-of-the-art report on the use of non-bibliographic databases in the fields of economics and business studies.[7]

In discussing the producers of numeric databases, O'Leary distinguishes between time-sharing services, such as ADP Data Services, I. P. Sharp Associates' InfoService and GE Information Services, and econometric services, such as Data Resources Inc. (DRI), Wharton Econometrics, and Citicorp Information Services (CIS).[5] With many of the former group of companies, the database services comprise only a part of the companies' many activities such as time-sharing and other computer services. Fuller details of these companies are given in the next chapter. Suozzi and Woggon in separate papers have given an introduction to numeric databases, Suozzi's main emphasis being on DIALOG and I. P. Sharp; and Woggon's on Chase Econometrics, DRI, I. P. Sharp, Wharton and DIALOG.[8,9]

'Textual-numeric' databases consist of a combination of statistical information and text. Many of the databases giving company information are of this type; the following gives an excerpt from a record on such a database:

(ICC database on Data-Star)
AN 01110106 8803 Full Record
CO TOLONA PIZZA PRODUCTS LIMITED
Old Name: SPENDGRADE LIMITED
Date of Change of Name: 761231
RO Registered Office: 7 PRIORSWOOD PLACE
SKELMERSDALE
LANCS
WN8 9QB
HI Accounts Reference Date: 01/31
Date of Latest Accounts: 850831
Date of Last Annual Return: 861231
....................etc
FF Consolidated Accounts (000's ukl)
Independent Company

Date of Accounts	850831	840831	830831
Number of Weeks	52	52	52
Balance Sheet:			
Fixed Assets	571	482	550
Intangible Assets	0	0	66
Intermediate Assets	0	64	45
Stocks	243	130	137
Debtors	660	272	360

....................etc

'Properties' databases contain information on physical, chemical and mechanical properties of substances and compounds, examples being the Heilbron database (Dictionary of Organic Compounds and other Dictionaries), Beilstein's Handbuch der Organischen Chemie, the Martindale Extra Pharmacopoeia, the Kirk-Othmer Encyclopedia of Chemical Technology, and the DARC chemical structure searching system on Telesystemes-Questel.[10-12]

'Full-text' databases provide access to the complete text of documents, such as legal databases which contain the full texts of statutes and law reports, for example LEXIS, produced in the United States by Mead Data Central and marketed in the United Kingdom by its agent Butterworth (Telepublishing) Ltd. Another area increasingly covered by full-text databases is news, for example FT Information Online's Profile Information and Mead Data Central's Nexis, access to newswire services such as AP News and UPI News, and databases such as Business Dateline, Businesswire, and Financial Times Fulltext.

Increasingly many of the major directories and encyclopedias to be found on the library shelves are available online also; for example, the *Encyclopedia of associations* (Gale), the *Encyclopedia of chemical technology* (Kirk-Othmer), and the Thomas *Register of American manufacturers*.

Some databases are offered in forms other than online or printed form. Many are now appearing in CD-ROM format – a recent report from Knowledge Research claims that in the USA 40% of databases are being converted to CD-ROM, compared with 20% in Europe.[13] Some databases are appearing in floppy disc format – such as the Financial Datafile from Information Services Ltd, the producers of the Kompass commercial database, and Britain's Top 4,000 Privately-Owned Companies from Jordans.

There are several sources which give information about which databases are available. Each online host will give users details of the databases that are available via their service. More comprehensive sources, covering a number of online hosts, are given in Appendix 1; and a list of databases from the seven online hosts featured in Part Two is given in Appendix 2.

Chapter 3

The online information retrieval industry

The online information retrieval industry which has been developing since the early 1970s has four main sectors:

1 the producers of the databases;

2 the online service 'hosts' or suppliers, sometimes referred to as 'spinners', or 'vendors'; the term 'host' will be used in this book;

3 the users of the systems: libraries, information services, information brokers, and end-users;

4 the telecommunications sector which provides the important networks and gateways between the other sectors.

A newcomer to the industry is the 'intelligent' interface between the second and third sectors.

These sectors will be looked at individually, and then an overview of the industry will be presented.

1 The producers of bibliographic databases are typically the learned societies and institutions which have traditionally undertaken the responsibility of organizing the primary literature covering their fields, and the various national government departments active in science-based and other industries, which need to provide information services for their staffs and customers. Many of the abstracting and indexing services in the sciences are long established; for instance *Chemical abstracts* dates from 1907 and *Physics abstracts* from 1898. But the massive growth of the literature after the Second World War, as evidenced, for instance, by *Chemical abstracts* – 100,000 abstracts published in 1957, 392,000 in 1975, and over 476,000 in 1987 – has forced database producers to abandon traditional publishing methods and to turn to computer-aided production of their databases. With the recent rapid expansion of the online information retrieval industry commercial organizations such as Data Courier Inc., Predicasts Inc., and Harfax Database Publishing have also become active as online database producers. *Information world*

review has published profiles on some database producers, giving a behind-the-scenes look at their operation.[1-3] Cuadra listed 1,685 database producers in 1988.[4]

2 The machine-readable databases produced by the first sector of the industry are leased from the producers by the online service hosts – organizations with sufficient hardware capacity who have also developed software systems to enable users to search the databases on the hosts' computers. This interaction between host and searcher is effected by using remote computer terminals linked by standard telephone equipment over national and international communications networks to the hosts' computers. The database producer's magnetic tapes are converted into a format compatible with the host's retrieval system. In this process the tape data entry format is analysed and design specifications are developed to transfer the information from the tapes to the magnetic discs used in the host's system.

Among the principal online hosts who were the early pioneers of online services in the United States were the Lockheed Missile and Space Corporation, System Development Corporation (SDC), and the National Library of Medicine.

In 1966, the Lockheed Missile and Space Corporation introduced its DIALOG system, an upgraded version of which became operational in 1969. In 1972 it was launched as a commercial venture with just a few databases. By 1988, as DIALOG Information Services Inc., since 1982 an independent subsidiary of Lockheed Missile and Space Corporation, the service was offering over 300 databases, and is estimated to have over 88,000 passwords.[5] In 1972 DIALOG's estimated value was $500,000; in 1981, around $70m, and in 1988 it was sold to Knight-Ridder for $353m. DIALOG is important for bibliographic databases, but over 50% of databases currently available are 'source' databases, and the service is targetting business and financial communities as its chief market – for example, its introduction of the DIALOG Business Connection (an end-user service for business), gateways to the stock exchange etc. – while still maintaining strong ties with the general user.[6] DIALOG introduced DIALOG Version 2 in 1984; this was a major upgrade of the retrieval system. DIALOG Versions 1 and 2 ran side by side until Version 1 was dropped, and the system is again called simply 'DIALOG'. Feldman says that in 1986 DIALOG had 80,000 users in 76 countries, nearly double the figure three years previously; the system used 340 gigabytes of disc storage and had 150 million records on 270 databases.[7] DIALOG has diversified in recent years – as well as the main DIALOG service DIALOG have introduced Knowledge Index (an after-hours end-user service introduced in 1982, which currently offers over 70 databases), Dialorder (document delivery), Dialmail (electronic mail service), the DIALOG Business Connection and the DIALOG Medical Connection (end-user services), DialogLink (software for accessing DIALOG), and DIALOG OnDisc products (databases on CD-ROM). Shortly before the sale of DIALOG in 1988 Pemberton wrote of DIALOG: 'It is the supermarket of databanks . . . its technical sophistication makes it the system against which all others are measured . . . and the online world – no matter who the buyer turns out to be – will never be the same again.'[5,8]

The System Development Corporation (SDC) was developing online information retrieval systems as long ago as 1965. SDC developed the ORBIT (Online Retrieval of Bibliographical Information Time-Shared) retrieval software, and in 1967 was co-operating with the National Library of Medicine in developing their online system (see below). In 1986, SDC's ORBIT Search Service was acquired by Pergamon Infoline, the new company being known as Pergamon Orbit Infoline, with the renamed ORBIT Information Technologies being a division of the main company. ORBIT currently offers about 90 databases, mainly in the fields of science and technology.

Through the efforts of the US National Library of Medicine (NLM), MEDLINE (Medical Analysis and Retrieval System On-line) became one of the first online bibliographic databases to be developed and made generally available, and subsequently it has become one of the most heavily used of the wide range of databases which are now available online. The National Library of Medicine, following the example of the American Chemical Society, started using a computerized system to produce its monthly subject index to the world's medical literature, *Index medicus*, in 1963, and shortly after this date on-demand, one-off, retrospective searches were being run on the database in batch mode. In the autumn of 1967 the NLM began to experiment with online access to its database, when a contract was signed with SDC, who installed and evaluated their ORBIT system at the NLM, using a small database in the field of neurology. A pilot online experimental service offering access to a subset of the *Index medicus* database became operational in June 1970 to about 90 medical institutions in the United States, giving access to Abridged Index Medicus (AIM) which covered 100 of the most important medical journals. This project utilized SDC's IBM 360/67 computer linked by the Teletypewriter Exchange Network (TWX) to remote terminals in medical institutions throughout the country. The response from users was enthusiastic, and a fully developed MEDLINE system giving access to a database containing records from 1,200 of the journals covered by *Index medicus* in one online database was introduced in October 1971. The current MEDLINE database which covers nearly 4,000 source journals is now marketed throughout the world by a variety of hosts as well as NLM, including BLAISE-LINK in the United Kingdom, DIALOG from the United States and Data-Star from Switzerland. NLM offers about 20 databases.

BRS Information Technologies, formerly the Bibliographic Retrieval Service (BRS), began operating in 1977 with ten databases. Today, with over 120 databases which are mainly bibliographic but with some full-text, it is still filling the niche of the academic librarian's principal online service, but is also after the 'medical dollar'.[6] In 1987 they established a gateway to Pergamon Financial Data Services (PFDS). The gateway works both ways; the next stage of this co-operative venture will be to allow customers to use either PFDS or BRS commands on either system. There is also a gateway to BRS via the Online Computer Library Center (OCLC). BRS introduced BRS After Dark, the first out-of-hours service, which is menu-driven and aimed at the home user; and also BRS Colleague, a menu-driven service for medical practitioners, engineers etc. The parent company of BRS until recently was TGB (formerly Thyssen-Bornemisza, which purchased BRS in 1980).[9] In December 1988 BRS was bought by Maxwell Communications Corporation.

Mead Data Central offers over 200 legal and 160 non-legal sources, and is accessed by 170,000 subscribers. The service originated in the efforts of the Ohio Bar Association to computerize state legal records in the 1960s and was taken over by the Mead Corporation in 1970. The LEXIS database was commercially launched in 1974, and Nexis in 1983. Mead's marketing agent in the United Kingdom, Butterworths, provides marketing, training and customer support for LEXIS in Britain. Mead has diversified with other databases, including Lexpat and NAARS (National Automated Accounting Research System), and includes abstracting services such as Abi/Inform and the Information Bank.[10]

The H. W. Wilson Company introduced its Wilsonline service in 1984, giving access to its own databases, such as Applied Science and Technology Index, Biography Index etc., and became a significant competitor to DIALOG and BRS. It currently offers about 27 databases, including some, such as LCMARC, not published by the Wilson Company. About 20 of its databases are also available on the CD-ROM Wilsondisc service.

ADP Data Services, a company which began in 1949, provides a wide range of computing services in North America and Europe and currently offers over 30 financial and economic databases via its TSAM (Time Series Analysis and Modelling System) software for retrieving and manipulating data. Databases offered include the Central Statistical Office (CSO) Databank, the Bank of England Databank, and the IMF International Financial Statistics.[11]

I. P. Sharp Associates, a Canadian company, was founded in 1964, and in 1987 was bought by Reuters for $48m.[12] Through its Infoservice it offers over 150 databases in finance, economics, aviation and other fields, via the MAGIC software for retrieving, analysing, manipulating and reporting both time-series and non-time-series data. The company have also developed INFOMAGIC, an alternative menu-driven system for the casual user. Databases offered include three IMF databases, 12 OECD databases, as well as several covering aspects of the US, Canadian and Australian economies.[11]

Data Resources Inc. (DRI), founded in 1968, offers over 125 databases in the field of economic analysis and forecasting. Its EPS Plus software allows the building up of in-house databases and econometric models, and has a range of statistical features. Databases offered include the Bank of England Databank, CSO Databank, DRI Europe Databank, Exstat, and IMF, US and OECD databases.[11]

GE Information Services, a subsidiary of the General Electric Company, is a worldwide computing system which offers a variety of programs for financial reporting and analysis through its Mark III system. Databases include the BI/DATA Time Series and Forecasts, IMF International Financial Statistics and Citibase, which gives time-series statistics on the US economy. The Mark III system uses MAP (Management Analysis and Projection System) software which is designed to provide planners and managers with specialized programs designed to manipulate international economic data.

Wharton Econometric Forecasting Associates – CISI-Wharton EFA in Europe – offer a number of business and economic databases, using AREMOS software for data management analysis and reporting. Databases include CSO, CRONOS-EUROSTAT, the Bank of England Databank, and econometric databases such as US Macro, Latin America and World Model. Chase Econometrics/Interactive Data Corporation, founded in 1978, offers over 60 databases giving economic data and forecasting modules worldwide.

In the United Kingdom there were 132 online hosts in 1987 listed in the *Britline* directory.[13] Some examples of British hosts are: BLAISE, Pergamon Financial Data Services, Reuters, Profile Information, and British Telecom's Business Direction.

BLAISE currently offers about 20 databases via BLAISE-LINE, and gives access to about 20 databases in the biomedical field via BLAISE-LINK; it also offers a facility for online production of catalogues – BLAISE Records. The British Library's BLAISE (British Library Automated Information Service) was introduced in April 1977, based on the ELHILL software developed for the US National Library of Medicine's MEDLINE service by SDC. The initial databases to be made available were in the biomedical field – MEDLINE, CANCERLINE, TOXLINE, etc. – and these were soon followed by the British and American MARC databases and later by other databases including Conference Proceedings Index and British Education Index. In 1982, BLAISE divided their service into BLAISE-LINK – a link with the National Library of Medicine for searching the biomedical and related databases – and BLAISE-LINE, which continues to offer the non-biomedical databases from Harlow, United Kingdom. The *BLAISE newsletter* of June 1987, reviewing the ten years of BLAISE's existence, states that 'from its inception, BLAISE was envisaged as a complete online bibliographic facility, supporting many library functions including cataloguing, information retrieval, acquisitions, bibliographic checking, and inter-library loans and photocopy requests'. In 1987 there were over 800 subscribers to BLAISE-LINE, and over 400 to BLAISE-LINK.[14]

Pergamon Financial Data Services currently offers about 40 databases. The service began as Infoline Ltd in the late 1970s and, after a faltering start, was taken over by Pergamon Press in 1980 and renamed Pergamon Infoline Ltd. In 1986, Pergamon acquired the ORBIT Search Service of the System Development Corporation (SDC), owned by Burroughs Corporation, and the company was renamed Pergamon Orbit Infoline, with two divisions, namely Pergamon Infoline (renamed Pergamon Financial Data Services in 1988) in the United Kingdom, and ORBIT Information Technologies in the United States. Pergamon Orbit Infoline operates both as a database producer and as an online host. As Pergamon at that time owned two services – Pergamon Financial Data Services in the United Kingdom and ORBIT Information Technologies in the United States – the databases of the two services are gradually being rationalized so that the ORBIT service will offer mainly scientific and technical databases, while Pergamon Financial Data Services will concentrate more on business oriented databases. Gateways have been established with both the European Space Agency's Information Retrieval Service (IRS) and BRS Information Technologies. The November 1987 issue of *Online* has an interview with the President of Pergamon Orbit Infoline, Jim Terragno.[15]

Reuters, currently with an estimated 90,000 customers, was established as a news agency in the nineteenth century, and since 1964 has also been involved in the computerized transmission of financial data. It acquired Finsbury Data Services in 1987 for about £11m. Finsbury had been offering online business information since 1979, principally through its Textline database – an index to business newspapers and journals across the world – and later also through Dataline, which gives detailed company information, and Newsline, which gives records on the last week's news. From June 1988 it was offering the full text of *The Independent* newspaper. Finsbury was said to have about 2,000 customers worldwide, with half in the United Kingdom, when it was taken over. Reuters also purchased I. P. Sharp Associates (see above) in 1986 for $48m.

Profile Information is another online host offering databases giving business information. Formerly called Datasolve Information Online and owned by Thorn-EMI, it was taken over by FT Information Online Ltd, part of the Financial Times group, in 1987 for £10m. It offers access to over 40 full-text databases, including McCarthy Online. The service is also available via a number of gateways, such as ESA-IRS, Telecom Gold, InfoSearch, Mercury Link and EasyNet.

A relative newcomer in the United Kingdom is British Telecom's Business Direction (formerly BT Hotline). Hotline was launched in September 1986, and offers over a dozen databases, including INSPEC, ICC company information and some full-text databases such as Marketing Week and Wall Street Journal.[16] Business Direction also offers a gateway to the Dow Jones News/Retrieval Service, Infocheck, Jordans, Information Services Ltd (Kompass Online) and Profile Information. British Telecom is planning a fuller integration between Business Direction, its videotex system Prestel, and its electronic mail service Telecom Gold, under British Telecom's company Dialcom.[17]

In Europe, as well as the United Kingdom hosts mentioned above, some of the major hosts are:

The European Space Agency's Information Retrieval Service (ESA-IRS) currently offers over 100 databases relating to science and technology. The European Space Research Organization (ESRO) Space Documentation Service (SDS) established in 1965 was one of the first centres to provide online searching facilities. The service gave access to a number of databases of relevance to space research and technology, e.g. the NASA database, Chemical Abstracts, Biological Abstracts etc., from a host computer located at Frascati, near Rome, using the RECON software developed under contract by Lockheed. In the United Kingdom the Department of Industry's DIALTECH service began to make dial-up access available to the 12 RECON databases in October 1970 via a minicomputer at Orpington, Kent. The European Space Agency was founded by 12 member states in 1975 to supersede ESRO, and the RECON software was replaced by the more sophisticated QUEST programs in the Information Retrieval Service (IRS) which replaced SDS late in 1979.

Data-Star, which began in 1980, currently offers over 100 databases, principally in the physical sciences, life sciences, social sciences and business, including full-text and company information databases. In 1985 it became the most-used European online host.[11] Radio-Suisse, the parent company of Data-Star, was reorganized in January 1988 and an independent company set up, with Motor Columbus AG replacing the Swiss government as the principal shareholder.[18] Data-Star markets its services throughout Europe from offices in Switzerland, the United Kingdom, France and Germany, and in 1987 made considerable investments towards entry into the North American market, and opened its first American office.[19] In 1986 for the first time it assumed the role of database producer when it purchased Tradstat – a database of European trade statistics – from the European Petrochemical Association.

The Deutsches Institut für Medizinische Dokumentation und Information (DIMDI) was founded in 1969 with the purpose of collecting, evaluating and storing national and international literature and other information in the field of medicine and related subjects, by the use of electronic data processing. A profile of the organization was given recently in *Information world review*.[20]

Telesystemes-Questel, established in 1979, is the largest French online host, with nearly 70 databases, and offers bibliographic and source databases, mainly in the fields of science and technology, but with some business databases.

The planning of the European online network and retrieval service EURONET/DIANE began in 1971 and the service became operational in 1980, with 90 databases from 15 online hosts. EURONET was the data transmission facility developed by the post, telegraph and telephone authorities (PTTs) of the EEC countries to provide users inside the Community with the means of access to databases while DIANE (Direct

Information Access Network for Europe) is the ensemble of the online hosts available within the Community. Among the first online hosts in the new network were ESA-IRS and the British Library's BLAISE system.

The Aslib survey of 1987[21] gives some information about the usage of various online hosts in the United Kingdom; the survey included Aslib members only. The following table shows the percentage of users who used a particular online host, compared with usage reported in the 1982 survey.[22]

Table 1 Usage of online hosts by Aslib members

Hosts	1986 users (%)	1982 users (%)	Change, %
DIALOG	75	87	−13
BLAISE	47	67	−29
ESA-IRS	55	61	−10
SDC	–	51	–
Pergamon	66*	35	+89
Data-Star	54	25	+116

* includes both Infoline and ORBIT

Usage of other hosts in the survey was as follows: Agdex 2%, Butterworth Telepublishing 4%, Datasolve 17%, DataStream 2%, DIMDI 4%, Echo 5%, Inkadata 3%, Kompass Online 7%, Leatherhead Food Research Association 3%, Mead Data Central International 3%, Scicon 12%, STN International 9%, Telesystemes-Questel 5%, Textline 13%. There were 24 other online hosts accessed by between two and five users. 13% of users accessed more than 10 hosts.

A detailed guide to searching on the systems of the following seven online hosts is given in Part Two: DIALOG Information Services Inc., ESA-IRS, BLAISE-LINE, National Library of Medicine (BLAISE-LINK), ORBIT, Pergamon Financial Data Services and Data-Star. There are several sources which give information about which online hosts exist; these sources can be found in Appendix 1. The databases offered by several online hosts are listed in Appendix 2.

3 The third sector of the online industry embraces libraries, information services and information brokers, who utilize the services offered by the online hosts to provide information, both bibliographic

and source, for their users in the industrial, commercial, public, medical, legal and academic sectors; this sector includes also end-users themselves, i.e. those who ultimately use the information retrieved. The survey of online usage in the United Kingdom by Aslib gives the following breakdown of organizations using online information retrieval systems in 1987 compared with the earlier survey in 1982.[21,22]

Table 2 Usage of online hosts by type of organization

Type of organization	1987 %	1982 %
Industrial/commercial	78	39.7
Academic	80	25.2
Government	80	19.7
Local government/public library	63	8.6
Research/trade/professional assoc.	55	6.8
Private individuals	50	–

Information brokers have increased in number during the 1980s – these services offer to conduct online searches on a commercial basis for end-users.[23-9]

To an increasing extent, both database producers and online hosts are marketing their services directly to the end-user. By developing 'user-friendly' software they are endeavouring to encourage the end-user to search databases directly rather than to use the services of an intermediary, such as a librarian, information officer or information broker. Some instances of this are shown in the introduction of multi-level access to databases – i.e. both menu-driven and command-driven access, via both the online version and, where it exists, the CD-ROM version of a database; and by the introduction of special end-user services such as BRS After Dark, DIALOG's Knowledge Index, DIALOG Business Connection[30] and DIALOG Medical Connection,[31] and BIOSIS' BIOSIS Connection.[31] O'Leary states that 'although databanks have been available for several years, they are still used primarily by specialized groups – the professional databanks by information specialists and the consumer databanks by personal computer users. To reach much larger audiences, online services will have to adopt content, design and marketing innovations of the kind already being carried out by GENIE

(General Electric Network for Information Exchange) and BIX (Byte Information Exchange)' – two end-user (consumer) databanks.[32] Arnold states that in 1983 the online industry realized that its systems were too difficult for new markets, and began a crusade for user-friendliness in systems to attract what he calls the 'new intermediaries' (i.e. end-users) – those who perform many of the functions of special librarians, but who have non-library backgrounds, and such titles as 'market researcher', 'corporate planner' etc.[33]

Cotton gives an 'intelligent estimate' that in 1986 less than 13% of online searches were conducted by end-users, excluding financial services such as Reuters.[34] Like Arnold above, he believes that the end-user will figure more in searching, but it will be a slow process. The Aslib survey of 1987 showed an increase in end-user searching since the 1982 survey (11% compared with 4%), but the majority of searching was done by the library/information professional.[21, 22] Nicholas also discusses the slow uptake of end-user searching, except in the case of Reuter Textline.[35]

Cotton believes that the main reasons for the slow uptake by end-users are that the appropriate communicating hardware has not penetrated very far; host systems have not been designed for amateurs; the habit of relying on specialists for information-gathering is deeply entrenched; the 'information habit' is not yet well established, at least outside the USA; product development and marketing have been poor.[34] The author continues by listing some factors that will facilitate, but not necessarily bring about, more usage by end-users: increasing availability of full-text databases; increasing availability of the 'communicating micro'; improved and friendlier interfaces; the proliferation of networks, including gateways; simplifying mechanisms such as 'integrators' and 'translation' devices. Dutton believes that end-user searching is the only practical way to meet the increasing demand for information – most organizations will not increase their information staff. If the information group does not promote end-user searching, then either end-users will start experimenting themselves, or another department will step in.[36]

These developments are leading to a reassessment of the role of the intermediary in online searching. Dutton sees the intermediary's role as complementary to that of the end-user; where a complex or exhaustive search is required, then the intermediary, in the role of a searcher or adviser, will usually be essential; the two areas most appropriate for end-user search are where a small group of databases is being searched regularly, and where a shallow scan is required. He believes that end-user searching does not release professional intermediary time for other activities because it leads to an enhanced appreciation of both the scope and the complexities of the search process and hence to an increased demand for intermediary searches; and it also causes an increased call on administrative services – training programmes, back-up user support facilities, and ongoing administration. He states that it is the common experience that the amount of money spent on online searching rises quite considerably with end-user search.[36] Cotton believes that the role of the intermediary will change to that of 'information manager' – while the role of searcher will diminish, the intermediary will advise on systems and sources, co-ordinate resources, organize training, and oversee research projects.[34]

4 The online searcher has access to a highly developed worldwide telecommunications system to link with the appropriate online host. If the online host is close by, the searcher would dial direct; but in many cases the online host is more remote, often at the other side of the world. In this case, national and international networks would be used, such as British Telecom's Packet SwitchStream (PSS) and International Packet SwitchStream (IPSS), Mercury Communications' services, Tymshare's Tymnet, Telenet Marketings' Telenet; these and other similar networks are high-speed data transmission networks linking users with computer systems throughout the world. Some online hosts make available private networks for users to link in with them, e.g. Dialnet for access to DIALOG. EURONET, which became operational in 1980, was a data transmission network developed by the post, telegraph and telephone authorities (PTTs) of the countries of the European Economic Community (EEC) to provide users in the Community with access to databases available on hosts within the Community.[37] The physical EURONET network ceased at the end of 1984, as users were by that time connected to their own national networks; the national PTTs now provide a fully European service. JANET (Joint Academic Network) is a network set up in 1984 to provide networking facilities to universities, polytechnics and research councils in the United Kingdom; BLAISE-LINE became available via JANET in 1987.[38,39]

To gain access to these networks, the searcher dials the nearest node (i.e. point for connection to the network), gives an identification number for using the network, and enters the address (usually in the form of a number) of online host required. In the United Kingdom, there are about 27 packet-switching exchanges on PSS, and in the United States, services such as Tymnet and Telenet have hundreds of access points. Networks employ packet-switching technology where discrete packets (of a certain character length) of data are transmitted along special high-grade paths between computer and the user's terminal. A message from a user's terminal travels to a PAD (packet assembler/disassembler), where the message is divided up into packets – each packet with its own address, control and data signals; these are then sent individually to their destination (sometimes along different routes), where the message is reassembled in the correct order. The reverse process takes place when the computer sends a message to the user. Packet-switching technology reduces the cost of telecommunications, for 'the communications channels are only occupied during the transmission of a packet as compared with conventional circuit switching in which a connection is made and maintained for the duration of the complete message transmission'.[40] The cost to the user of telecommunications is dealt with in Chapter 7.

The mode of transmission from the terminal to network node or computer is variable; the searcher selects either half-duplex or full-duplex, according to the requirements of the system being used. In half-duplex mode, communication will take place over the line in either direction but in only one direction at a time, from terminal to network node or computer, or vice versa. Full-duplex mode permits communication to take place simultaneously in both directions over the line. When the terminal is set at half-duplex, a character is printed or displayed on the terminal as it is typed. When in full-duplex mode, the terminal does not print or display input characters immediately, but only when they are echoed back from the network node. This echoplexing provides the searcher with a degree of input error detection. If the character is received and echoed correctly by the network's node, it will almost certainly be received correctly by the host's computer. If a character is echoed in error, it can be corrected immediately. As most online hosts' computers are not, like network nodes, equipped with echoplexing facilities, the searcher will need to set the terminal at half-duplex when dialling direct to a host's system.

Quality of service of telecommunication services is an important issue. Zuther gives details of a European Association of Information Services' (EUSIDIC) survey in 1985, which included replies from 100 organizations in Europe. The conclusions included: many users found public data networks an obstacle course; communications technology is not designed with the average user in mind; users were presented with coded and therefore unintelligible messages; and congestion and local difficulties left users stranded. 'Considering 100 different organisations in a large number of countries were involved, there is a large degree of unanimity that even by 1985, public data networks in Europe seem to arouse a great deal of antagonism amongst so many of the smaller users.' Partly as a follow-up, the European Online User Group, under the aegis of EUSIDIC, held the EUROLUG Monitoring Week in January 1986 for monitoring calls within Europe.[41] Another Monitoring Week, organized by EUSIDIC, was held in 1987 and found that on 5,223 calls, the failure rate for connections was 3 in 10; a further Monitoring Week took place in March 1988, where, of the 5,669 calls monitored, 1,439 failed – a 25% failure rate. Some of the results of the three Monitoring Weeks, relating to successful or unsuccessful connections made to telecommunications networks, are given in Table 3.[41-3]

Table 3 Success/failure rate of calls via telecommunication networks in Europe

Country	Success 1986	Failure 1986	%Fail 1986	%Fail 1987	%Fail 1988
UK	708	296	30	28	28
Italy	151	78	34	43	35
Belgium	362	245	40	32	14.5
Denmark	289	93	24	30	23
Switzerland	66	3	4		0
Sweden	272	101	27	35	20
Norway	80	30	27	17	33
Ireland	70	32	31		
Spain	123	55	31	47	27.5
Finland	410	118	22	19	18.5
Portugal	17	2	10		
Germany					15.5
Netherlands				23	14.5

EUSIDIC produced a report, 'European telecommunications – the information industry perspective', in October 1987.[44]

Gateways are a relatively new concept in online information retrieval. A gateway interfaces 'networks so that a terminal on one network can communicate with a terminal or computer on another';[40] 'the gateway takes messages, strips each transmission down to a level that the systems are the same and then builds up the message in the form required by the receiving system'.[45] For example, users of British Telecom's viewdata service Prestel have the ability to use gateways via that system to the Stock Exchange Automated Quotation (SEAQ) service, the Securities and Investment Board (SIB) register and the Educational Counselling and Credit Transfer Information Service (ECCTIS); DIALOG Information Services offer a gateway to American stock exchanges with the Quotes and Trading service.

A recent innovation is that of online hosts making gateways available through their own systems to other hosts' systems in reciprocal agreements; some examples of this are: BRS and Pergamon Financial Data Services (PFDS), and also the agreement between PFDS and ESA-IRS – a sophisticated inter-host connection protocol devised by members of the European Host Operators Group (EHOG). These gateways usually require knowledge of each system, though BRS and PFDS are hoping to develop the facility for using either BRS or PFDS commands on either system.

More often the gateway is one-way. Some examples of this are (with the 'host' system first – i.e. the system offering the gateway, followed by the 'guest' system (this terminology is used by Conger in her introduction to gateways):[46] Business Direction – Dow Jones News/Retrieval Service, Toxnet – NLM Elhill files,[47] One to One – Profile Information (Datasolve),[48] OCLC – DIALOG,[49,50] RLIN – DIALOG,[49,50] ALANET – Dow Jones News/Retrieval Service,[51] Kompass Online – Infocheck,[48] and many more.

Another type of gateway is the intelligent 'front-end' system, such as Istel's InfoSearch, Searchlink produced jointly by CW Communications Inc. and Telebase Systems Inc.,[52] InfoMaster,[53] Telebase Systems' EasyNet,[54] and Intelligent Information, developed on the Geomail electronic mail system.[55] Services such as these act as an intelligent link between the searcher and databases on a variety of hosts, and have been programmed to make decisions like choosing appropriate databases and hosts and converting a subject request into a statement acceptable to a particular host and database. Istel's opening menu is shown in Fig. 2.

Istel's InfoSearch began in the United Kingdom in 1987, and the company was reported to have suspended temporarily issuing of passwords early in 1988 due to unexpectedly high demand.[55] In mid 1988, the company was valued at £35m.[56] Istel grew from the data processing facilities of British Leyland.

```
PRESS                TO SELECT
  1    *MHA-I           We choose the database
  2     MHA-II          You choose the database
  3     Database Directory
  4     News, Instructions
  H     Help
        (* = Multi Host Access)
```

Fig. 2 Opening menu from Istel's InfoSearch

Tucker speaks of a 'world-linking gateway concept' using electronic mail (e-mail) services to interconnect private and commercial networks; for example Western Union offering InfoMaster to its EasyLink e-mail users. With the acceptance of the X.400 set of international electronic mail interconnection standards recommended by the Consultative Committee on International Telephone and Telegraph (CCITT), it is hoped that the interconnection of e-mail services will be as straightforward as the interconnection of telephone systems.[45]

The growth of the online information retrieval industry has been marked since its infancy in the early 1970s. According to Cuadra's *Directory of online databases*, the number of online hosts has increased from 59 in 1979/80 to 555 in 1988; in the same period there has been an increase in database producers from 221 to 1,685; see Fig. 3.[4] According to the same source, there were 59 gateways available in 1988, compared with 35 in 1986. The directory of British databases entitled *Britline* gives the figure of 132 online hosts in the United Kingdom in 1987, and 220 database producers.[13]

The number of databases online continues to increase at a high rate. Cuadra lists 3,669 databases in 1988, compared with 400 in 1979/80; see Fig. 3.

Many of the larger online hosts claim large numbers of users: DIALOG is said to have over 80,000 users in 76 countries[7] and Mead Data Central 170,000 users.[10]

Some indications have been given of the value of the online database market. Hawkins, referring to the report 'Information market indicators' by M. Williams, notes that online databases generated over \$210m in revenues in 1984, an increase of 90% over the figure for 1982.[57] Arnold reckoned that the online bibliographic industry was worth \$300m in 1986, deriving the bulk of revenue from about 3,000 firms, with large organizations contributing the bulk of revenue.[33] DIALOG alone was said to have a sales volume of \$100m in 1988[58] and was bought by

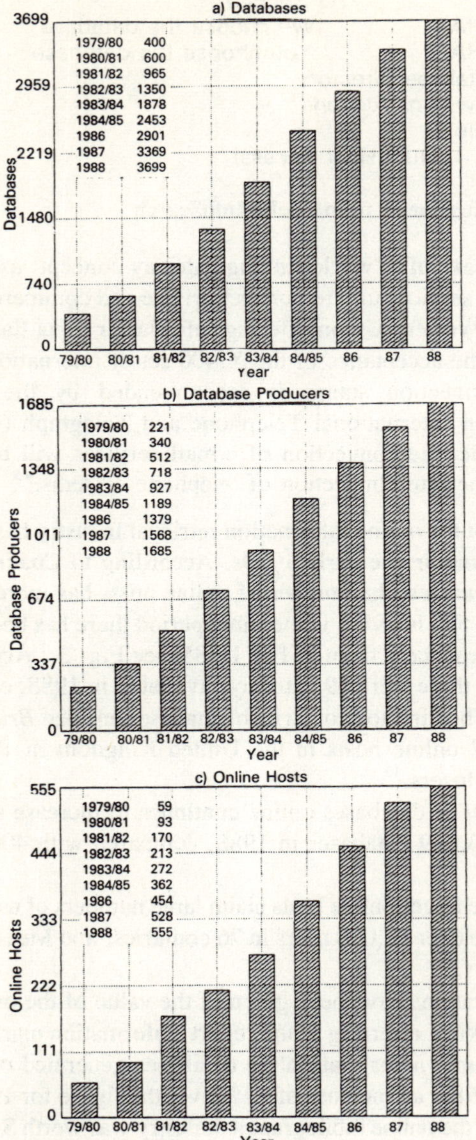

Fig. 3 Growth in the number of Databases, Database Producers and Online Hosts 1979–1988. (Source: *Directory of online databases*, Cuadra/Elsevier.)

Knight-Ridder in that year for $353m.

A Keynote report gives a figure of $600–$700m for the size of the West European market for online databases, with an annual growth rate of between 28% and 32%, leading to an estimated market of $2,000m in 1990.[59] The report gives the market figure for the United Kingdom as $245m, and notes that bibliographic databases account for only a small proportion of the market estimate; of the $245m mentioned for the United Kingdom, $12m was for bibliographic databases, and $233m for source databases, of which about $180m was for financial databases. In discussing an Action Plan for European information services, a report in *Information market* states that the European domestic information market employed some 100,000 people in 1988; these generate 1.25b ECU of annual revenue; within a decade this revenue should be 10b ECU, due to a growth rate of 20–30%.[60]

The online industry is open to the same market forces as other industries – competition, mergers, takeovers, etc. There have been a number of examples of this in recent years: the acquisition of I. P. Sharp by Reuters, who also acquired Finsbury Data Services; Data Courier was acquired by UMI, who were themselves bought by Bell & Howell; Pergamon Infoline took over the ORBIT Search Service from the System Development Corporation (SDC) in 1986; Datasolve (now Profile Information) was purchased by FT Information Online Ltd from Thorn-EMI for £10m in 1987; Disclosure was purchased by VNU Publishers; and the largest sale of all was that of DIALOG, which was purchased by Knight-Ridder from Lockheed Missile and Space Corporation for $353m in 1988.

Many of the parent companies are extremely large, with the subsidiary company associated with the online industry contributing only a small part of their revenue. For example, in 1986 Datasolve's turnover was £32,990,000, but this represented only 1.0% of the total turnover for the parent company Thorn-EMI. Similarly, Pergamon Infoline's turnover in 1985 was £1,972,000, merely 0.4% of the turnover of the parent company Pergamon Press. Derwent Publications in 1986 had a turnover of £21,449,000 – only 1.8% of the turnover of the parent company, the International Thompson Organization.[61]

Uneconomic databases are being withdrawn, as are databases which do not fit in with the image the online host is attempting to portray. Conger believes that there is a new look in the online environment; instead of a number of online hosts competing for the same audience with different versions of the same databases, each seems to be trying to create its own corporate image and to define its own market niche. As a result, each is dropping databases that are not paying their way or do not fit in with the image to which they aspire.[6] For example, BRS is the academic librarian's principal online service; DIALOG is currently targetting the business and financial communities, while retaining its ties with the general user; Pergamon Orbit Infoline is reorganizing its databases so that the scientific and technical databases are being offered via ORBIT, and the business databases by the renamed Pergamon Financial Data Services (PFDS).

Marketing is taken very seriously. Hawkins notes that the major online hosts advertise in consumer-oriented as well as information-related publications; they have learned about the 'niche' markets and specialization mentioned above; they have become more sensitive to customers, establishing newsletters, customer service desks, toll-free enquiry lines, full training courses etc. Data-Star opened an office in the USA in 1987, and BIOSIS and Newsnet have established European help desks.[57]

Fierce competition is not the complete story of the online industry; there is a degree of co-operation between some online hosts in that they have introduced gateways that allow one host's system to be made available through another. Some examples of this are: two-way gateways between Pergamon Financial Data Services and Information Retrieval Service (IRS), and between BRS and Pergamon – these two systems also hope to move towards using either command language on either system; Profile Information is available through a number of gateways, including Telecom Gold; Infocheck is available via Kompass Online.

Conger, in an article describing the 'plateau' that she considers the online industry to have reached, describes the move from the dumb terminals and low speeds to microcomputers and high speeds; the development of bigger and better mainframes; the 'explosion' in the number of online hosts' databases; the development of different ways of searching – 'front-end' programs as well as command languages.[6] On the subject of microcomputers, Arnold estimated that the value of personal computers in the USA in 1986 was $14.6 billion; and it was with the boom in computers from the early 1980s that the online hosts sought a new user community – the end-users – to increase revenue and meet growth predictions. Arnold believes, however, that even with more user-friendliness in online systems, including menus and 'front-end' software, the reality has not lived up to the dream in terms of the 'new intermediaries' using online services.[33] Deunette and Anthony believe that the computer age has not lived up to expectations, the main problem being the enormous gap between information, or data, which is what computers deal with, and knowledge, which human beings create by original thinking and which, ultimately and hopefully, leads to wisdom; a major activity of the next ten years is to bridge this gap. Also, the concept of the 'global village' is unlikely to reach fruition without worldwide compatibility and standardization, which are essential if the information industry is to survive.[62] Another development will be moves to improve the 'quality' of information, a theme also highlighted by Jewitt.[63]

On the subject of the future of databases in the online industry, Arnold sees the continued proliferation of databases in online and CD-ROM form; the reshaping of the information industry with the emergence of new information 'powerhouses' — banks, consortia of companies in particular industries, and global information providers; distribution alternatives, including online, CD-ROM, read-write optical discs and other as yet not commercial technologies; the increasing intelligence of retrieval software; hybrid retrieval systems combining online, CD-ROM; and significant quality differences in electronic products.[64]

Chapter 4

Hardware and software

1 Hardware

The hardware (i.e. physical equipment) needed for online searching consists of a terminal, a modem, a printer, and a telephone line.

The word 'terminal' is used to describe a number of different types of equipment used for sending and receiving data in online searching and other applications. The most common terminal today is the microcomputer; in the Aslib survey of 1987 mentioned previously over 70% of the 376 respondents used a microcomputer compared with only 4% in the 1982 survey.[1,2] The microcomputer has a number of advantages over other types of terminal: it is so common today that an organization is likely to possess at least one already; it is comparatively cheap; it can be used for a multitude of other applications as well as acting as an online terminal (e.g. word processing, internal database creation, accounts etc.) and, depending on the software chosen, can considerably enhance the facilities available for the online search itself.

Other types of terminal in use are 'dumb' terminals (i.e. they can send and receive data but have no additional facilities such as programmable memory). These may take the form of a teletypewriter terminal without a visual display unit (VDU) giving a hard copy printout of the whole search; or a keyboard and VDU screen, to which is attached a printer – the search is displayed on the screen and the searcher prints out only those parts of the search needed in hard copy. On all terminals instructions are given to the host's computer via the keyboard, the layout of which is identical to that of a standard typewriter, but which normally incorporates specific keys for particular online functions; for example, the 'break' key enables the searcher to interrupt the search at any time on most systems.

'Intelligent' terminals send and receive data, but also have additional facilities such as programmable memory, so they can do much more than the 'dumb' terminal. By using a combination of the memory and user-definable function keys on the keyboard, it is possible, for instance, to pre-record and edit search statements, before uploading them to the host's computer; in addition to economizing on the time connected to the computer online, this can avoid the typing errors which can occur during the online search. This facility, when used selectively, does not impede the interactive character of online searching. Frequently used data (e.g. passwords for logging-on to the different systems) can be pre-recorded and when required uploaded by pressing a single function key. The results of the online search can be downloaded into the memory of the terminal for subsequent editing and printing.

'Videotex' terminals can also be used for online searching, but many organizations use microcomputers which can access the videotex services.

Some sources giving guidance on choosing terminals are: *Online terminal/microcomputer guide and directory*, published by the journal *Online*; and *Going online*, published by Aslib (see Appendix 1).

A modem (MOdulator/DEModulator) is necessary to convert the digital signals sent by the terminal into analog signals for transmission over the public telephone lines; this process is reversed when receiving data from the host's system. Similarly, there is a modem connecting the computer and telephone lines at the host's end. The modem may be a separate piece of equipment connected to the terminal and telephone line, it may be incorporated in the terminal itself, or it may be incorporated in an organization's mainframe computer, if online searching is conducted via that equipment. Before the advent of the plug-in telephone socket, the acoustic coupler type of modem was popular – this used the telephone handset itself as the connection between the terminal and the telephone network; the handset was placed into a cradle fitted with rubber caps to insulate it from interference. The development of modems, the widespread use of plug-in telephone sockets, and the non-standard nature of telephone handsets in recent years, have made the acoustic coupler largely obsolete. In the Aslib survey, the following percentages of respondents used the various types of modem: British Telecom (34%), Dacom (14%), Case (11%), Miracle Technology WS 2000 (8%), Racal (7%), and more than 17 other types were in use.[1] Even the days of the current modems are numbered, with the imminent advent of digital telephone networks, such as the Integrated Services Digital Network (ISDN).

The most common speeds at which online systems operate are either 300 baud (30 characters per second), or 1,200 baud (120 characters per second), although higher speeds are becoming more common. The baud rate is the number of times per second that a system changes state; in the particular case of a binary channel, the baud rate is equal to the bit rate, i.e. one baud equals one bit per second.[3] Harris gives details of a survey of users of Predicasts' databases which shows that up to 20% of their searchers have moved to searching at 2,400 baud, and discusses the effects this could have on producers' revenues and charging policies, perhaps causing them to move towards 'baud rate pricing'.[4] The Aslib surveys show the speeds used by members (see Table 4).[1,2]

Table 4 Baud rates used by Aslib members

Baud rate	Organizations, % 1987	Organizations, % 1982
300	52	100
1,200/75*	43	–
1,200/1,200	33	20
2,400	8	–
4,800	2	–
9,600	5	–

*i.e. receive at 1,200 baud, send at 75 baud

Teletypewriter terminals do not need a separate printer, as all data sent and received is printed anyway. Some VDU terminals have a built-in printer, but normally a separate printer is required to attach to the terminal. Printers suitable for online searching today are of four main types: dot matrix, daisywheel, thermal and laser.

On the dot matrix printer each character is made up of a series of dots. For most online purposes a dot matrix printer is sufficient; it is relatively cheap, it is fast and can normally work at close to the speed of the terminal up to 1,200 baud, and it often has a slower speed giving 'near letter quality' printing if this is required.

'Daisywheel' printers use a wheel with each of the characters at the end of one of the 'spokes'; these impact on the paper, giving a very good, clear and firm impression, of superior quality to the dot matrix printers. They would normally be more expensive, noisier and much slower than the dot matrix printers.

'Thermal' printers use a heat process to produce an image of whatever is on the VDU screen. These printers are cheap and quiet, but the quality is not normally as good as the two types mentioned above.

In laser printers, the laser is used as a scanning light source to build up the image on an electrostatic drum; toner is then released onto the surface of the drum, transferred electrostatically to the paper, and finally melted on by hot rollers. The advantages of laser printers are their quietness, speed and very good quality; but they are more expensive than other types of printer to buy and maintain.[5] A recent online application requiring a laser printer is DIALOG's graphic images on Trademarkscan, on which it is possible to produce graphic images of trade marks.

The other piece of hardware necessary is a telephone line. The terminal may plug straight into the public telephone network, or into a private exchange which in turn will be connected to the public network, or into a local mainframe computer which is connected via a modem to the public network. It is inadvisable to use a private exchange if there is any likelihood of being disconnected accidentally by a switchboard operator.

2 Software

When using a microcomputer as a terminal for online searching, software (i.e. a computer program or programs) is needed to make the microcomputer work like a terminal. This software may be built-in to the microcomputer already, or it may have to be purchased separately and loaded each time the microcomputer is to be used for online searching. The types of software available vary, but the following gives some indication as to the types of functions which may be available.[6]

(i) Basic functions

(a) The ability to work in teletype mode, and also viewdata mode if accessing services such as Prestel.

(b) The ability to access any online host via the same software.

(c) The ability to configure the microcomputer for telecommunications – choose the appropriate speed of working (baud rate), full- or half-duplex, stop bits and parity.

(d) Have function of 'break' key to interrupt flow of data from computer.

(e) The ability to store data – phone numbers, log-on information (user identification numbers and passwords), and search statements and automatically upload it when required (modems might do some of this).

(f) The ability to receive data from the computer, display it on the screen and print on printer.

(ii) Enhanced functions

(a) Relating to log-on procedures: automatic responses to questions from the computer, the use of time delays, use of function keys.

(b) Relating to search preparation: the use of an editor to prepare search statements before going online, the ability to upload information either line by line or as a continuous stream of text, and the ability to edit information while online.

(c) Relating to receiving data from the computer: the ability to download (see Chapter 6) data onto a disc for subsequent processing – e.g. editing, and/or permanent storage in a local database (which would often employ different, though, hopefully, compatible software).

(d) 'Front-end' software gives help with all the above, and also gives varying amounts of extra help, e.g. choice of online host, of database/s, use of menus to avoid using command languages etc. O'Leary puts forward the possibility that systems such as DIALOG Business Connection and EasyNet, who offer a host-based search assistance interface, may foreshadow the end of the disc-based front-end search assistance interfaces.[7]

The software may be of several types: general purpose software which may be available for a particular microcomputer; software which is applicable to a particular host's system; or software especially prepared for the library/information community.

The Aslib survey of 1987 showed that 70% of respondents used communications software, the main packages being: Headline (17%), Assist (12%), Connect (7%), Crosstalk (6%), Kermit (4%), and a further 17 other types were used.[1]

On the question of evaluation of software, Niewwenhuysen gives guidelines for information and documentation work, classifying the programs into:

(a) those for terminal emulation/communications/uploading/downloading;

(b) those for reformatting/converting downloaded and manually created data;

(c) those for local storage and retrieval of information;

(d) those for word processing. (The full paper, available from the author Niewwenhuysen, covers over 40 software packages.[8])

Some sources which may help in the choice of software are: Burton, Paul and Petrie, J. Howard, *Librarian's guide to microcomputers for information management*, 2nd edn, London, Van Nostrand Reinhold (UK) Co. Ltd, 1986; *Text retrieval: a directory of software*, 2nd edn,

Aldershot, Gower, 1987; Dyer, Hilary and Brookes, Alison, *Directory of library and information retrieval software for microcomputers*, 2nd edn, Aldershot, Gower, 1986. Also: Library and Information Technology Centre; Aslib Technology Centre; Aslib Information Resources Centre. (See Appendix 1, which also lists journals which often include reviews of software.)

Chapter 5
Searching – general principles

This and the following chapter deal with searching. In this chapter some general points about searching will be dealt with, and the following chapter will deal with all the steps in the searching process, from the initial request for information to the delivery of the search results.

1 Principles of information retrieval

The act of retrieving information depends on information having been stored, so we should think in terms of information storage and retrieval. Both the storage and retrieval functions consist of three operations:

(a) Storage

(i) Subject analysis of a document by an indexer.
(ii) The translation of the subject analysed into the indexing language of the database.
(iii) The organization of the files of which the database is comprised.

(i) The documents, the records of which are to be entered into the database, are analysed to determine their subject content. Traditionally this has meant that indexers scan each document, decide on its subject content and then determine the concepts they wish to store. The 'depth' of indexing refers to the number of concepts and the index terms describing them which are used for each document, and this will be the result of a management decision dependent on the amount of indexing effort available, so that the depth of indexing will vary from one database to another. On MEDLINE, up to 15 Medical Subject Headings (MeSH) may be used, usually three to four of these being concepts central to the paper and the headings under which the record may be found in the printed *Index medicus*.

(ii) The concepts isolated by the indexer are then translated into the indexing language of the particular database; the indexing language is the words and phrases used to describe concepts found in a document. The indexing language often employs a 'controlled' vocabulary, i.e. a fixed list of words and phrases which the indexers must adhere to; with ample help by such means as cross-references and annotations, this form of controlled indexing can be most helpful to both indexers and searchers. Some examples of controlled vocabularies are: INSPEC Thesaurus (Fig. 4), Medical Subject Headings (Figs. 5–6) and the ERIC Thesaurus of Descriptors.

Some databases rely wholly or partly on 'natural' language indexing, i.e. they dispense with the intellectual process of concept indexing and employ the actual words used by the author of the paper in the title, and abstract where this is available. Full-text databases use the actual text of the original document as the basis of retrieval. Natural language can be deficient as a medium for information retrieval because it is rich in synonyms, and the same concept may be described in different ways by different writers. There is some substance in the generalization which divides terminology into the two categories 'hard' and 'soft'. 'Hard' terminology is almost always used by authors in science and technology – they use clear and unambiguous titles for their papers, using terminology specifically defined in their individual disciplines. However, in the social sciences and humanities the terminology used is often 'soft' – it can be ambiguous. For example, a literature search on drug abuse retrieved serious contributions to the literature with such titles as 'From potty to pot: a giant leap backwards', 'Grass: the modern tower of Babel', 'Potted dreams' and 'Mary Jane faces the identity crisis or three blind mice in search of an elephant'. In the field of librarianship, useful contributions on information retrieval have been published with the titles 'How golden is your retriever?' and 'On the construction of white elephants', and a book on a famous national library was entitled 'Out of the dinosaurs'. Thus, when searching a database which employs natural language indexing, it is important to think of all the synonymous terms which might have been used, and also to make use of any other searching features available, such as classification categories (see Fig. 6, Medical Subject Headings – Tree Structures). It is also necessary to accept the fact that usually at least some of the retrieved records are going to be 'false drops', i.e. irrelevant.

As a consequence of such linguistic idiosyncracies many database producers employ a controlled vocabulary as an aid to concept indexing. This controlled vocabulary standardizes the terminology by limiting the choice of words available to the indexers as indexing terms.

1989 Thesaurus 219

INEPT
USE nuclear magnetic resonance

inert anodes
USE anodes

inert gas compounds
NT argon compounds
helium compounds
krypton compounds
neon compounds
radon compounds
xenon compounds
DI January 1975
PT *none*

inert gases
UF noble gases
rare gases
NT argon
helium
krypton
neon
radon
xenon
DI January 1973

inertial navigation
BT navigation
TT navigation
RT inertial systems
CC B7630 B7650 C3360L
DI January 1973

inertial systems
RT inertial navigation
CC C3200 C3300
DI January 1973

inference engines
USE inference mechanisms

inference mechanisms
UF inference engines
inference techniques
BT knowledge engineering
TT cybernetics
CC C1230 C6170
DI January 1989
PT knowledge engineering

inference techniques
USE inference mechanisms

infinite dimensional systems
USE multidimensional systems

infinite impulse response filters
USE digital filters

infinite series
USE series (mathematics)

inflammability
USE combustion

information analysis
UF citation analysis
NT abstracting
cataloguing
classification
indexing
vocabulary
BT information science
TT computer applications
RT information centres
information retrieval
information services
information storage
information use
CC C7240
DI July 1973
PT information science

information analysis centers
USE information centres

information analysis centres
USE information centres

information centers
USE information centres

information centres
UF information analysis centers
information analysis centres
information centers
BT information science
TT computer applications
RT information analysis
information services
libraries
CC C7210
DI January 1973

information dissemination
UF dissemination of information
SDI
selective dissemination of information
BT information science
TT computer applications
RT document delivery
CC C7220
DI January 1973

information needs
BT information science
TT computer applications
RT information services
information use
libraries
CC C7220
DI January 1985
PT information use

Information Network System
USE ISDN

information retrieval
UF document retrieval
online literature searching
query processing
retrieval, information
BT information science
TT computer applications
RT bibliographic systems
information analysis
information storage
query languages
records management
CC C7250 C7260
DI January 1973

information retrieval languages
USE query languages

information retrieval system evaluation
BT information retrieval systems
TT computer applications
CC C7250
DI January 1973

information retrieval systems
UF information storage systems
online databases
NT bibliographic systems
information retrieval system evaluation
BT information science
TT computer applications
CC C7250
DI January 1973

information science
UF documentation
librarianship
library science
NT document delivery
information analysis
information centres
information dissemination
information needs
information retrieval
information retrieval systems
information services
information storage
information use
vocabulary
BT computer applications
TT computer applications
RT language translation
libraries
microforms

Fig. 4 Excerpt from INSPEC Thesaurus 1989 (reproduced by courtesy of INSPEC)

MANUSCRIPTS
L1.178.682.608+
IM; includes books prepared by hand before invention of printing; also handwritten or typescript drafts of pre-print papers, correspondence, diaries, notebooks, memoranda, etc.; no qualif; check century tag; Manual 33.12: relation to BOOKS

MANUSCRIPTS, MEDICAL
L1.178.682.608.526
see note above

MAPLE SYRUP URINE DISEASE
C10.228.140.163.608 C10.496.560
C18.452.648.66.608 F3.709.346.569
do not use /congen /drug eff /physiol /rad eff
X BRANCHED-CHAIN KETOACIDURIA
XR URINE

MAPPINE see BUFOTENIN
D3.438.473.914.237.150+ D3.438.473.914.814.150+
D15.236.372.163 D24.185.965.33.163

MAPROTILINE
D4.615.117.600 D15.236.122.140.573
do not use /biosyn /defic /physiol; /analogs NIM only
(75)
see under ANTHRACENES

MAPS
L1.178.147.426
avoid: a cataloging term; possibly GEOGRAPHY might apply; no qualif
XR GEOGRAPHY

MARASMUS see PROTEIN-CALORIE MALNUTRITION
C18.654.223.708.626+

MARBURG VIRUS
B4.909.777.750.490
do not use /blood-csf-urine; infection = MARBURG VIRUS DISEASE (75); was see under Rhabdoviruses 1978-80, was see under RNA VIRUSES 1975-77
see under RHABDOVIRIDAE
X FRANKFURT-MARBURG SYNDROME VIRUS

MARBURG VIRUS DISEASE
C2.782.417.560 C22.576.500
disease of monkeys transmissible to man; do not use /vet but check tag ANIMAL
75

MARCHIAFAVA-MICHELI SYNDROME see HEMOGLOBINURIA, PAROXYSMAL
C15.378.71.141.510.460 C15.378.190.625.460

MAREK'S DISEASE
C2.256.466.650 C2.928.489
C4.557.386.480.545 C4.619.935.489
C15.604.515.569.480.545 C20.683.515.761.480.545
C22.131.546
do not use /vet; don't forget also BIRDS or POULTRY (NIM) or specific bird or fowl (IM); check tag ANIMAL
73(72)
X FOWL PARALYSIS
X NEUROLYMPHOMATOSIS

MAREK'S DISEASE VIRUS
B4.909.204.382.675 B4.909.574.204.525
do not use /blood-csf-urine /cytol; infection: see heading & note above
75
X FOWL PARALYSIS VIRUS
X NEUROLYMPHOMATOSIS VIRUS

MARFAN SYNDROME
C5.116.99.674 C16.131.77.550
C23.205.200.441
do not use /congen
85; was ARACHNODACTYLY 1963-84
use MARFAN SYNDROME to search ARACHNODACTYLY back thru 1966
X ARACHNODACTYLY

MARGARINE
D10.516.212.302.651 J1.341.637
only /ad-poi-tox /anal /class /hist /rad eff /stand /supply

MARGINAL ULCER
C6.405.613.489
(64)
see under PEPTIC ULCER

MARGUERITE see PYRETHRUM
B6.781

MARIANA ISLANDS see MICRONESIA
Z1.782.680+

MARIDOMYCINS see LEUCOMYCINS
D9.203.408.51.485 D20.85.60.480

MARIE-BAMBERGER DISEASE see OSTEOARTHROPATHY, SECONDARY HYPERTROPHIC
C5.116.758 C5.550.684

MARIE-STRUEMPELL DISEASE see SPONDYLITIS, ANKYLOSING
C5.550.69.680 C5.550.114.154.856
C5.799.114.856 C5.878.805.680
C20.111.199.856 C23.205.200.732.99.856

MARIJUANA see CANNABIS
B6.560.139

MARIJUANA ABUSE see CANNABIS ABUSE
F3.709.597.780.610.200

MARIJUANA SMOKING
F1.145.466.753.488
only /drug eff /rad eff; consider also CANNABIS ABUSE
88
X CANNABIS SMOKING

MARINE BIOLOGY
G1.273.476
SPEC: SPEC qualif; IM; marine = ocean or sea, not inland waterways, lakes, ponds (= FRESH WATER (IM) + organism (IM))
see related
OCEANOGRAPHY
PLANKTON
XR OCEANOGRAPHY

MARINE TOXINS
D24.185.926.580+
includes toxins from marine flora or fauna; do not use /analogs /defic /diag use /physiol; /antag permitted but consider also ANTITOXINS; coord IM with specific source (IM with no qualif); does not include venoms of sea snakes (= SEA SNAKE VENOMS)
74
XU CIGUATOXIN

MARINESCO-SJOGREN SYNDROME see SPINOCEREBELLAR DEGENERATIONS
C10.228.140.252.253.871+

MARITAL RELATIONSHIP see MARRIAGE
F1.829.263.315.526 I1.880.225.423.526
N1.824.308.526

MARITAL THERAPY
F4.754.500
SPEC qualif
76; was MARRIAGE THERAPY 1973-75
use MARITAL THERAPY to search MARRIAGE THERAPY back thru 1973

MARKER ANTIGENS see ANTIGENS, DIFFERENTIATION
D24.611.216.301.264+

MARKER, DNA see GENETIC MARKER
G5.735.450

MARKER, GENETIC see GENETIC MARKER
G5.735.450

MARKETING OF HEALTH SERVICES
N3.219.463.548
do not use /educ /methods
80(79); was see under HEALTH RESOURCES 1979
X HEALTH SERVICES MARKETING

+ INDICATES THERE ARE INDENTED DESCRIPTORS IN MESH TREE STRUCTURES AT THIS NUMBER
-73

Fig. 5 Excerpt from Medical Subject Headings – Annotated Alphabetical List 1988 (reproduced by courtesy of the British Library)

C6 – DISEASES-DIGESTIVE

DIGESTIVE SYSTEM DISEASES
GASTROINTESTINAL DISEASES
INTESTINAL DISEASES
INTESTINAL POLYPS
GARDNER SYNDROME

Heading	Tree number	Other tree numbers
GARDNER SYNDROME	C6.405.469.583.393	C4.700.392 C4.799.411. C16.131.77. C16.466.700.
PEUTZ–JEGHERS SYNDROME	C6.405.469.583.598	C4.700.705 C4.799.411. C16.466.700.
JEJUNAL DISEASES	C6.405.469.600	
JEJUNAL NEOPLASMS	C6.405.469.600.523	C4.588.274.
MALABSORPTION SYNDROMES	C6.405.469.637	C18.452.603
BLIND LOOP SYNDROME	C6.405.469.637.145	C18.452.603.
CELIAC DISEASE	C6.405.469.637.250	C18.452.603.
LACTOSE INTOLERANCE	C6.405.469.637.506	C18.452.603. C18.452.648.
LIPODYSTROPHY, INTESTINAL	C6.405.469.637.598	C18.452.603.
SHORT BOWEL SYNDROME •	C6.405.469.637.832	C23.814.777
SPRUE, TROPICAL	C6.405.469.637.850	C18.452.603.
MESENTERIC VASCULAR OCCLUSION	C6.405.469.675	C6.772.510 C14.907.137.
PNEUMATOSIS CYSTOIDES INTESTINALIS	C6.405.469.778	
PROTEIN–LOSING ENTEROPATHIES	C6.405.469.818	C18.452.805
LYMPHANGIECTASIS, INTESTINAL •	C6.405.469.818.521	C18.452.805.
RECTAL DISEASES	C6.405.469.860	
ANUS DISEASES	C6.405.469.860.101	
ANUS NEOPLASMS	C6.405.469.860.101.163	C4.588.274.
FISSURE IN ANO	C6.405.469.860.101.430	
PRURITUS ANI	C6.405.469.860.101.752	C17.685.544
FECAL INCONTINENCE	C6.405.469.860.300	
HEMORRHOIDS	C6.405.469.860.401	C14.907.449
PROCTITIS	C6.405.469.860.622	
PROCTOCOLITIS •	C6.405.469.860.622.790	C6.405.469. C6.405.469.
RECTAL FISTULA	C6.405.469.860.704	
RECTOVAGINAL FISTULA	C6.405.469.860.704.642	C13.371.894.
RECTAL NEOPLASMS	C6.405.469.860.767	C4.588.274.
RECTAL PROLAPSE	C6.405.469.860.829	
PEPTIC ULCER	C6.405.613	
DUODENAL ULCER	C6.405.613.216	C6.405.469.
CURLING'S ULCER •	C6.405.613.216.200	C6.405.469.
ESOPHAGITIS, PEPTIC	C6.405.613.306	C6.306.780.
MARGINAL ULCER •	C6.405.613.489	
PEPTIC ULCER HEMORRHAGE	C6.405.613.627	C6.405.348. C23.542.516.
PEPTIC ULCER PERFORATION	C6.405.613.698	
STOMACH ULCER	C6.405.613.860	C6.405.748.
POSTGASTRECTOMY SYNDROMES	C6.405.650	C23.814.617
DUMPING SYNDROME	C6.405.650.310	C23.814.617.
STOMACH DISEASES	C6.405.748	
ACHLORHYDRIA	C6.405.748.45	C18.452.42
DUODENOGASTRIC REFLUX	C6.405.748.240	
BILE REFLUX •	C6.405.748.240.140	C6.130.140
GASTRIC FISTULA	C6.405.748.297	
GASTRIC MUCOSA PROLAPSE	C6.405.748.333	
GASTRITIS	C6.405.748.369	
GASTRITIS, ATROPHIC •	C6.405.748.369.394	
GASTRITIS, HYPERTROPHIC •	C6.405.748.369.410	
PYLORIC STENOSIS	C6.405.748.597	
STOMACH DILATATION	C6.405.748.717	
STOMACH DIVERTICULA	C6.405.748.753	
STOMACH NEOPLASMS	C6.405.748.789	C4.588.274.
STOMACH RUPTURE	C6.405.748.824	C21.866.17. C21.866.761.
STOMACH ULCER	C6.405.748.860	C6.405.613.
STOMACH VOLVULUS	C6.405.748.895	
TUBERCULOSIS, GASTROINTESTINAL	C6.405.831	C1.252.40.
VISCEROPTOSIS	C6.405.890	
VOMITING	C6.405.937	C23.888.821.
HEMATEMESIS	C6.405.937.378	C6.405.348. C23.542.516.
HYPEREMESIS GRAVIDARUM	C6.405.937.562	C13.703.799.
LIVER DISEASES	C6.552	
ACUTE YELLOW ATROPHY	C6.552.45	
CHOLESTASIS, INTRAHEPATIC	C6.552.150	C6.130.450. C23.888.498.
LIVER CIRRHOSIS, BILIARY	C6.552.150.250	C6.130.450. C6.552.630. C23.888.498.

• INDICATES MINOR DESCRIPTOR

83

Fig. 6 Excerpt from Medical Subject Headings – Tree Structures 1988 (reproduced by courtesy of the British Library)

The standardized list of indexing words and phrases – variously referred to as index terms, controlled terms, descriptors etc. – used to describe things, actions and concepts, can be a simple list, with 'see' and 'see also' references directing the indexer, or the searcher, to preferred terms; or it can be in the form of a thesaurus, which also shows the relationships which exist between the preferred terms. An example of a database employing a thesaurus is INSPEC (see Fig. 4). The INSPEC Thesaurus shows not only 'Use For' (UF) and 'Use' references, but gives Broader Terms (BT) – those above the preferred term in the hierarchy; Narrower Terms (NT) – those below the preferred term in the hierarchy; and Related Terms (RT) – those which are horizontally rather than vertically related to the preferred term.

Most bibliographic information retrieval systems allow the searcher to search on natural language terms or 'free-text' terms (i.e. words and phrases from title, abstract etc.) even when the database employs a controlled vocabulary as the main basis of retrieval. This gives the searcher extra searching power. Newly coined words and phrases will not be present in the thesaurus and therefore could not be expressed other than in terms of natural language. In addition, fringe subjects and concepts from outside the main discipline covered by the database might not be well represented in the controlled vocabulary. Thus, as will be seen later, the searcher will often employ a mixture of controlled vocabulary and natural language in a search strategy. Dubois assesses some advantages and disadvantages of free-text and controlled vocabularies.[1]

(iii) When the documents have been analysed and the concepts to be stored are identified and translated into the language of the database, the records are entered into the database. In online information retrieval, all systems employ 'inverted' files, i.e. all searchable terms, codes etc. from all the records on the database are put into one file, usually called the index file. The full record is held in a print file; the two files are linked by a postings file. When a searcher enters a search term or terms, the computer searches the index file for the terms, and locates the number of records with those terms from the postings file; when the searcher asks for the actual records to be displayed or printed, this information is obtained from the print file. When searching, it is possible to look at sections of the index file to see what terms are available for searching (see Chapter 6 and Part Two, Section 2.1).

The number of fields in a record varies from one database to another but there are a number of fields which are common to the majority; these are shown by the following examples, one from a bibliographic database (ERIC), and one from a source database (Shops):

(ERIC database on DIALOG)

Accession Number:	EJ340582 SO515537
Title:	Roman Catholic Secondary Schools: Falling Roles and Pupil Attitudes.
Author:	Francis, L. J.
Source:	Educational Studies, v12 n2 p119–27 1986.
Language:	English
Abstract:	Investigated the respective influence of a Catholic home and distance from school on attitudes of pupils in Roman Catholic secondary schools ..... etc.
Index Terms:	*Catholic Schools; *Declining Enrolment; *Religious Education; School Administration; Secondary Education; Student Attitudes.

(Shops database on Pergamon Financial Data Services)

Accession No.	:	445823072
Shop Name	:	Tandy
Activity Code	:	F654
Activity	:	COMPUTERS & AUDIO
Address	:	96 Kirkgate WAKEFIELD WEST YORKSHIRE
Post Code	:	WF1 1TB
Chain Size:	:	6, over 100 branches
Centre Name	:	WAKEFIELD
Review Date	:	01-APR-87

(b) Retrieval

The stages involved in the retrieval of information are analogous to the storage functions mentioned above.

(i) The analysis of the search question.
(ii) The translation of the concepts contained in the question into the indexing language of the database.

(iii) the formulation of the search statement – the order in which the terms chosen are to be sent to the computer, the relationships between these terms, and the commands to be used.

(i) As those who seek information do not always specify their information needs precisely, defining the exact scope of a search can be difficult. It is usually necessary for the intermediary undertaking the search to liaise in some depth with the end-user, often in a face-to-face reference interview, to elucidate and define the scope of the search, and to establish the basic concepts which are to be related in the search statement. The reference interview is dealt with in some detail in the next chapter.

(ii) This accomplished, the scope of each concept is translated into the language of the database; recourse would now be made to printed lists of subject headings or thesauri where these are available, if a controlled vocabulary is employed by the database; natural language terms would also be employed where necessary. If the database does not utilize a controlled vocabulary, the search statements would be expressed wholly in natural language terms with each concept defined as specifically as possible.

(iii) The relationships between terms are usually expressed in 'Boolean' logical statements, after the mathematician George Boole. The principal 'logical operators' are AND, OR and NOT.

George Boole (1815–64) devised a system of symbolic logic in which he used three operators (+, ×, –) to combine statements in symbolic form. His work was later developed by John Venn (1834–1923) who expressed Boolean logical relationships diagrammatically adopting Euler circles. Leonhard Euler (1707–83) was a Swiss mathematician who introduced the technique of expressing logical relationships graphically a century before Boole devised his logical operators. Boole's three operators are: logical sum (+), i.e. OR logic, logical product (×), i.e. AND logic, and logical difference (–), i.e. NOT logic. John Venn, in his book *Symbolic logic* (1881), used shading of segments of circles to show areas that were excluded from, as well as areas that were included in, the main logical expression.[2] All online information retrieval software is designed to allow the searcher to develop search statements using these three operators to link terms which have been selected to circumscribe the scope of the search.

Only rarely will a searcher wish to retrieve information under a single term; most subjects require a number of terms describing concepts which are related to each other, forming parts of a complex search statement. Logical product (AND logic) allows the searcher to specify the coincidence of two or more concepts; e.g. MUMMIES AND (BLOOD GROUPS) – both the term MUMMIES and the term BLOOD GROUPS must appear in a record before that record can be retrieved. Logical sum (OR logic) allows the searcher to specify alternative terms within a concept; e.g. (FALLING ROLLS) OR (DECLINING ENROLMENT) – records will be retrieved with either the term FALLING ROLLS or the term DECLINING ENROLMENT. Logical difference (NOT logic) gives the searcher the facility for excluding a set of records from the search; e.g. SEMICONDUCTORS NOT SILICON – this will retrieve all records with the term SEMICONDUCTORS except those which also have the term SILICON. Venn diagrams are helpful as part of the search strategy in demonstrating Boolean logical relationships. The terms to be ORed are represented as a group enclosed by a rectangle or circle (see Fig. 7(a) – ONLINE OPERATION OR REAL-TIME SYSTEMS etc.); ANDing is demonstrated by the intersection of superimposed rectangles or circles (see the shaded area in Fig. 7(a) where the concepts overlap); NOT logic is illustrated by Fig. 7(b) – (HYPERTENSION AND THERAPY) NOT DRUGS.

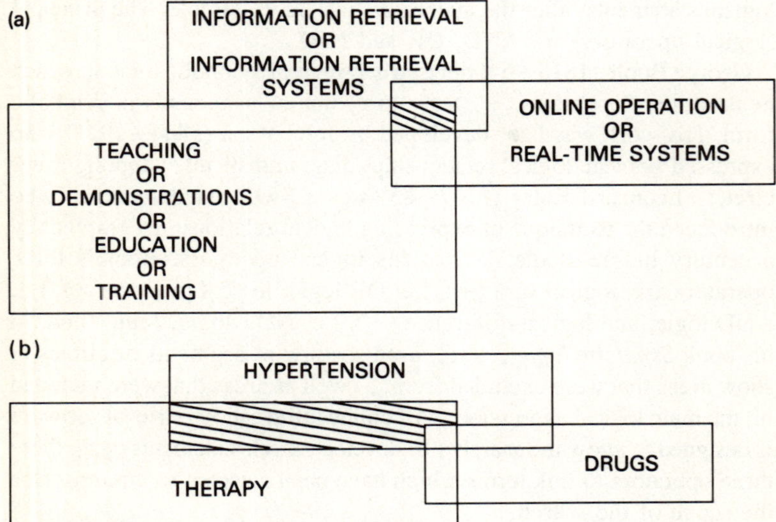

Fig. 7 Venn diagrams illustrating Boolean AND and NOT logical relationships

2 Command languages and menus

A command language is a set of operators which the searcher uses to instruct the computer to perform certain functions. Menus provide the searcher with a list of functions, from which one choice is made by pressing a specific key, thus avoiding the training needed to learn and use a command language.

The details of a command language will vary from one system to another, but the command language will contain the commands necessary to perform the basic search functions. These were conveniently grouped under five headings by Negus in a study which sought to devise a standard command language for EURONET in the late 1970s.[3] These headings are still valid, though the details have been brought up to date, reflecting advances over the last ten years. These headings are:

(i) General functions – instructions which are not strictly commands but rather functions of the terminal which allow the searcher to exercise control over the progress of the search, e.g. to erase a character wrongly typed, to interrupt the terminal's output when additional information is not needed etc.

(ii) Entering and leaving the system – logging-on and logging-off; requesting tutorial help online when in difficulty.

(iii) Selecting a particular database from the range of databases available on a system; changing databases; searching a number of databases either simultaneously or sequentially.

(iv) Formulating the search, e.g. entering the search terms to create sets of records; combining search terms and sets; obtaining displays of index terms, related terms; limiting the search by particular fields, e.g. language.

(v) Displaying the search product – choosing the format in which the records are to be displayed; choosing which records to display and whether they are to be printed online or offline (i.e. a command is entered requesting that records be printed by the online host and mailed to the searcher or end-user (see Chapter 6 and Part Two, Section 3.3 for more details)); downloading records onto microcomputer disc.

Negus identified 14 basic commands, most of which can be further modified. His set of commands, which became the basis for the Common Command Language (CCL) for EURONET/DIANE, is a useful summary of command functions:

CONNECT	to provide for logging-on
BASE	to identify the database to be searched
FIND	to input a search term
DISPLAY	to display a list of alphabetically linked terms
RELATE	to display logically related terms
SHOW	to print records online
PRINT	to print records offline
FORMAT	to specify the format to be displayed
DELETE	to delete search terms or print requests
SAVE	to save a search formulation for later use on the same or another database on the same system
OWN	to use a system's own command (e.g. those of ESA-IRS) in preference to the Common Command Language
STOP	to end the session, and log-off
MORE	to request the system to display more information, for instance to continue displaying an alphabetical list of terms
HELP	to obtain guidance online when in difficulty

The newcomer need not be put off tackling a command language, thinking that all the commands need to be learned before going online. As will be seen from working through the Units for each online host in Part Two, a good search can be conducted using a very few different commands. Indeed, some online hosts have attempted to reduce the number of commands needed; for example, DIALOG Information Services Inc. allow the searcher now to use one command – SELECT – in the place of three commands which were needed formerly, i.e. SELECT, COMBINE and LIMIT. The difference in the commands used to perform similar search functions when using different systems can cause difficulty to experienced and inexperienced searchers alike. However, some online hosts have made efforts to overcome these difficulties by allowing the searcher to use a variety of commands, some of which the searcher may be familiar with from using other systems, for the same function; for example, on Pergamon Financial Data Services (PFDS) the searcher can use either SELECT, COMBINE or FIND when searching for particular terms. On some systems, such as BLAISE, National Library of Medicine and ORBIT Search Service, terms are generally input without a preceding command; this is similar on Data-Star when the searcher is in search mode. On most systems, most searches can be conducted with the use of about five or six different commands only. PFDS and BRS, who have established a two-way gateway between their systems, hope shortly to allow customers to use either PFDS or

BRS commands on either system.

It is advisable for the newcomer to online systems to become familiar with one system before attempting to learn another; once the various functions and features of one system have been mastered using that system's command language, it should be relatively easy then to learn the commands to use similar functions and features on another system. If each system is not mastered, however, confusion can arise: for example, the command PRINT on the ORBIT, BLAISE, Wilsonline and other systems is used to display records online at the terminal, or 'offline' at the host's computer; whereas on DIALOG the command TYPE or DISPLAY is used to display records online, and PRINT to print records offline. Many online hosts now publish 'quick reference' guides to their commands and system features in a handy form which can be kept by the terminal; and for those who use several systems, there are guides which list the commands used by these systems, grouped under common headings. Two of these guides are: *Online international command chart 1987–88*, giving commands from the systems of 31 host systems, including CD-ROM retrieval systems; and the *Quick guide to online commands 1987*, giving commands from 12 host systems – related commands and features are grouped under seven main headings, with subheadings.[4,5] (Full bibliographic details are given in Appendix 1.)

Part Two of this book gives the principal commands from the seven systems covered, introducing the commands gradually throughout the three Units.

Menus are not new in online information retrieval (Finsbury Data Services introduced Textline – an index to business and related information – using menus in 1979), but an increase in the introduction of menu-driven systems has gone hand-in-hand with the online hosts' attempts at marketing their services direct to end-users; information specialists do not become redundant as a consequence of this, but their role changes to include training, help and advice, and conducting the more sophisticated searches. Menus are easier to use than command languages; the searcher does not have to learn and remember the commands and the many facilities available for searching. However, Conger believes that even menu-driven systems should offer some kind of command language option, because growing familiarity caused by frequent use usually generates a desire for the speed and flexibility provided by search commands.[6] As well as speed and flexibility, there are other considerations such as cost, and the type of database being searched – menus may be more suitable on company databases, for example, than on bibliographic databases. Pergamon Financial Data Services introduced a menu option for searching the JordanWatch database in 1984, and more recently have added other databases, e.g. BIS Infomat Newsfile, which can be searched on a menu basis – part of a complete programme to make online searching easier for the occasional user. BRS has menu-driven alternatives for all its databases; DIALOG's Business Connection and Medical Connection are menu-driven end-user services, as are some of their other databases, such as Quotes and Trading. On a wider scale, a new type of service has recently been introduced, the intelligent 'front-end' system, which gives access to over 1,000 databases from several online hosts, with the option of using menus or the command languages of the individual systems. A complete novice can request the service to search for information on a specific subject, and the rest is left up to the system, including choosing the database and online host to be used. They also provide an SOS service, where the searcher can communicate, via the terminal, with an information professional for help.

Chapter 6

The search

The basic principles of searching were outlined in the previous chapter; the search itself will now be analysed in more detail. The applications of the various commands and features described here, for individual host systems, can be found in Part Two.

1 Analysis of the enquiry

It has already been said that the end-users of information retrieval systems do not always specify their information needs precisely, and this situation is not unfamiliar to librarians and information officers whatever retrieval methods are available. Lancaster states the importance of defining precisely what is required:

> While the requester himself might successfully browse through the literature on the basis of an ill-defined need, it is impossible to prepare a successful search strategy for machine search on the same vague basis. If a machine search is to yield useful results, we must do as much as possible to obtain request statements that explicitly delineate the actual information need. The wider the gap between stated request and information need, the less successful the search is likely to be.[1]

Where the online search is being conducted by an intermediary on behalf of an end-user, the request for an online search may come in a number of different ways – from a personal call, by telephone, telex, letter, special online request forms, electronic mail or other electronic media. Whichever way is used, it is important for the intermediary to obtain as much information about the enquiry as possible. This will often involve a face-to-face reference interview with the end-user where this is possible, and sometimes it is helpful to have the end-user present during the search. A combination of the precise subject knowledge of the end-user and the system knowledge of the intermediary will normally produce the best results. If the enquiry is not well articulated before the search by the end-user the intermediary needs to help in clarifying and analysing the enquiry. Knapp has observed that all too often search analysts merely replicate the end-user's statement rather than gain the sense of the underlying meaning.[2]

Many online search services operate at a distance from their end-users and it is not always possible to conduct a face-to-face interview. Where this personal contact is not possible, it is important for the end-user to give precise information relating to the enquiry, whichever method is used to convey the enquiry to the intermediary. The type of information that is normally required may be illustrated by the 'Computer Search Request Form' (see Fig. 8) used by the Lancashire Library, the public library serving the county of Lancashire in the United Kingdom. The form is designed to elicit the type of information most helpful to the intermediary responsible for analysing the enquiry and constructing a search statement. Under 'Statement of the specific subject of the enquiry' or similar wording, the end-user is given the opportunity to elaborate on what is required and, equally important sometimes, what is not required. Keywords under which the end-user has found useful records previously or which are known to be used by authors in relation to the subject of the enquiry are of particular importance. The end-user will often have searched the subject manually before, and the keywords found can be especially useful if the online search is to be conducted on the database corresponding to the indexing or abstracting publication used previously by the end-user. Records retrieved previously from other sources can suggest additional keywords which can be incorporated into the search statement and they will also be the basis for an author search if particular authors are known to have contributed significantly to the subject being explored. They can also be used during a search when making relevance judgements on records retrieved; and they can be used on citation indexes, such as Science Citation Index and Social Science Citation Index – by inputting the known reference, it is possible to retrieve records to any more recent papers that have cited the known reference. Any limitations on the search – such as language (English only, or not Russian), publication date (only papers published since 1984), number of records that can be handled by the end-user (a complete state-of-the-art search involving hundreds of records, or a handful of the most recent records), or cost, should be decided where possible before the search commences.

Even when all this information is gathered together, there are still things to do before commencing with preparing the actual search.

THE LANCASHIRE LIBRARY
REFERENCE AND INFORMATION SERVICE

Harris Library,
Market Square,
Preston PR1 2PP
Tel: Preston 53191

Ref No.________

COMPUTER SEARCH REQUEST FORM

Name: ______________________________
Company/Organisation: ______________________________
Address: ______________________________
____
Tel. No: ______________ Date: ______________

Please tick boxes below where appropriate

Statement of the specific subject of the enquiry:
(Please give specific and detailed information about the subject of your enquiry; it would help if you could also give the level or purpose of the enquiry, e.g., patient care, industrial use, graduate research, etc.)

(continue over if necessary)

Keywords: (Words or phrases under which the information may be indexed)

Relevant references already known to you:
1.
2.

**Language:* English only | Any language | The following languages only: ______________ ______________

***Time span* (the years to be covered by the search):______________

Type of search:

A. *Limited search.* No charge will be made. Search limited to about 15 minutes online time and up to 25 references.***

B. *Full search.* A charge will be made where search exceeds the limits of A. above. (£1 per minute and 10p per reference)†

***Maximum number of references required, including the first 25 free references ☐

Your limit on the cost of the search, e.g. £5, £10, £30, etc. ☐

Please state the last date on which this information would be of use: ______________

Would you like to be present during the search? YES NO
If YES, we will contact you to arrange a convenient time.

Please give details of any special requirements for this search: ______________
____
____

* The ability to limit references to a particular language is available on many, but not all databases.
** The time span covered by databases varies: normally the whole database will be searched unless you specify a particular time span.
*** There is no guarantee that any particular number of references will be found.
† Subject to change.

Please return this form to the nearest branch of the Lancashire Library, or to the Harris Library, from which further information may be obtained.

For office use only:

Date received	Date searched	Date despatched	Searcher	Cost

Fig. 8 Lancashire Library computer search request form

One question that has to be answered is: is the enquiry suitable for an online search? End-users may ask for an online search, being unaware both of what is available online and often of what is available in other forms in their library or information service. The intermediary has to decide the sources to use to answer the enquiry in the best possible way – sometimes the enquiry will be answered from non-online sources wholly, sometimes from online sources wholly, and often from a combination of both.

Whatever sources are being used, the intermediary needs to have as good an understanding of the subject as possible, particularly in the context of a face-to-face interview. Some intermediaries are subject specialists, searching in a specific discipline only, such as chemistry; some may be subject specialists conducting searches in a wider field such as the sciences; others may be required to search in many or all subject fields. It would be impossible for the intermediary in the last category to be a subject specialist in everything, but some background reading, coupled with the help from the end-user, will avoid the situation of typing in a number of unintelligible terms and hoping the unintelligible records coming out of the computer are the correct ones! End-users are invariably happy to explain their requirements to the intermediary, realizing that the intermediary cannot be a subject specialist in everything, but can, with a sound knowledge of the online systems, help produce the required result. Somerville has listed a number of 'Dos and Don'ts' of the reference interview, among them being: do 'ask questions of the user to ensure your understanding of the subject'; don't 'try to save time by not doing the background reading'.[3]

The next stage in the search process is normally defining the concepts which are to be related in the search ('normally', because there are different approaches to conducting a search – see below). This information would become apparent in the preparation and/or reference interview detailed above. For example, 'Blood groups of Egyptian mummies' has three basic concepts – blood groups, mummies and the geographical concept Egypt. Only rarely will a subject search be conducted under a single concept; such enquiries can usually be answered conveniently from printed abstracting and indexing sources and will therefore not usually be the subject of an online search; however, there are occasions when the end-user does require 'everything there is' on one specific concept – such a recent enquiry searched by the author was on Carpal Tunnel Syndrome, which retrieved literally hundreds of records from just one database; often this type of enquiry can be limited by such things as language, date of publication, or where the term is a major concept only. The majority of online searches on bibliographic databases are research-oriented enquiries which exhibit complex subject relationships which are difficult to locate in printed sources, whose subject access points are limited to perhaps two or three subject index entries, or classified displays of related items. Normally the number of concepts required to co-occur in a search is between two and three. In a report by Houghton et al., the average number of concepts required to co-occur by members of a group learning to use MEDLINE was 2.21, and 2.46 by more experienced searchers using the database for retrieval of drug-related information.[4] In a study at the Ames Centre described by Lancaster and Fayern, the average number of concept groups was 2.7.[5]

2 Database selection

The next question in the search process is: which database or databases do I use? This is not always an easy question to answer today, as the number of databases available is so great; in the last edition of this book, published in 1984, we quoted 762 bibliographic databases and 1,083 databanks listed in the *EUSIDIC database guide*; Cuadra lists 3,699 databases in 1988. (Please see the overview of the online industry in Chapter 3 for more details.) Many databases are to be found on two or more online hosts; the subject matter covered by these databases on the whole is vast, and the subject matter within each database often includes fringe subjects which the searcher without the necessary background information and experience would not expect.

What databases exist? Each online host provides lists of the databases on that service; further details of each individual database are usually available in a manual, and often online also. Many online host systems have online indexes to their databases – all the basic indexes from all the databases are amalgamated into one index, so the searcher can use keyword searching to ascertain which databases are likely to be the most fruitful in retrieving records on the subject of the enquiry. An example of such an index is DIALOG's Dialindex: (The enquirer is interested in the easter egg market; this example shows only a few databases – further databases could have been chosen):

```
File 583: BIS INFOMAT WORLD BUSINESS
          84 – 88/MAY 20
File  16: PROMT  –  72 – 88/MAY, WEEK 3
File 196: FINDEX DIR. OF MARKET RESEARCH
          JAN 82 – FEB 88
File 635: BUSINESS DATELINE –
          85 – 88/MAY, WK 4

File        Items     Description
-----       -------   ----------------
```

The searcher first chooses likely databases.

```
? s easter(f)egg? ?

583: BIS INFOMAT WORLD BUSINESS
     84 – 88/MAY 20
              280 EASTER
              640 EGG? ?
               69 EASTER(F)EGG? ?
```

This command asks the system to SELECT any records with the words EASTER and EGG or EGGS in the same field (F) anywhere in the complete record.

```
 16: PROMT  –  72 – 88/MAY, WEEK 3
              178 EASTER
             3765 EGG? ?
               27 EASTER(F)EGG? ?

196: FINDEX DIR. OF MARKET RESEARCH
     JAN 82 – FEB 88
                1 EASTER
                8 EGG? ?
                0 EASTER(F)EGG? ?

635: BUSINESS DATELINE  –  85 – 88/MAY,
     WK 4
              207 EASTER
              953 EGG? ?
               29 EASTER(F)EGG? ?
?
```

From this search, the searcher can obtain a good idea of those databases which might, with further modification to the search, retrieve useful records.

There are sources that give details of databases from several or most online hosts, including databases in specific subject areas; some of these are in printed form, many with an online equivalent (see Appendix 1). Once you have drawn up a short list of databases using the sources available, how do you narrow down this list to the one or more databases which you will actually search and in what order of priority? There is a need at this stage to look at the databases in some detail, using the sources supplied by the hosts and any of the other sources available which give detailed information about databases. The following gives some criteria for selecting a database:

(i) Subject coverage

What subject matter does the database aim to include? Is it discipline oriented, such as CA Search or BIOSIS? Is it problem oriented, such as TOXLINE, Enviroline? Is it mission oriented, such as Nasa? Does it set out to be multi-disciplinary, such as Scisearch, Social Scisearch, NTIS? Reference to the documentation supplied by the host, and/or the other sources mentioned above, will give an indication of the scope of a database, together with any information available from the database producers themselves. This latter information may take the form of a user guide, or a list of controlled terms, or a combination of these. Articles on particular databases can be found in such journals as *Database* and other online journals (see Appendix 1). Where the online host offers an online index to its databases, this can be the most precise way of finding out whether a particular subject is covered or not.

(ii) Comprehensiveness

How comprehensively is the subject matter covered? Does the database include the principal journals in the field? Often a publication separate from the database manuals produced by the online hosts is necessary for a list of journals covered. Are all the papers in the journals indexed or only some? For example, in most journals covered by MEDLINE all papers are indexed, but some of the journals are only indexed selectively. What is the size of the database? Though quantity is no substitute for quality, this can often help in deciding which database might be the most fruitful. When searching retrospectively it is important to know when the database coverage begins. Many of the databases have online coverage now for 15 to 20 years, and more in some cases: CA Search begins in 1967, BIOSIS and INSPEC in 1969, Commonwealth Agricultural Bureaux Abstracts in 1972 and Dissertation Abstracts Online in 1861! On the other hand, many databases, particularly those without a hard copy equivalent, cover just a few years.

(iii) Currency

How current is the database? The majority are updated monthly or more often; others are updated quarterly or less often. With the great increase in the last two years in the provision of business-related information – company information, indexes to business publications including newspapers, access to stock exchanges, newswire services etc. – the updating of these sources is down in some cases to minutes. For example, DIALOG's Businesswire and Reuters are updated every 15 minutes, DIALOG's access to US Stock Exchange is delayed 20 minutes. Ojala makes the important distinction between 'timeliness' and 'time-lag' in the field of business information, giving examples on Nexis, Dow Jones News/Retrieval and DIALOG. On DIALOG's First Release news service, updating is every 15 minutes, but 'time-lag' is 30–45 minutes – considered very good; on Dow Jones there is continuous updating, with a time-lag of about 90 seconds.[6] A database may be updated monthly, but how much time has elapsed since the papers were published? Some databases have their records online weeks in advance of the hard copy equivalents finding their way on to the shelves of libraries. For example, the National Library of Medicine introduced twice monthly updating of MEDLINE in April 1988 on an experimental basis; previously both MEDLINE and SDILINE were updated at the beginning of each month with records not to be found in the printed *Index medicus* until the following month. Updating of a particular database may vary from one online host to another. Records on MEDLINE can be online within four or five weeks of the paper being published.

(iv) Subject overlap

How much overlap exists between databases? For instance, the problem oriented database TOXLINE is made up of a number of subfiles, one of which is the Toxicity Bibliography from MEDLINE, another the National Institute for Occupational Safety and Health (NIOSH); and its companion database TOXLIT includes Chemical Biological Activities (CBAC) from CA Search, and International Pharmaceutical Abstracts (IPA), which appears also on other services as a separate database. Many of the same cancer-related records would appear in MEDLINE, EMBASE and CANCERLINE. About 50% of Exceptional Child Education Resources would appear in ERIC; there is about 37% overlap in journal coverage between MEDLINE and EMBASE – of the 6,030 unique titles covered by both databases, EMBASE covers 4,349 and MEDLINE 3,881, with an overlap of 2,206.[7]

(v) Record content

How much information is included in an individual record on a particular database? The online host's manual will give this information, calling each part of the record variously a field, an element, a category or a paragraph. All bibliographic records would give author, title, source (journal title, volume, number, date); after that, there can be a wide variation in what information is available. Most databases would have at least one field with index terms (see (vi) below); many have abstracts; they are useful, not only because each word in the abstract is normally searchable as a keyword, but they give more help to the end-user when deciding whether to read the original paper or not, and sometimes they may even contain sufficient information to make it unnecessary for the end-user to obtain the original paper. Is the corporate source given – i.e. the company, educational establishment or other organization where the author is employed? On company databases, is just the name and address given (e.g. the ICC database covering all UK registered companies gives company name, registered address, registered company number, and brief (unsearchable) details), or does the record give further information helpful in identifying particular groups of companies suitable for a marketing mail-shot (e.g. Dun & Bradstreet's Dun's Market Identifiers, which has 200,000 records of UK companies, giving company name, address, telephone and telex number, directors, ownership, sales figures, number of employees, and Standard Industrial Classification (SIC) code for type of business)? Industrial Market Locations is a similar database. Where financial information on a particular company is required, does the database give brief information (e.g. Dun's Market Identifiers, Trinet, Key British Enterprises (KBE)), or more detailed information (e.g. ICC Financial Datasheets, JordanWatch, or Dun's Financial Records Plus)? Some databases have a large number of 'elements' in each record – MEDLINE has a maximum of 38; LCMARC and BNB have more possible elements; Dun's Financial Records Plus has up to 50. In Social Scisearch, any citations made by the author at the end of the original paper are included in the online record.

(vi) Indexing

How comprehensive and exhaustive is the indexing? On Social Scisearch there is title word searching only, with no index term fields. Most other databases have in addition to that an index term field, usually for controlled language indexing terms – for example, ERIC, COMPENDEX, INSPEC, MEDLINE – and often a further index term field, variously called Supplementary Terms, Identifiers, Uncontrolled Terms, Free Terms, Textwords, which normally contain proper names, geographical terms, or subject terms important in the record but not covered by the controlled language. Other databases employ natural or uncontrolled terms, for example CA Search, BIOSIS and CANCERLINE. On MEDLINE most papers are indexed in depth – at least 12 index terms from the controlled language Medical Subject Headings, though some papers are less thoroughly indexed, using about five index terms. Does the database employ some form of classification scheme for searching wider concepts (e.g. MeSH Tree Structures, see Fig. 6)?

(vii) Types of publications included in the database
What types of publications are included? Sometimes, only one type is included, for example patents on World Patent Index, or standards on BSI Standardline or IHS International Standards and Specifications, or conference proceedings on Conference Papers Index or Conference Proceedings Index. On bibliographic databases, are journal papers only included, or are there other types of publication included also, such as monographs, theses, patents, newspapers? On business news databases, are only newspapers included, or are business journals included also?

(viii) Cost
Consideration must be given to the cost of using different databases. If your short list of databases has been narrowed down to two databases using the criteria detailed above, either of which might answer the enquiry satisfactorily, then cost can play a part in your choice of which database to search first. If it is likely that an enquiry will be answered adequately on ERIC at $30 an hour, would it be wise to search Social Scisearch at $120 an hour when the expected results from both are similar? In practice, you might search both to ensure comprehensive coverage, but as the time taken online on the initial database is normally longer than on subsequent databases (the initial input of the search, and any modifications to the search statements as a result of records retrieved, printing out records and saving the search for use on subsequent databases are done on the initial database; after that, the saved search can be recalled and executed on subsequent databases in a much shorter time), it is advisable to search the cheaper database first. Online hosts and database producers give information about the cost of their databases, and such publications as *Clover comparative cost chart*, covering 19 online hosts, give prices of all the databases on several online hosts, so a quick comparison can be made of the cost of different databases.[8] An example from the *Clover chart* gives the cost of a 'standard search' (10 minutes online, five online displays and 50 offline prints) for Analytical Abstracts as £17.86 on Data-Star and £25.34 on DIALOG – but in many cases

choice would be affected by other criteria used for selecting the online host (see below).

A number of online hosts are making some of these decisions about selecting appropriate databases easier by introducing the facility for searching a number of databases at once. For example, on ESA-IRS the searcher can 'Cluster' up to eight databases together and search them all at the same time; some of these Clusters on certain topics are predefined, e.g. Foodscience (File 251) includes the databases Food Science and Technology Abstracts, Packaging Abstracts and Vitis. There is a set charge of 115 Accounting Units (AU) per hour – offline and online print costs are charged according to the normal charges for the constituent databases. DIALOG have introduced 'OneSearch', where up to 20 databases can be searched at the same time; DIALOG's accounting software tracks the time spent in each file and charges accordingly – there are no additional charges.[9]

3 Online host selection

Cuadra lists 555 online hosts in 1988;[10] this and other sources giving online hosts are given in Appendix 1. In practice an organization would have decided to sign up with one or a few online hosts, and the decision in terms of a particular enquiry is to choose from the small number of different online hosts which the organization uses. Sometimes the database required can only be accessed on one online host, and therefore the problem as to which host to use does not arise. However, often the same database will be available from a number of different hosts, and the decision as to which is the most appropriate must be made. What criteria should be used?

(i) Retrospective coverage

Do the online hosts have all the database, or just part of it? How many years are covered by the database on different host systems?

(ii) Currency

Does one online host update the same database earlier than another? If very current information is required, days, hours or minutes could be important.

(iii) Separate files for large databases

Do online hosts offer the large databases, such as CA Search, MEDLINE and BIOSIS, in one complete file, or in several smaller files, or both?

For example, on Data-Star CA Search is available as one complete file and is also available as separate files, corresponding to the Collective Indexes 8–12. From a searching point of view, it is quicker to search smaller files, particularly the current file when you require the most recent records only; the main advantage of searching the complete file is that there is no necessity to save searches and change files; there is comprehensive coverage where currency is not necessarily an important consideration, but it can be slower than searching smaller, separate files.

(iv) Record content

Do all the online hosts make available all the elements of a record which are available for a database? An important example is CA Search – abstracts are available only on CAS Online via STN International; the leasing agreement of this producer with other online hosts does not allow the latter to offer abstracts for this database.

(v) Search features

The searching features offered by different online hosts often determine which host to use. If a particular search requires the use of proximity searching, or stringsearching, or both (see later in this Chapter), which online hosts offer these features? A chemical search may require the capability of left-hand truncation (see later in this Chapter); which hosts make this feature available? Can a search on a particular database be limited to a certain language on one online host and not on another?

(vi) Cross-file searching

This can take a number of forms: saving a search on one database and searching it on one or more other databases; saving a search on one database and transferring elements of records on to another database, for example PRINT SELECT (ORBIT) and MAP (DIALOG), and then conducting a further search on the new database using these elements;[11, 12] and finally multi-database searching, mentioned above, where a number of databases can be searched at the same time.

(vii) Cost

What is the cost of the same database on different hosts? This is a complex problem. It cannot be resolved by simply selecting the host who levies the lowest connect time charge for searching a particular database; other factors must be considered:

(a) The telecommunications charges to access the online host; a searcher in California may have local, toll-free access to one online host, but have to pay international telecommunications rates to access a system in the United Kingdom, even though the connect time charge for accessing that system is less than the one in California.

(b) The charges for printing retrieved records, online or offline, and for downloading records on to an in-house database; do these vary from one host to another?

(c) Most online hosts offer discounts on high usage of their databases; if the amount of searching done in a year is sufficient to make discounts an important consideration and presuming all the databases you require are on the one host system, it may be worth concentrating all your searching on one system to maximize the advantages of the discounts offered.

(d) If a searcher is more familiar and at ease with a particular host system, it is often more cost effective to use this system, even though the database being used has cheaper charges on another system.

(e) Response time on one system may be much slower than on another, particularly when complex search statements are entered by the searcher.

It can be time-consuming continually checking all the different elements of costs for a database on different hosts; publications such as the *Clover comparative cost chart* mentioned above seek to assemble all this information in one place.

The above criteria relate to the choice of an online host for a particular database, assuming that the searcher is equally familiar with the systems of all the online hosts providing that database. Often the searcher will be more familiar with, and more at ease with, one system than another, and this can be a very important consideration, particularly when working under pressures of time. Ojala has observed of the searcher seeking business information (but this could equally well apply in other information environments)

> you can overdo the planning. Often in the business environment, you don't have time to thoroughly plan a search. When the fast paced business world demands an immediate answer, the searcher who sits down and carefully writes out an elaborate search strategy will soon be replaced. Logon 'while' thinking. Pick a database you could search in your sleep, and hope for the best.[13]

Familiarity with a particular online host's system might provide a quicker, more efficient search, thus overcoming any cost differences vis-à-vis another host with whose system the searcher is less familiar; but this would not necessarily give the best search result, for the search could suffer from the lack of some of the advantages (such as those mentioned in (i)–(vii) above) offered by other online hosts. On this subject, Bawden, looking at the history of the choice of online host, comments that initially the choice was commonly enforced by the unique availability of a required database; somewhat later, system performance and telecommunications reliability were predominant factors; more recently costs, differing implementations of databases, and the subjective preferences of the searcher have been the main considerations.[14]

4 Search strategy

Once decisions have been made about the concepts involved in the enquiry, and which database(s) and online host(s) to use, the searcher needs to decide what strategy to adopt, and to prepare that strategy accordingly. The 'strategy' is the overall plan for the whole search, and 'operates above specific term choice and command use'.[15] The most common strategy involves translating the concepts involved in the enquiry into the language of the database(s) to be searched, using whatever system features are appropriate, using Boolean operators to show the relationships between different terms in the search strategy, and keeping some ideas in reserve for possible modification of the search while online after seeing the results from the initial search statement entered. This approach is described by Hawkins as the 'building blocks' type of search.[16] Other strategies described and illustrated by him include the 'successive fractions' and 'citation pearl growing' approaches. In the 'successive fractions' approach, the searcher works from the general to the particular, beginning with the whole database and gradually breaking down the whole into a smaller and smaller fraction until to narrow the search further would begin to omit relevant records. The 'citation pearl growing' approach works in the opposite direction; beginning with a key record already known (a 'citation pearl' of great price!), this is first retrieved on the database and then the search extended in a number of ways: using the keywords ascribed to the 'citation pearl' to see if other records use the same keywords; finding other records by the author of the 'citation pearl' on a similar or closely related subject; finding, from the 'corporate source' field (if it exists) of the 'citation pearl', if any other records on a similar subject have emanated from the same organization under different authors; finding, where citation searching exists on the database (e.g. Scisearch), which authors have cited the 'citation pearl' at the end of their papers. In these ways a body of records is gradually built up, all connected with the original key record.

Returning to the 'building blocks' approach, each concept identified in the enquiry requires to be translated into the language of the database chosen. If the database employs a controlled language, reference can be made to the appropriate thesaurus or list of subject headings, where these are available; if they are not available in hard copy, they can be found online by looking at the basic index for the database. As an alternative to, or in addition to, the controlled language, it is possible to enter 'natural language' terms – any terms which the searcher thinks an author might have used to describe a particular concept; the system would normally search all the fields of each record where there are keywords, i.e. title, keyword fields, abstract etc. The INSPEC database employs a controlled language – the INSPEC Thesaurus;[17] an enquiry on the teaching of online information retrieval involves three concepts: information retrieval, teaching and online. The INSPEC Thesaurus gives the following terms which might be used for this search: INFORMATION RETRIEVAL SYSTEMS, INFORMATION RETRIEVAL, TEACHING, DEMONSTRATIONS, EDUCATION, TRAINING, ONLINE OPERATION, REAL-TIME SYSTEMS. The MEDLINE database employs a controlled language – Medical Subject Headings (MeSH);[18] an enquiry on the use of meditation to treat hypertension involves two main concepts: meditation and hypertension. MeSH gives HYPERTENSION as a term (this can be EXPLODEd to include the more specific terms HYPERTENSION, MALIGNANT and HYPERTENSION, PORTAL as well – see Part Two, BLAISE-LINK, 2.3) but not MEDITATION (there are MeSH terms for YOGA, RELAXATION, RELAXATION TECHNICS, THINKING but not for MEDITATION specifically), but this can be entered as a 'natural language' term or 'textword'; the concept 'treat' in this enquiry might be presumed, but could be included as a 'subheading' relating to HYPERTENSION on the MEDLINE database.

While choosing the appropriate terms, the searcher would also be applying Boolean logic and showing the relationships between the terms. The logical operator OR would join together each term within a concept, for example, in the 'online' concept of the above enquiry:

ONLINE OPERATION OR REAL-TIME SYSTEMS

i.e. the system would retrieve all the records to EITHER of those two terms. Each separate concept would be arranged in this way, and then the logical operator AND would be used to join the concepts together;

this would have the effect of retrieving records which contain at least one term from each of the three concepts, as shown in the shaded area of Fig. 7(a).

The way the searcher would enter this on the system would depend on the online host being used; Part Two of this book gives this information in some detail for the seven systems covered.

Terms, whether from a controlled language or not, are not all that can be used as part of a search strategy. Sometimes a concept cannot be described adequately by a term or terms; a concept covering a wide subject area may require some form of classification code; these are available on most databases. For example, it is possible on CA Search to use a section code in a search. There are currently 80 sections on CA Search; section 4 covers toxicology – the toxic effects of chemicals, venoms and toxins on plants, nonmammals and mammals, including subcellular studies. A more comprehensive search would be conducted by using such a code to describe the concept of toxicology than by merely using the term TOXIC? (the question mark on some systems is a truncation symbol; the use of this symbol would retrieve any word beginning with the word stem entered – in this case TOXIC, TOXICOLOGY, TOXICOLOGICAL etc. (see Part Two, 2.2 for more details of truncation symbol)). If a narrower search is required on CA Search, subsections can also be searched. When searching LCMARC and BNB, it is possible to use Dewey Decimal Classification numbers in a similar way; if a wide search is required on beverage technology, the broad class number 663: could be used (the colon (:) is the truncation symbol on BLAISE-LINE) – this would retrieve all records beginning with 663. If a more specific search is required, a more precise number could be used – for wines and wine-making this would be 663.2:. A similar feature is available on the MEDLINE database; the list of controlled terms used on that database, the Medical Subject Headings,[18] is arranged in an hierarchical structure and it is possible by using one of the subject headings to retrieve records, not only with that heading, but also with any other more specific terms lower down the hierarchy; for example, by prefixing the term PEPTIC ULCER by the word EXPLODE, the searcher can retrieve not only records with PEPTIC ULCER as a MeSH heading, but also the more specific terms such as DUODENAL ULCER, ESOPHAGITIS, PEPTIC etc. – see Fig. 6. Most databases have some form of classification code which can be searched, and some others also have subsections, e.g. TOXLINE and Commonwealth Agricultural Bureaux Abstracts. Some databases have search fragments already stored on the system, and these can be recalled and used in a search, e.g. education topics on British National Bibliography (BNB) on BLAISE-LINE,[19] and 'pre-explosions' on MEDLINE, where some of the most commonly used MeSH headings are EXPLODEd in advance and stored, e.g. ENZYMES, NEOPLASMS.

In the field of chemistry, an important element used in searching particular substances is the Chemical Abstracts Service's Registry Number – a unique number assigned to individual substances, e.g. the registry number for borax glass is 1330-43-4. In the field of life sciences, the BIOSIS database uses 'concept codes', e.g. 15002 Blood and Lymph Studies.

There are features also for narrowing down a concept – sometimes even one word covering a concept is too wide or retrieves too many records. Sometimes these features may be applicable to specific databases; for example, subheadings on MEDLINE (ASPIRIN/AE will narrow down the term ASPIRIN to papers dealing with Adverse Effects (AE) of Aspirin only); on COMPENDEX subheadings can be applied to controlled language terms from Subject Headings for Engineering (SHE), e.g.

COMPUTER SYSTEMS, DIGITAL(L)MULTIPROCESSING;

on CA Search RN=1330-43-4U would retrieve only those occurrences of the registry number for borax glass relating to its Uses. On some databases it is possible to limit a search to where a term is a major concept in the original paper; for example, *ASPIRIN on MEDLINE would retrieve only those records where Aspirin is a major concept in the index term field, and hence in the paper.

Word proximity is a feature which is offered by most online hosts; two or more words are input with an appropriate proximity operator, and the system will retrieve records accordingly; for example, the two words FISH and FARMING can be entered in a variety of ways (a few examples only are given below; fuller details are given of these proximity operators for individual systems in Part Two, Section 2.2):

(a) As a phrase FISH FARMING; e.g. on DIALOG, ORBIT and IRS this would appear as FISH(W)FARMING – the (W)ord proximity operator indicates that the words input should be adjacent to each other and in the order in which they were input. On Data-Star this would be input as FISH ADJ FARMING and on Pergamon as WN 2 FISH,FARMING.

(b) The words appearing adjacent to each other, but in any order – on DIALOG this would appear as FISH(N)FARMING; (N=near).

(c) The words appearing in the same sentence in any order anywhere in the record – on ESA-IRS this would appear as FISH(S)FARMING.

(d) The words appearing in the same field in any order anywhere in the record – on Data-Star this would appear as FISH SAME FARMING.

(e) The words appearing anywhere in any order in the same record – on DIALOG this would appear as FISH(C)FARMING; (C=citation).

Another feature available on all systems is truncation, i.e. the stem of a word is input, followed by the appropriate truncation symbol, and the system will retrieve any word beginning with that word stem. For example, on Data-Star where the symbol is a dollar sign, inputting TOXIC$ will retrieve TOXIC, TOXICITY, TOXICOLOGY etc. There are methods for limiting the number of letters after the word stem; on DIALOG, inputting ION? ? will retrieve only the word ION and words with one more letter only, e.g. IONS, but not IONIZATION etc. Truncation symbols can be used within words; e.g. on DIALOG WOM?N will retrieve both WOMAN and WOMEN. Examples of truncation are given in Part Two, Section 2.2.

The search statement may need to incorporate limitations such as the language of the original papers, the date of entry into the databases, the date of publication etc. These limitations could form part of the original statement or be selected simply to use later in the search if a large number of records needs to be reduced in size.

Much planning, therefore, can be done before going online, but it must always be remembered that the searcher is dealing with an interactive system and will often have to modify the search, change tactics[15] while in the middle of a search, as a result of what has been retrieved by the initial search statement; indeed, the interactive nature of online systems is one of their main strengths. What tactics can be employed to modify the search while online if the results of the original strategy are unsatisfactory? The amount of modification will depend on the complexity of the search, the content of the database, and other variables. In the report previously cited, the number of modifications made after the original search formulation had been entered and processed was 3.21 by the group learning to use MEDLINE and 6.61 by the more experienced users.[4]

What are the occasions when modification is necessary and what are the options open to the searcher?

(a) Sometimes modifications are not needed, or no modifications would be appropriate; e.g. if a pharmacist wished to know of any papers showing that treatment with a particular drug induced a specific side effect and the search retrieved no relevant records, there might be little point in trying from a different angle, apart from searching a number of different databases; this is presuming that the original search statement included any variations on the drug's name, its registry number if available, etc.

(b) If the initial search statement realizes too many records, however, there are several courses of action which could be adopted:

(i) The searcher might introduce another concept using one or more terms, and AND the result with the retrieved set of records. If extra terms used in this context have not been considered and checked earlier it is often helpful to display the index terms used in one or two relevant records from the retrieved set; these lists of index terms will often suggest additional relevant terms which could be used to narrow down the search and make it more specific to the enquiry. For example, the end-user might have requested all information relating to problems of radioactivity; using the Health and Safety Executive's database HSELINE the searcher would be overwhelmed by the number of records retrieved; it might be helpful to introduce another concept, e.g. a geographic or environmental concept, to reduce the number of records.

(ii) If more than one term has been used to describe a concept in the original search statement in an attempt to achieve maximum recall (i.e. the retrieval of every possible record which includes the concept) the number of records listed for each term might indicate that one or more of these terms is used to describe a very broad subject area and might encompass too wide an area for this particular search. A new combination of sets, omitting one or more of these terms, would result in a smaller, possibly more precise set of records.

(iii) Most databases offer the searcher the option of limiting a set by certain criteria, e.g. by range of publication dates, accession numbers, volume numbers; and by language of the original paper, by corporate source (i.e. the organization where the author works), and other criteria to narrow down the original set of records retrieved (see Part Two, Section 3.1).

(iv) When indexing papers for their databases, some producers adopt a policy of 'weighting' terms which describe the most important concepts in the original paper; the searcher can then limit a set of records to those occasions when the term chosen describes a major concept only in the original paper (e.g. ERIC, MEDLINE) (see Part Two, Section 2.1).

(v) When displaying records from a retrieved set, the order in which they are displayed is in reverse-chronological order, i.e. the latest records input on the database are displayed first. If no other way of modifying a large set of records is apparent, and presuming that the records in the set are as precise as possible to answer the enquiry, the searcher can limit the search by printing out the first 'n' number of records from the set – these would be the latest records input on the database, and usually the latest published papers.

(c) If the original strategy realizes no records, or fewer than expected, some possible courses of action could be:

(i) On average, in the initial search statement, between two and three concepts are required to co-occur in a record; sometimes this might be four or even five; rarely would it be one. If no records are retrieved, it might be possible to dispense with the concept which is least important, and combine the other concepts. For instance, if there are three concepts:

		ELECTRIC EQUIPMENT		
FISH		OR		
		ELECTRONIC TEST		
OR		EQUIPMENT		EFFECTIVE-
FISHERIES	AND	OR	AND	NESS
OR		ELECTRIC MEASURING		
FISHES		INSTRUMENTS		

(from NTIS)

and when they are ANDed together the result is nil retrieval, the third concept described by the term EFFECTIVENESS could perhaps be omitted, as it could be too restrictive.

(ii) Perhaps the terms chosen to describe a concept are too specific; can other terms be introduced to more fully describe a concept? If the searcher has been using terms from a controlled language and no other terms from it seem appropriate, does the database include the use of natural language terms? If so, these could be ORd to those already chosen to widen the search while still maintaining its relevance to the enquiry. If one or more records have been retrieved, a list of the terms used to index the records might prove useful, as was seen earlier when considering methods of narrowing down a search. This can be achieved by displaying the records in a format which includes index terms, or by using one of the features such as ZOOM on ESA-IRS or GET on ORBIT for analysing search results (see Part Two, Section 2.3).

(iii) Does the database employ a classification scheme or similar feature for including a large number of subject-related terms with just one input? For example, as shown above, selecting section 4 of CA Search might describe the concept more comprehensively than attempting to OR together all the terms relevant to toxicity (see Part Two, Section 2.3).

(iv) When using natural language, all the different variations of a term must be used; truncation might help here, where the searcher inputs the stem of a word, e.g. FISH, followed by the truncation symbol. This would have the effect of retrieving records indexed under such terms as FISH, FISHERIES, FISHING etc. (see Part Two, Section 2.2).

(v) Does the system offer any other retrieval methods unused so far, such as proximity searching, stringsearching etc.? (See Part Two, Unit Two.)

(d) The quality of the search result is all-important – one 'pearl' may be worth a hundred less important records. How does the searcher modify the search when the records retrieved are not sufficiently precise to the enquiry, or there are too many irrelevant records included in the search result?

(i) This could result from imprecise or inappropriate terms being used, or the inclusion of terms which could be used in more than one context. This could be remedied by displaying the index terms from any relevant records retrieved, or by requesting a display from the index file, which would give an alphabetical list of terms adjacent to the term the searcher inputs. It is not always possible to develop a strategy which eliminates 'false drops' (i.e. completely irrelevant records often retrieved because of the ambiguity of terms used). Some further help in this respect is given by Wagner, who cites the following as potential problem areas: reverse concepts, homographs, truncation, acronyms and negatives.[20]

(ii) Where a controlled language is used, the terms available from this language may not be adequate to describe the concepts required. An answer to this problem may be found in using natural language terms or phrases.

Unsatisfactory online searches may result where incomplete or inadequate search strategies have been employed, with inappropriate levels of specificity or exhaustivity; where inappropriate search terminology has been employed; where not every reasonable approach to the problem has been considered; and where the enquiry has not been fully understood and analysed. According to Knapp, the searcher's failure to cover all reasonable approaches may be an indication that the searcher has failed 'to explore with the user all the logical possibilities that could be considered'.[2]

Fig. 9 is arranged to aid the searcher in developing a search and is a reminder of the various features, on both the database and the online host system, which might be helpful in formulating and modifying the search.

Database features: CONTROLLED LANGUAGE//NATURAL LANGUAGE// SUBJECT CODES//STORED SEARCH FRAGMENTS// DATABASE-SPECIFIC FEATURES//

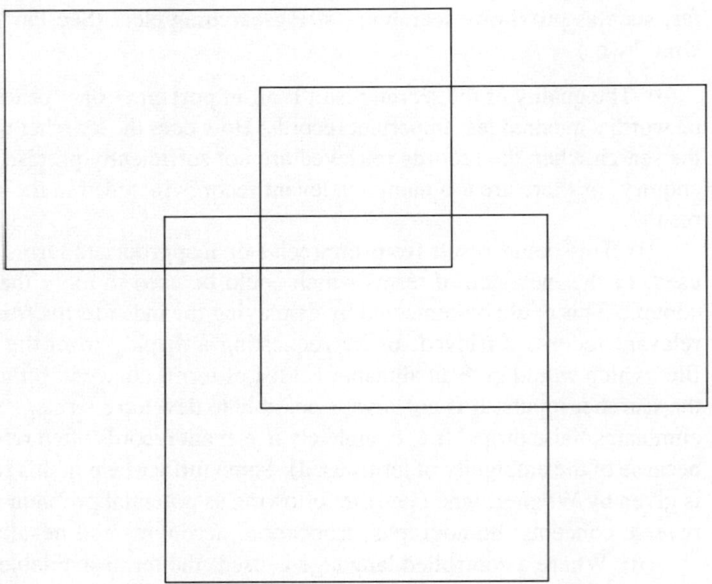

System features: 'AND' LOGIC//'OR' LOGIC//LIMIT BY FIELD//WEIGHTING//WORD PROXIMITY//DISPLAY INDEX FILE// TRUNCATION//LIMIT BY LANGUAGE ETC//CROSS-FILE SEARCHING//'NOT' LOGIC//LINK SUBJECT TERMS//STRINGSEARCH//ANALYSE SEARCH RESULTS//MULTI-FILE SEARCHING//

Fig. 9 Online search planner

5 Output of search results

When the searcher has arrived at a set or sets of relevant records, how are these records reproduced in a format suitable for the end-user to use? Most online searching today is conducted using a VDU screen, which severely limits the amount of information which can be viewed at one time; some other form of reproducing large amounts of data is needed. Some of the options are:

(i) Printing the whole search, or parts of it (i.e. just the required records) on a printer attached to the terminal while the online search is taking place. Using the greater transmission speeds which have been introduced on public data transmission networks in recent years (1,200 baud and very recently 2,400 baud) this has become more of an economic proposition than formerly. However, there is normally an online charge for each record printed in this way; this charge varies from one database to another.

(ii) Printing sets of records 'offline' (i.e. a command is entered requesting that records be printed by the online host; these records are then mailed to the searcher or end-user). Two advantages of this method are cost and presentation: although there is a charge for each record or for a page of information, by printing offline the online connect charges are being saved; and the presentation of the records tends to be better offline than from many online printers. Williams, however, in his paper on costs, concludes that the differences between the costs of online and offline printing are not significant.[21] This study was a comparison of search costs for online and offline printing on two online hosts – DIALOG and BRS – based on a consistent set of assumptions. The Clover Publications *Online comparative cost chart* gives comparative costs for online and offline printing and downloading of all databases on 19 systems. The main disadvantage of offline printing is that the records are not immediately available for the end-user, but in many cases, where large numbers of records are being printed, this is not an important consideration. Some online hosts have introduced other methods that give the cost advantages of printing offline, while at the same time reducing the time between ordering the offline prints and the searcher or end-user receiving them. DIALOG introduced an electronic mail service – Dialmail – in 1985; it is possible to request that offline prints be transferred to Dialmail; these are then available the following morning for printing online at a greatly reduced connect time charge. It is also possible to edit the records before printing them, but spending time editing in this way may erode any cost benefits if telecommunications charges are a significant element.[22] In 1986 ORBIT introduced their 'Electronic Offline Prints' feature, whereby offprints are available in less than two hours after a search,[23] and Data-Star introduced their electronic mail service early in 1989.

(iii) Another method is for the searcher to store the records in electronic form at the terminal, with the object of reprocessing the records in some way. The term used for retrieving and storing the records in electronic form is 'downloading'. The Aslib survey of 1987 showed that 35% of respondents were downloading records.[24]

There are a number of considerations involved in 'downloading'. Firstly, there are the legal implications. Database producers and online hosts are concerned about how the information downloaded is to be used; copyright laws are involved here. Nicholls examines unlicensed downloading in relation to criminal law, dealing in some detail with the concept of ownership of information, and concluding that granting the right of exclusive ownership of information would have unacceptable social and legal implications.[25] Some publishers even claim that by abstracting their articles the electronic information industry is depriving them of potential revenue and royalties.[26, 27] Davenport questions whether the downloading argument is such an important one as some producers and users make out; he calls the idea that downloading presents a threat to the livelihood of database producers and online hosts 'a myth'.[28] Some online hosts have introduced commands specifically for downloading, the charge for each record downloaded being higher than the normal offline print charge. Saksida has described the introduction by ESA-IRS of a downloading command to give a legal means for a user to download information and have the 'right to re-use the data for his own use'; the user 'shall not transfer, retransmit, duplicate or resell any of the data received by download to any third party without the prior approval of ESA-IRS', and the user 'shall not use the download data to combine with other information to create a consolidated file to be offered on-line or in any other way to third parties'. Downloading on ESA-IRS in 1986 represented just under 1% of the total online hits recorded by ESA-IRS, but the trend was largely exponential. ESA-IRS managed to get the approval of all database producers 'with the exception of one or two', for their downloading policy.[29]

Some database producers require users to apply for a licence to download. It also depends on the hardware and software used by the searcher as to whether it is possible or advantageous to download. 100K bytes of RAM memory on a terminal or microcomputer will soon be used up, but may be useful for storing and editing (e.g. eliminating irrelevant records) the results of a brief search before forwarding them to the end-user. If the searcher has much more RAM available, on a microcomputer, minicomputer or mainframe, the possibilities of reprocessing the information downloaded are increased: the information can be stored locally in an in-house database; new information can be downloaded at intervals and merged with the local database, so that this database, specific to the interests of the end-user, can be searched locally at no further cost. In (i) and (ii) above, the end-user is presented with a printed list of records. By capturing the information in electronic form the searcher may have the capability of forwarding the information to the end-user in electronic form, either with or without editing, perhaps via a local area network, a national network, or an electronic mail service. Having received the information in this form, the end-user can then print out the information in full or selectively, and/or store it in electronic form temporarily or permanently. EUSIDIC is producing a Code of Practice on downloading and electronic mail.

One decision to be made, whichever of the above methods is used, is how much of a record is to be printed or downloaded – will it be the full record, or only part of it? Normally, the less information asked for, the less the cost. For example, a full record – including all the fields – on the INSPEC database on ESA-IRS costs 25.20p to print online, and 35.30p to print offline, while just the bibliographic details (author, title and source) costs less in each case. Some online hosts have pre-defined formats (see Part Two, Section 1.2); others have these but also allow you to choose particular fields which meet your requirements more precisely. For example, on BLAISE the command PRINT is a pre-defined format giving author, title and source, but the searcher can include other fields as appropriate; e.g. PRINT INCLUDE DC on the BNB files will give author, title, publisher and Dewey Decimal Classification Number. The decision about which format to use will normally be made in the preparation stage of the search, for it would be costly looking up suitable formats while online.

Where the search is being conducted by an intermediary, the presentation of the results of the search to the end-user may be important. Some of the methods that might be adopted have been mentioned above; it is also helpful to let the end-user know when the search was conducted, which databases were used etc. An example of the 'Search Report Form' used by the Lancashire Library in England is given in Fig. 10. This is prepared on a word processor and attached to the results of the search.

THE LANCASHIRE LIBRARY
REFERENCE AND INFORMATION SERVICE

Computer Search Report

Harris Library
Market Square
Preston
PR1 2PP
Tel: Preston 53191

Number: 7343

Name: A. N. Other
Company: Postgraduate Medical Centre – Preston
Date: 21st March 1989
Databases: Medline, Embase
Subject: Salivary gland antibodies
Cost: £0.00

N.B. We do not normally keep copies of references. When ordering items resulting from this online search, it would help us if you could supply photocopies of the appropriate references; please order through your local District Library.

If there has been a charge for this search, we will send an invoice to you shortly.

Thank you.

If there are any enquiries arising from this search, please contact Joe Bloggs at the Harris Library, Reference and Information Service,

Tel. : Preston 53191.

THE INFORMATION ENCLOSED HAS BEEN OBTAINED FROM THE DATABASES MENTIONED ABOVE AND IS THE COPYRIGHT OF THE PRODUCERS OF THOSE DATABASES

Fig. 10 Lancashire Library Computer Search Report Form

Most organizations would require some kind of 'log' to be kept of online searches; there may be a requirement to keep a very detailed log, but this can take as long to fill in as the search itself takes! The search summaries produced by the online hosts each month are very detailed – down to 1/100th of a second! – and are generally very accurate. The log kept by the Lancashire Library includes: search number, date, online host, database(s) and subject of search, and can be completed in about

30 seconds; it is recorded in electronic form using a program on the same terminal as used for online searching.

6 Document delivery

When the end-user has decided which papers are required to be read in full, these would be ordered often through well-established inter-library loan sources unconnected with online – a local, regional, national or international source may be used. Many online hosts offer online ordering facilities, whereby the user can order particular documents from a number of document delivery suppliers. DIALOG introduced online ordering in 1979, with 14 suppliers; they currently have about 75 suppliers available for online ordering of documents. Online ordering is particularly useful for end-users in areas where local or national sources of document supply are less well developed.

An important consideration is speed of delivery – many suppliers have different rates for priority and non-priority orders (e.g. of 'rush' service). In a brief review of ten years of document delivery, Colbert gives four main reasons for increased speed of delivery and a comparative reduction in cost: overnight delivery services, full-text databases, facsimile transmission ('fax') and online ordering.[30] For example, The Genuine Article advertises document delivery via fax in 30 minutes or less.[31] In the Colbert article, Randy Marcinko gives the following forecast for document delivery: the average document will routinely be supplied within 24 hours; paper copies will continue to account for well over half of documents delivered; the cost of an article, relative to other products and services in the industry, will probably be the same or become less expensive. Publishers and document delivery centres have attempted to harness new optical disc technology to provide document delivery more economically; in the Adonis project, the contents of about 220 mainly biomedical journals are held on CD-ROM, and requests for articles from these journals are printed directly from the CD-ROM disc.[32,33]

7 The intermediary

What requirements and qualities are desirable in the intermediary – the person conducting the online search on behalf of the end-user? These may be divided into two categories: skills and knowledge which may be acquired, and qualities which are largely innate in the searcher's personality.

(a) Acquired knowledge and skills

(i) Subject expertise. Subject expertise is most certainly desirable when the searcher is operating in a specific subject field, particularly in the sciences, where a limited number of databases related to that field will be used; the searcher can then liaise with the end-user on the basis of a common subject knowledge and vocabulary. The concepts to be searched can thus be analysed more meaningfully on the basis of the common language possessed by both searcher and end-user. In the social sciences and humanities the possession of particular subject expertise is not as critical, for these subject fields are more penetrable to the non-specialist; the concepts to be searched are more likely to be familiar and the terminology used to describe them will be less esoteric. For searchers providing a more general service in academic and public reference libraries, as broad an educational background as possible allied to the traditional skills associated with literature searching will provide the best basis for successful searching.

(ii) Knowledge of the databases to be searched. An awareness of the peculiarities of specific databases: the fields which can be searched directly, a familiarity with the indexing languages, a knowledge of how the search product may be limited – these and similar features will allow the searcher to make decisions quickly both before and during a search; it is costly having to consult database manuals while online. It is easier for the searcher working in a specific subject field to acquire this knowledge as the number of databases used intensively will be fewer than those of the more general subject searcher whose search load will be spread over a far greater variety of databases.

(iii) Detailed knowledge of command languages. A detailed knowledge of the command languages of the systems being used is required to enable the searcher to utilize each system to its fullest potential. As the command language is the basis of the communication with the system, an interactive search cannot be conducted in the best way unless the searcher has a good knowledge of all the commands that are likely to be needed. The initial training on each system will often be obtained by attendance at an introductory course run by an online host or other organization, but complete facility with each system can only be acquired by extended use of the system under real search conditions.

(iv) Typing skills. The importance of adequate typing skills should be emphasized. Although the searcher today can be required to do less typing online than in the past – the use of menus and of uploading information prepared offline are two instances of this – when it is considered that the searcher communicates with the online host via a terminal keyboard, it is difficult to see how the searcher can operate with anything approaching efficiency unless a reasonable level of typing proficiency has been acquired.

(b) Innate qualities

(i) Logical thinking and analytical skills. The searcher needs to be able to think logically and possess the analytical skills necessary to identify the essential nature of the enquiry under consideration. All search statements for the online search will be expressed via the command language as Boolean logical relationships; the searcher must be able to interpret the analysis of the enquiry within these conventions.

(ii) Curiosity and persistence. The searcher should also possess a natural curiosity in order to pursue the analytical approach so essential in the searching process. This curiosity should be supplemented by a persistence which will persuade the searcher to follow up all possible approaches to the enquiry under consideration – the 'dogged perseverance (for wringing the last citation out of intransigent databases)' required in the famous job advertisement on the front of *Online* magazine.[34]

(iii) Self-confidence. Online searching requires the searcher to make decisions while online; these must be made quickly if the search is to be conducted economically. The searcher then must possess the self-confidence to make decisions while under the pressures both of being online and, in some cases, of having the end-user present.

(iv) Communication skills. The searcher must possess the communication skills to allow effective liaison with the end-user. The approach to the end-user must inspire confidence during the search interview, where there is one; and during the search itself the searcher must be able to interpret the progress of the search and communicate this to the end-user, and then where necessary elicit feedback from the end-user as to any modifications necessary in the search. Tenopir gives some views on the subject of the online searcher.[35]

Chapter 7

Costs

The costs involved in online information retrieval relate to hardware, software (if applicable), telecommunications access to the remote online host, online hosts' charges, and in some cases subscriptions or other charges direct to the database producer.

The cost of hardware will depend very much on the requirements of the organization using online services. A personal computer (PC), quite adequate for online searching, can be purchased for less than £500. More expensive and sophisticated PCs, perhaps with modem and telecommunications software built-in, and with more memory, are available. In many cases an organization will already possess a suitable terminal, but may have to rent or buy a modem. Modems can be purchased from about £200, depending on the facilities required; often a modem will be built-in to the PC. A printer is a necessity; a dot-matrix printer working at up to 1,200 baud can be purchased from about £300; more finance will have to be allowed for this item if the intention is to use databases with graphics, using a laser printer. Additional costs include such items as maintenance of equipment, stationery and printer ribbons.

The cost of software will depend very much on what facilities are required (see Chapter 4). It is possible to purchase a basic software package for the PC to emulate a teletype terminal from about £100, but usually a more sophisticated package will be required. Additional costs involved would be for updates of the software and annual charges for use of the supplier's help desk, where available.

Telecommunications costs include the use of a telephone line to the online host's computer or to the nearest node of the communications network linking the user with the online host's computer. There would usually be an annual standing charge for such a line, as well as usage charges. For example, in the United Kingdom, the rates are as follows:

(i) quarterly rental for business telephone line – £22–55 + VAT

(ii) phone rates per hour – these range from £0.51 per hour (including VAT) for local calls in the cheap period, up to £10–12 per hour (including VAT) for national calls in the peak period.

Some online hosts make available toll-free telephone lines into their systems, so (ii) above would not apply in their case.

Where the online host's computer is not a local telephone call away, one or more communications networks will be used. These would normally make an annual standing charge, as well as usage charges, for use of the network. The usage charges would include either a time charge, or a data volume charge, or both. The standing charge on British Telecom's Packet SwitchStream (PSS) is £10.00 per quarter; there is no charge for the volume of data transmitted, but there is a time charge of £1.80 per hour for use of the network. British Telecom's International Packet SwitchStream (IPSS) makes the following volume charges (time charges have been discontinued from June 1989):

From the UK to:	*Volume charge (per segment)*
Europe	0.28p
North America	0.7p
Rest of the world	0.82p

Again, some online hosts will allow users to use the host's password for a network, the usage costs for that network thereby being met by the host. Some hosts have implemented their own international networks, such as DIALOG's Dialnet, and ORBIT's Orbitnet.

The charges levied by the online hosts normally include a connect time charge, charges for retrieved data (online, offline or downloaded) and, in some cases, annual subscription charges. Part of the revenue received in this way is passed on to the database producer by the online host. Connect time charges for access to a particular database may vary from one online host to another, and the charges from one database to another vary considerably. Currently database charges start from $30.00 per hour, with an average of around $70.00–$80.00 per hour.

There have been moves by online hosts to reduce the amount charged for connect time and to charge more for records displayed. BLAISE have done this to a certain extent, but the most radical change is that instituted by ESA-IRS on 1 January 1989. On this date ESA-IRS introduced their 'pricing for information' policy, which involves a small connect time charge of £6.65 per hour, with higher charges than previously for printing out actual records; there is also a charge for entering a database. By the introduction of this policy, it is hoped to enable searchers to spend more time searching to achieve the best search result before displaying or printing records. It remains to be seen whether this heralds a new era in pricing for online searching.

Wilsonline in 1989 introduced free online connect time to subscribers to their Wilsondisc (CD-ROM) databases; this enables searchers to switch from the CD-ROM version to the online version of a database to obtain the most up-to-date information, without incurring online connect time charges – only telecommunications charges would be incurred.

The charges for data retrieved constitute a significant element in the total cost of online searching. Charges are levied for records printed online, offline or downloaded in electronic form for processing later. The charges vary, depending on how much information is required for each record. The average cost for a full record on a bibliographic database would be about 20–25p, but would be much higher on source databases such as those giving company information – some of these charge several pounds for a full record. These charges would be higher than previously on ESA-IRS, because of their new charging policy. When using 'download' commands, the user can normally expect to pay more per record than for online or offline prints.

Other costs would be charged for subscriptions to online hosts, where these are levied: some charge a minimum amount per month, others charge an annual subscription to cover such things as a regular newsletter; some do not charge either of these. Other costs include purchase of hosts' and database producers' manuals and search aids, where these are needed and helpful.

The overall cost of an average online search on a particular database on a particular host, including telecommunications charges, is given in the *Clover comparative cost chart* ('average' is taken to be ten minutes online connect time, five online displays and 50 offline prints); for example, an 'average' search on Analytical Abstracts on Data-Star was £17.86.[1] The average time taken to complete an online search varies considerably, depending on its nature. In a recent survey by Aslib, most searches took 6–36 minutes to complete, with an average of 18 minutes per online search; these figures were very similar to those in the earlier survey by the Online Information Centre.[2,3] In an analysis of 340 searches on drug information undertaken on a research project using MEDLINE and Excerpta Medica (EMBASE) on DIALOG, the average search time was about 12 minutes.[4] In the BIROS project in the Lancashire Library, the average search time for 412 searches was 18.2 minutes.[5]

Chapter 8
CD-ROM

As we have seen, abstracting and indexing services have been produced in printed form, in computerized form for batch searching, and later for online searching; some database producers have also published sections of their databases on floppy discs for searching on the user's PC (see Chapter 2). The latest form in which some databases are appearing is in Compact Disc—Read Only Memory (CD-ROM). These small 4.72″ discs can store up to 600 megabytes of information (or 200,000 pages of text). This capacity gives the database producers the ability, in some cases, to put the whole of an online database on one of these discs; and larger databases can be divided up over two or more discs if necessary. The disc is read in a CD player attached to a PC; the online database is no longer 'remote'; it is next to the terminal! Most people agree that at this time – 1989 – it is still too early to see how databases on CD-ROM will fare in relation to databases accessed remotely online.

(a) What are the advantages of CD-ROM?

(i) It does away with the necessity to pay telecommunications charges to access remote online systems, and the connect time charges levied by those systems; by-passing telecommunications problems could be quite a significant advantage, bearing in mind the failure rates in telecommunications noted in Chapter 3. Does it, however, save money? Apart from having to pay an annual subscription (see (b)(i) below), there are other financial considerations. Kollin estimates that for every online dollar spent by a library, about 8% goes to telecommunications, about 52% to the online host and about 40% to the database producer; much of that saved from telecommunications and online hosts' costs could be eaten up in costs of hardware, maintenance, staffing, end-user training, disc storage, general logistical costs, space, security etc.[1]

(ii) It gives the searcher all the power of the retrieval software of major online systems – this software is normally included on the disc with the database. All the commands and features described in Chapters 5 and 6 would normally be available for searching CD-ROM products. The current approach uses multi-level software, i.e. both menu-driven and command-driven. Schwerin sees the next generation products including intelligent front-end software, graphics associated with text (see CD-I below), full-text in either ASCII or digitized page image form associated with citations, and generally more products designed expressly for the medium.[2]

(iii) It gives unlimited access for one annual subscription, thereby simplifying costings, and also eliminates financial pressures while searching – the searcher can have as much 'thinking time' as needed.

(iv) It has a large storage capacity, durability, and low cost of reproduction.

(v) It can help to introduce more people, particularly end-users, to computerized literature searching, and so the overall market for databases should expand.[3,4]

(vi) It can combine text, graphics, audio and moving images.

(b) What are the disadvantages and problems of CD-ROM?

(i) The cost of the databases. As with printed abstracts and indexes, an annual subscription would normally be required for each database on CD-ROM; this would have important consequences for the financing of information retrieval in the library/information centre. For example, the Library and Information Science (LISA) database on CD-ROM as produced by Silverplatter Information Ltd costs $995 per year. The costs of databases on CD-ROM ranged from £250–£3,200 in 1987, with predictions that the range would fall to £100–£500 in 1988, and the lowest cost might be £20 by 1990.[5] These predictions for 1988, however, did not materialize. There is also the considerable cost of buying hardware – Personal Computer(s) and CD player(s); and other costs mentioned in (a)(i) above. This may be reduced if the organization already owns suitable PCs. The cost of a CD-ROM drive was about £1,000 in 1987, with a forecast that the price would reduce to about £600 in 1988 and to £250 by 1990; for a PC with a built-in CD-ROM drive, the prices were £2,200 in 1987, with a forecast reduction to £1,500 in 1988 and £600 by 1990.[5] The Library and Information Briefing on CD-ROM from the British Library covers all aspects succinctly – hardware, software, applications, standards, costs and the market.

(ii) The number of sources available is much greater online than would be possible for an organization to finance in CD-ROM form. It would be more economical to search infrequently used databases online rather than to subscribe to the CD-ROM format.

(iii) CD-ROM creates logistical problems – access is limited to one person per CD installation; this could be remedied in the future by the use of Local Area Networks (LANs) and multi-user systems, but response time could be severely affected. Silverplatter introduced 'daisy-chaining' software in late 1988, which supports the linking of multiple CD-ROM drives to a single PC; multi-disc drives allow users to search across a multi-disc database such as MEDLINE, and to switch quickly from one database to another. CD-ROM also creates problems of security.

(iv) Currency of CD-ROM products is not as good as the online version; it falls between the online and printed products; the online version will almost always be the most current.

(v) Lack of compatibility of equipment and software; the problem of standardization is being sorted out.[6]

(vi) Other possible disadvantages are: slower response time than online, for more complex searches; not all features available online are always available on the CD-ROM version of the database; lack of standard retrieval software – searchers need to learn different systems; an increase in staff involvement, particularly in training and overseeing end-users.

It would seem that, in relation to online searching, CD-ROM products would only be viable if heavy use was made of that source. In practice, searchers would make use of both remote online searching and CD-ROM searching. Most people seem to agree that it is online 'and' CD-ROM, rather than online 'versus' CD-ROM.[4] This raises important issues for the managers of library and information services.

It is too early to say what impact CD-ROM will have on both online and printed products. Database producers have been the prime movers in developing CD-ROM products – Conger says that 'in large part, database producers may desire to regain control over the dissemination of their product'[7] – but some online hosts are producing some of the databases they offer in CD-ROM form also; is this part of the future role of online hosts? Arlen Raedeke, Vice President of Reference Technology, has been reported as estimating that the cost to a publisher of creating one CD-ROM product is $15,000 to $20,000, plus an additional $15–$20 for each disc replicated.[8] Gates, at Microsoft's 3rd CD-ROM Conference, is reported to have estimated the cost of producing a CD-ROM product to be $1m.[9] Arnold holds the view that the CD product must offer more than its online counterpart, or be substantially different in a significant way; highly specialized information for specific markets can be configured into a CD product.[8] One such product is the

Adonis project, where CD-ROM is used as part of a document delivery service. The contents of about 220 journals, mainly in the biomedical fields, are stored on CD-ROM and individual articles are printed out by laser printer from the CD-ROM as required.[10]

Looking at market projections for CD-ROM, Herther states that early estimates of the growth of CD-ROM markets were not realized.[9] CD-ROM is in a sensitive position, affected by consumer tastes and pressures, available hardware and the state of the economy, and is also dependent on the maturation of the computer and publishing industries, and the growth of the emerging information industry. CD-ROM is greatly affected by the lack of standards, the introduction of new media such as DAT, DVI, CD-I and WORM discs. The author further states that the optical publishing industry does not have a clearly defined leader, and publishers are cautious – they would like to see more drives sold before committing themselves; projected growth rates in the installed base for CD-ROM drives are given, from five market forecasts in the US; however, the estimates vary so widely that it is difficult to see what value they have – the lowest estimate for worldwide is 1,120,000, and for the US 983,000 in the year 1990.[11] This latter estimate (from Link Resources), which includes CD-I installations also, is dealt with in more detail by White, who gives the total value of all installed systems in the US as being $1,283,093,400 in the year 1990.[12] However, Gates reports that there were less than 50,000 drives in the market place in the USA in early 1988.[13] A later report by Link Resources gave the installed base for CD-ROM drives as 25,100 in Europe in 1988, with 2,400 in the United Kingdom, and projects a total of 284,000 for Europe by 1992, with 54,000 in the United Kingdom. Julie Schwerin of Infotech gave the figure of 78,750 for the world installed base of CD-ROM drives in 1988.[14] Herther, writing in 1988, states that over 200,000 CD-ROM drives had been sold worldwide altogether, and that there were about 200 CD-ROM products available for public use; data preparation sources reported that over 1,300 separate disc titles had been made.

It would seriously curtail the services which some libraries and information centres could offer if some databases ceased to be made available online, because of CD-ROM.

Perhaps the era of CD-ROM will be short-lived. The advent of Write Once Read Many (WORM) technology allows organizations to write information onto their own laser discs. The erasable laser disc is being developed and another technology which might compete with CD-ROM is Digital Audio Tape (DAT); these cassettes, not unlike audio cassettes, can be erased and used many times, and each tape could hold up to 2–3 gigabytes of data (four times that held on CD-ROM). Compared with CD-ROM it is less durable, gives slower access, and is more expensive initially, but it does allow re-writing, and it can store any digitized information – data, voice or music.[15] Compact Disk Interactive (CD-I) is a standard for a fully interactive system being developed by Philips and Sony, which provides for handling of music, speech, still pictures, graphics, computer programs and computer data.[16] In late 1988, Philips, Sony and Microsoft announced a joint development of CD-ROM Extended Architecture, or CD-ROM XA; this new format would incorporate audio and graphics technology from CD-I format and serve as a bridge between CD-ROM and CD-I.[13]

Some sources giving further information are: the *Electronic and optical publishing directory, Eusidic database guide, The CD-ROM directory* and *CD-ROMs in print* (see Appendix 1). Miller gives some help in evaluating CD-ROMs, under the headings of descriptive, comparative and use evaluation.[17]

Chapter 9

Advantages and disadvantages

The advantages of online information retrieval are considerable; the following gives details of some of them.

(i) The amount of time spent searching the literature is vastly reduced. An experienced online searcher can conduct an online search in between 15 and 20 minutes on average, depending on the complexity of the search. Managers of information services may be concerned when they learn that the cost of searching online may amount to £1 per minute on some host systems, but against this they must compare the total staff cost, as well as subscription charges, of extended manual searching and the recording, proof-reading and duplication of search results.

(ii) While online it is possible to search at once the entire contents of a database, which may contain millions of records covering literature published over 20 years or more.

(iii) It is possible to search a number of databases during the same search session, either together, or consecutively by saving the search on the initial database and then processing the same search on related databases on the same host system. In this way a number of databases can be searched in a matter of minutes. The state-of-the-art search which formerly might have taken one or two days or longer to complete manually, can be undertaken online in minutes.

(iv) The online searcher can undertake detailed multi-concept searches which because of their complexity could not be searched manually other than by extended and laborious scanning of the text of abstracts.

(v) Searching online offers much enhanced capabilities over manual searching: more access points per record are available – when searching manually the searcher is limited to the choice of alphabetic subject index headings provided by the indexer, which are usually limited to two or three per record; online searching gives, in addition to these headings, the full range of index terms chosen by the indexer, and the natural language of the text, e.g. title words, words in the abstract etc. Other capabilities include searching other fields such as corporate source and language, proximity searching, truncation, searching using classification codes, analysing search results, sorting records.

(vi) The manager of the online service is not usually faced with large subscription charges for using online hosts, particularly those offering bibliographic databases, although a small subscription may be required to cover the costs of regularly updating literature. This compares favourably with the in-house provision of printed or CD-ROM abstracting and indexing services, where ongoing subscriptions for the titles needed must be placed, and these subscriptions are not variables dependent on use. Apart from purchasing printed or CD-ROM titles which are essential for the provision of a particular information service, the manager will often acquire fringe and lesser used titles which must be available as an insurance against what may be needed; it is in accessing these online as an alternative that considerable savings may be made. As the online information retrieval industry expands, more databases are becoming available in online form only.

(vii) Online searching ensures file integrity; the searcher cannot be inconvenienced by missing or misfiled issues, or by non-receipt of an issue.

(viii) Online search results are presented in a concise and standardized format, where the detail can be predetermined by the searcher. The command languages of the various online hosts allow the searcher to specify the required form of output: this may be titles only when sampling the results of an initial search, or it may be to display the bibliographic details with indexing terms of records in a set which has proved relevant from the evidence of titles displayed, or it may be to display the full records including abstracts, where available. Some online hosts have special report formats for printing numeric information. This presentation contrasts starkly with the convoluted processes involved in selecting and presenting the results of a manual search with all the inherent possibilities of errors in transcription and delays in typing and proof-reading.

(ix) The problems of geographical location as barriers to the transfer of information are eliminated through online information retrieval, particularly when the benefits of multi-database searching are considered. The room in which the terminal is located becomes an information centre in itself, giving access to millions of records on hundreds of databases. The smallest organization in the remotest rural location can obtain access to databases which could previously only have been accessed by visiting national or larger regional libraries and other libraries with major subject collections. This has helped the emergence of the 'information broker' – the entrepreneur who undertakes to provide information for fee-paying clients.

(x) Searching databases online usually gives the searcher much earlier access to new records than when searching manually or on CD-ROM.

(xi) Having access to online sources enables the library or information service to serve more users. As the amount of time spent searching the literature is reduced for an enquiry, the staff time saved can be used to deal with more enquiries. A survey conducted in the United States by SDC showed that in almost every case where online searching was introduced into an organization, the number of literature searches undertaken increased rapidly; furthermore a large percentage of organizations which previously did no literature searching at all began searching online after being persuaded of the benefits that may be obtained.[1]

What are the possible disadvantages of online information retrieval?

(i) Budgeting can be more difficult than for printed or CD-ROM publications, as much online searching is on a pay-as-you-use basis, and it can be difficult to estimate how much online usage there will be in a particular year.

(ii) Costs can seem higher than for other publications if they are looked at in isolation; however, this might not seem such a problem when seen in relation to such things as the vast sources available, the staff time saved, the enhanced service provided. Initial hardware and software costs could be seen as a disadvantage, if these were not already available in the organization.

(iii) Access might seem more restricted than for printed publications – a number of people can search a printed index at the same time, whereas there may be only one terminal for online access and the search may have to be performed by an intermediary; efficient timetabling for online searching could overcome this problem; where there was a great demand for a particular index, this would probably be held in printed form as well anyway.

(iv) Staffing – are there sufficient staff trained and available to perform online searches if and when required? Is the online service an 'on-demand' service, or can it be provided only when certain staff are available? Are end-users encouraged to perform their own searches, and is training for this provided by the library staff? A particular end-user could find it a disadvantage to work through an intermediary.

(v) How can the end-user be sure that important records have not been missed in the search? This would depend very much on the way the search had been conducted, the databases chosen, and whether information on the subject was available online at all. Online information retrieval in no way includes the whole of human knowledge. It is limited mainly to information published in the last 20 years; some subjects, e.g. chemistry, are covered very comprehensively, while other subjects, e.g. history, are covered well, but in no way comprehensively – other sources would need to be explored for a complete search. A recent report from the UK Scientific Documentation Centre reviewed in *Online review* claims that online searching compares unfavourably with other methods of information retrieval in locating scientific and technical information.[2]

(vi) Browsing, and spending sufficient time online to ensure that all relevant records have been retrieved, is more difficult online than manually, because of the pressures of time and money; recent moves by online hosts such as ESA-IRS to reduce drastically the cost of connect time could make this less of a problem.

(vii) Online host systems could be 'down' when required, and telecommunications faults might interrupt searches or prohibit a search from even beginning. Many online host systems have increased the hours of availability, some to 24 hours a day, and if a host system has an unscheduled break in service, which is relatively unusual, the service is normally resumed within ten minutes.

Chapter 10

Into the future . . .

Lewis, when asked to give views on where the online industry was heading over the next ten years, wrote that he was certain of only one thing: 'I'll be wrong!'[1] However, certain trends can be isolated relating to the major areas covered in the earlier chapters of this book.

The growth in the number of databases has been increasing steadily over the last ten years, without any apparent decrease in the rate of growth. This rate of growth will slow down as the market becomes saturated, uneconomic databases are dropped by host systems, and the gaps in subject coverage are filled. The number of full-text databases is set to increase substantially; and there will be more moves to repackage databases, in a similar way to Toxnet, BIOSIS Connection and DIALOG Medical Connection, aiming at particular user markets.

Quality of information will become of increasing importance; Jewitt has addressed this problem, stating that among the concepts present in the information world are 'the general perception that much of what is published is dross; and the suspicion (verified here and there) that what is found and used is not necessarily all, and only, the best'. More quality control can be applied at each stage in the information dissemination cycle.[2]

Henderson and Leamy see the evolution of fourth-generation databases, where the creation and processing of information products will be done online as well as the access and retrieval, as publishers develop their own online databases.[3]

The rate of growth in the number of database producers already shows signs of slowing down, and this trend is likely to continue. More producers may see advantages in becoming online hosts themselves, thus having more control over their products; similarly, this control is also increased by producing databases on CD-ROM, which is another trend likely to continue at an accelerated rate. There may well be a substantial change in the type of producer, with powerful organizations such as banks and telecommunications giants becoming more involved.

There has been a slowing down in the rate of growth of the number of online hosts also, a trend which will continue. There is likely to be more collaboration between online hosts, the 'horizontal integration' discussed by Pemberton, particularly in the area of gateways which enable a host service to be accessible via another host, similar to the ESA-IRS – Pergamon Financial Data Services link. This will hopefully lead to agreement on the use of any other host's command languages and menus, so that searchers can use the command language of their choice.[4] Online hosts are likely to offer an increasing range of services as well as online access, such as CD-ROM versions of databases, increasingly sophisticated software products, electronic mail services, and hybrid retrieval systems, i.e. incorporating CD-ROM and remote online access. Depending on the outcome of the ESA-IRS policy of 'pricing for information', more online hosts could introduce much lower connect time charges, with increased charges for retrieved records.

Both Holmes and Cuadra see a move away from centralized towards local control for users of databases.[5,6] Easier access, greater marketing efforts by host systems and the increasing use of menu-driven systems will make online searching more attractive to the end-user, and consequently the percentage of searches conducted by end-users will increase. Training of end-users will have more prominence, including targetting students in schools.[7] The role of the intermediary will change, as detailed earlier in this book, but, happily, Conger believes 'the online intermediary will survive'.[8]

Developments in telecommunications will have repercussions for use of online systems: Holmes reports that electronic mail has had a marked effect upon the use of Jordan's database;[5] the introduction of ISDNs with their greater speed will help the use of full-text databases; the number of gateways will increase, giving more and easier access, and possibly altering the economics of the online information retrieval industry. 'Intelligent front-end' systems will be used more, particularly by end-users, but also by intermediaries if the systems are sufficiently flexible. More use will be made of higher data transmission speeds, particularly 2,400 baud; this may cause producers and hosts to introduce 'baud rate pricing'; otherwise their revenues could be affected by searchers spending less time online.[9]

The terminal configuration will undoubtedly change, with such things as integrated CD-ROM drives, WORM drives, and other possible peripherals as yet not commercially available. Software for retrieval, downloading and database creation will become increasingly sophisticated, allowing better organization of results of searches.

As regards searching features, more developments will take place in multi-database searching, possibly to the extent of eliminating duplicate records across databases. Searchers one day may be able to search any host with just one favourite command language. More menus will be made available.

Laser disc technology, mainly at present in the form of CD-ROM, will tend to expand the market for database products, so it will complement remote online searching, rather than threaten its existence, so the two technologies should be able to exist side by side. CD-ROM may, however, have an effect on printed publications. CD-ROM gives producers the ability to repackage databases – Datext takes sections from five different databases and combines them into a single database.[9]

Lewis sees 'Information Management' (IM) as the key to effective information flow in the future, and online information retrieval is an important part of this: 'as online gathers unto itself many of the associated technologies, e.g. E-mail, teletext, videotex, CDROM, interactive systems, DBS, expert systems, robotics, reprographics, etc., so it will make itself even more indispensable to the future development of Information Management (IM) on the international scene'.[1]

PART TWO

Practical introduction to seven online host systems

Introduction

The aim of Part Two is twofold: firstly, to show practical applications of the principles outlined in Part One, showing the most important operations, with their commands and features, on the following seven online host systems:

1 DIALOG Information Services Inc.
2 European Space Agency Information Retrieval Service (ESA-IRS)
3 BLAISE-LINE
4 National Library of Medicine (BLAISE-LINK)
5 ORBIT
6 Pergamon Financial Data Services
7 Data-Star

Secondly, it is arranged in such a way that it can form part of a training programme for searchers new to online information retrieval, whether they be students, librarians, information scientists or information workers, or 'end-users'.

There are three self-contained Units for each online host system, each Unit covering a number of 'operations' with their accompanying system commands and features; the searcher can therefore concentrate on one host system without needing to refer elsewhere. Additionally, the 'operations' are numbered similarly for each host system, so that an operation such as 'truncation' can be found in Section 2.2 in each of the seven host systems. Each of the three Units introduces new commands and features, to enable the searcher to perform progressively more complex searches. The searcher can delve more deeply into the complexities of a host system by reference to the user manuals and regular newsletters produced by the online hosts (see Appendix 1).

The Units, including the examples, have been developed from experience gained in the day-to-day use of the online systems; therefore abbreviations, short-cuts etc. are used as a matter of course, and hints arising out of experience with a particular host system are included.

A list of the 'operations' covered in the seven online host systems, with the appropriate section numbers, is given below.

Appendix 2 includes the databases offered by the seven online hosts featured in this Part; these databases are arranged by subject for easier use.

Operations covered in each of the three Units for each online host system, where applicable:

Unit One	1.1	logging-on to the system; choosing a database (file)
	1.2	entering search statements and creating sets of records; using Boolean operators; displaying records
	1.3	reviewing a search; ending the search and searching session (logging-off)
Unit Two	2.1	displaying the index file; using both controlled and natural language terms; searching specific fields
	2.2	proximity searching (full-text searching); string-searching; truncation
	2.3	searching using classification codes, subfiles etc.; analysing search results
Unit Three	3.1	limiting a retrieved set of records by some criteria, e.g. language, date of publication; ranging
	3.2	saving a search on one database, changing to another database and conducting the same search on the new database; searching a number of databases at once ('multifile' searching); searching elements of records across databases
	3.3	printing 'offline'; sorting records; downloading records; transferring records to an electronic mail facility.

System 1

DIALOG Information Services Inc.

UNIT ONE

1.1 Operations: logging-on to the system; choosing a database (file)

Commands and features introduced: logging-on information; BEGIN (B)

DIALOG Information Services Inc. currently offers over 300 databases accessed either by direct dial, via one of the commercial data transmission networks such as Tymnet or Telenet, or via its own network Dialnet. From outside the United States, the system may be accessed via national post, telegraph and telephone services (PTTs) to link into one of the networks mentioned above. In the United Kingdom, users contact the nearest 'node' of British Telecom's Packet SwitchStream (PSS) network, and then make the link with DIALOG's computer in Palo Alto, California, either via British Telecom's International Packet SwitchStream (IPSS), or by Dialnet. The example below shows a log-on via the Manchester (UK) node of PSS, using Dialnet, and with a terminal working at 1,200 baud (120 characters per second (cps)).

For the purpose of clarity, the characters input by the searcher in the examples below are underlined; this is not the case when actually working online.

The searcher first dials the node of the network (in many cases the terminal or modem will be programmed to do this automatically), and after identifying the type of terminal being used, and the speed of transmission, will receive a response similar to the following from the node:

EXAMPLE:

MAN A002-6164340213 NDIALOGOOOOOO ↵	Response from the MANchester node of PSS. The Network User Identifier (NUI) is entered – a number unique to the user. In this case DIALOG lets users use DIALOG's own Identifier.
ADD? a21230012011 ↵	The network asks for the ADDress – to which online host does the searcher wish to be connected? ↵ = return.
23421230012011+COM DIALOG INFORMATION SERVICES PLEASE LOGON: XXXXXXXX ↵ ENTER PASSWORD: XXXXXXXX ↵	The ADDress is repeated by way of confirming the connection. The next response is from DIALOG, which requires a two-step log-on procedure (a user number and password is given to each new customer).
Welcome to DIALOG Dialog level 19.5.7A Last logoff 14feb89 05:08:09 Logon file 001 16feb89 07:35:34 ***	The 'Welcome' message confirms that the searcher is connected to DIALOG; the searcher is given immediate access to a database (file), in this case file 1 (ERIC). ***

COPR. (c) DIALOG INFORMATION SERVICES, INC. ALL RIGHTS RESERVED. NO CLAIM TO ORIG. U.S. GOVT. WORKS.

DIALOG NeWS (Enter ?NEWS for details):

****

Now available:

KNIGHT-RIDDER FINANCIAL NEWS (File 609)

AMERICAN MEN AND WOMEN OF SCIENCE (File 236) -- reloaded with 17th edition

MEDLINE (Files 152-155) -- 1989 annual reload completed; enter ?MEDLINE for details.

Free time in February:

Up to $70.50 of combined online connect time and TYPEs or DISPLAYs is available free for searching D&B – DUNS FINANCIAL RECORDS PLUS (File 519) during February.

etc. . . . . . .etc. . . . . . . ? b249 16feb89 07:36:40 User 000000 $0.36 0.012 Hrs File1 $0.36 Estimated cost File1 $0.12 DialnetE $0.48 Estimated cost this search $0.48 Estimated total session cost 0.012 Hrs	At this stage, the searcher is given any system news of immediate importance, and then given the question mark (?), which is the searcher's prompt to input something. The searcher selects the file required by its number, preceded by the command BEGIN, or its abbreviation B.

```
File 249:MIDEAST
FILE-1980-88/SEP
 (Copr. Learned Information 1988)
  Set  Items  Description
  ----- -------  ---------------
?
```

1.2 Operation: entering search statements and creating sets of records; using Boolean operators; displaying records

Commands and features introduced: SELECT (S); Boolean operators AND and OR; 'stacking' commands; TYPE (T); DISPLAY (D); PAGE (P)

The general principles and methods of searching have been discussed in Chapters 5 and 6. After the initial analysis of the subject of the search, the identification of the concepts involved and the selection of terms appropriate for those concepts on this database, the terms are input using the SELECT (S) command.

EXAMPLE: Mideast File

```
  Set  Items  Description
  ----- -------  ----------------
? s saudi arabia or iran
           5500 SAUDI ARABIA
           7874 IRAN
    S1    12345 SAUDI ARABIA
                   OR IRAN
? s crime or criminals
             98 CRIME
             91 CRIMINALS
    S2      112 CRIME OR
                   CRIMINALS
```

SET, ITEMS and DESCRIPTION are the headings for the subsequent search results, giving the SET number, the number of ITEMS (or records) retrieved for the DESCRIPTION (i.e. the terms or phrases input by the searcher).

The system will search the basic index for these two terms, find how many records (items) there are for each, display this information, and then, as the searcher has ORd the two terms, will create a set of records with EITHER SAUDI ARABIA OR IRAN in them. (NB As Saudi Arabia is a multi-word term, records will be retrieved only where SAUDI ARABIA has been used as an index term (descriptor) – see 2.2 below for other methods of searching multi-word terms and phrases.) Upon receiving the ? prompt, the searcher inputs the next statement CRIME OR CRIMINALS.

```
? s s1 and s2
          12345 S1
            112 S2
    S3       11 S1ANDS2
?
```

Using the logical operator AND, the searcher now requires a set that gives only those records that are included in BOTH set 1 AND set 2. Again the command SELECT (S) is used, with the set numbers prefixed by S. (COMBINE (C) can also be used, but without the S prefix, e.g. C1AND2.) Terms can be 'stacked' on one line, as long as each command is separated by a semi-colon (;), e.g. S SAUDI ARABIA OR IRAN; S CRIME OR CRIMINALS. The system will process each command in turn.

The details of the records retrieved in set 3 can be displayed online by use of the TYPE (T) or DISPLAY (D) commands. There are a number of different formats available and the searcher can choose whichever is most appropriate in the circumstances; some of the formats vary from one database to another, but the most common formats are:

Format number	*Record content*
1	DIALOG accession number
2	Full record (without abstract)
3	Author, title, source
4	Abstract and title
5	Full record
6	Title
7	Author, title, source and abstract
8	Title and subject indexing

The searcher would normally consult the appropriate database details when planning the search to verify which formats were available. A TYPE (T) command usually consists of these elements:

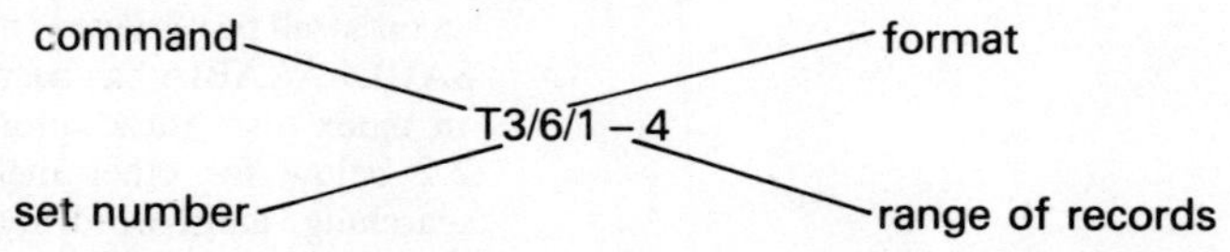

TYPE (T) gives a continuous output, DISPLAY (D) gives one screen at a time to facilitate searching on VDU screens; the command PAGE (P) brings up the next screen of a display.

EXAMPLE: Mideast File

```
  Set   Items  Description
  -----  -------  ----------------
  S3        11  S1ANDS2
? t3/6/1-4

 3/6/1
068733
  Amnesty to Prisoners Declared

 3/6/2
055373
  Saudi Arabia: Vigilance
    against Crime

 3/6/3
054904
  Protection of Public Utilities

 3/6/4
054446
  Islamic Moralities
```

The searcher will often at this stage browse through the titles to make sure the records retrieved are relevant. The command T3/6/1-4 asks the system to display the titles and accession numbers (format 6) of the first four (1–4) records of set 3. (NB – records in sets are displayed in reverse-chronological order, so that the first records displayed are the latest entered into the database.)

The second and fourth records look good, so the searcher asks for them to be displayed in full – format 5 – and will probably print them on the printer at the same time.

```
 ? t3/5/2,4
  3/5/2
 055373
   Saudi Arabia: Vigilance against Crime.
   Monday Morning  vol. 14 iss. 700  59-60p.  december 23 1985
   Document Type: a
   Languages: English
```

A commentary in December, 1985 on the low crime rate in Saudi Arabia. Under the Minister of the Interior, Prince Na'if Abd al-Aziz, and his deputy, Prince Ahmad ibn Abd al-Aziz, Saudi Arabia enjoys one of the highest levels of internal stability and security in the world. Crime in the kingdom is mainly attributable to the presence of foreign, unskilled workers who have repeatedly been found guilty of embezzlement. Although forgery has declined, practitioners using sophisticated technology have infiltrated Saudi society in an attempt to undermine it.

```
   Descriptors: Saudi Arabia-Society-Crime and criminals; Alien labour
   Historical Period: 1980-1990
   Section Headings: Saudi Arabia

  3/5/4
 054446
   Islamic Moralities
   Iran Press Digest  vol. 4 iss. 28 4p. july 16 1985
   Document Type: a
   etc.....etc.....
```

The options open to the searcher at this stage are numerous – one or more of them may be: to browse through the remainder of the set; to print out all the records in the set; to develop the search further and display the resulting records; to conduct a similar search on another database; to end the searching session.

1.3 Operations: reviewing a search; ending the search and searching session (logging-off)

Commands and features introduced: DISPLAY SETS (DS); LOGOFF

The searcher wishing to change to another database would normally use the BEGIN (B) command, followed by the number of the required database; this would erase all previous sets and enable the searcher to begin at set 1 again on the new database. In many cases, before changing databases, the searcher would save the search already conducted (see 3.2).

There are many occasions on which the searcher requires to see a display of the search to date – particularly when the search statements have scrolled off a VDU screen! To review a search, enter DISPLAY SETS (DS).

EXAMPLE: Mideast File

```
? ds                                    ←┘

Set     Items  Description
S1      12345  SAUDI ARABIA OR IRAN
S2        112  CRIME OR CRIMINALS
S3         11  S1ANDS2
?
```

To end a searching session and disconnect from the host computer, the searcher would type the LOGOFF command; no further input is required by the searcher.

EXAMPLE:

```
?LOGOFF                                 ←┘
        16feb89 07:43:14 User000000
            $5.78    0.07 Hrs File249
            $0.00 2 Types in Format 5
            $0.00 4 Types in Format 6
            $0.00 6 Types
    $5.78 Estimated cost File 249
```

The command LOGOFF HOLD will disconnect the searcher from the system, but will save the search on the last database used for at least ten minutes – giving the searcher time for a coffee! If the searcher reconnects within that time limit,

```
  $0.77 DialnetE
  $6.55 Estimated cost this search
  $9.50 Estimated total session
          cost      0.128 Hrs
Logoff: level 15.5.11 D  07.43.36

CLR PAD (00) 00:00:07:30 300 40
```

the search can be continued.

After disconnection from the host computer, a message from the network shows how long the network was used (7 mins. 30 secs.) and how many 'segments' of data were received (300) and how many were sent (40). A 'segment' holds up to 64 characters, half a 'packet'.

UNIT TWO

2.1 Operations: displaying the index file; using both controlled and natural language terms; searching specific fields

Commands and features introduced: EXPAND (E); searching for author with prefix AU=; limiting search statements to specific fields using a suffix, e.g. /DE, /TI

The ability to display terms from the index file, where all directly searchable terms are listed, is useful for finding out the occurrence of both controlled and natural language terms; and also for finding out the precise format of a term – for example, that of an author's name. For this operation the EXPAND (E) command is used. If no particular field (e.g. AU= for the author field) is asked for by the searcher, the EXPAND command will display the basic index only.

EXAMPLE: CAB Abstracts

```
  Set  Items  Description
  ---- -------- ---------------
? e edible fungi

Ref  Items  RT   Index-term
E1       0   3   EDIBLE FAT
E2       1       EDIBLE FILM
E3      48  66  *EDIBLE FUNGI
E4       1       EDIBLE
                  MUSHROOMS
E5       1       EDIBLE OILS
E6       1   3   EDIBLE PLANTS
E7     283   8   EDIBLE SPECIES
E8.........
```

The searcher searches the CAB Abstracts database, and EXPANDs the term 'EDIBLE FUNGI'. An alphabetical listing is given, each with a reference number, the number of items (records) containing that term, the number of related terms (RT) – this is available on a few databases only – and the term itself; normally 12 terms are listed. The searcher can SELECT a term or terms directly from the

```
            Enter P or E for more
?se3                            ←┘
        S1      48  "EDIBLE FUNGI"
?ee3                            ←┘
```

list, e.g. SE3, or SE3,E6,E8 or SE3-E6,E8,E10-E12; a set will then be established, as in the example. When a range of terms is being SELECTed from an EXPAND display (e.g. SE3-E8), this can be input in alternative ways – the following ways do not give intermediate postings, which can be an advantage if the range involves many terms: S E3:E8 or S E3 TO E8 or SS E3-E8.

```
Ref  Items  Type  RT  Index-term
R1     48         66 *EDIBLE
                      FUNGI
R2   9272     B   50  FUNGI
R3   4750     B  421  VEGETABLES
R4      0     N    2  AGARICUS ARVENSIS
R5     34     N    3  AGARICUS BISPORUS
R6      9     N    2  AGARICUS BITORQUIS
R7 . . . . . . . . . . .
            Enter P or E for more
?
```

Where a database has an online thesaurus, it is possible to display any related terms (RT) by EXPANDing the E reference number of the appropriate term. The display shows B(roader) and N(arrower) terms in relation to the first term in the display. The R numbers can be SELECTed directly, e.g. S R1, R4-R6.

EXAMPLE: INSPEC

```
 Set  Items  Description
 ---- ------- ---------------
? e au=sulman, dl              ←┘

Ref  Items  Index-term
E1       1  AU=SULLY, D.C.
E2       1  AU=SULLY, M.O.
E3       0 *AU=SULMAN, DL
E4       1  AU=SULMAN, D.L.
E5       3  AU=SULMONT, P.
E6       1  AU=SULOCKI, J.
E7       1  AU=SULONEN, M.S.
E8. . . . . . . . . . . . . . . . . . . . . . .
            Enter P or E for more
```

To search in a field which is not in the basic index, a field prefix is necessary, e.g. S AU=BLOGGS, J. However, it is important, particularly when searching authors' names, to EXPAND the name first, to find the exact format used, especially the format of the initials. An asterisk (*) indicates the item input by the searcher – the initials were correct, but without correct punctuation. E4 appears to be the author required.

```
? s e4
     S1       1  AU = "SULMAN, D.L."
```

The great majority of bibliographic databases use a controlled language for indexing records and these terms are held in one field in the record; on DIALOG they are called 'descriptors', and are directly searchable. In addition, most words taken from other fields within the record, e.g. title, abstract, are also directly searchable as natural language terms. Some databases, such as BIOSIS, do not have a controlled language. The searcher will normally find appropriate terms when planning the search either from manual sources or from EXPANDing terms online, as above.

EXAMPLE: ERIC

```
  Set  Items  Description
  ---- -------- ----------------
? s declining enrolment/de*
  S1    604  DECLINING ENROLMENT/DE* (DIMINISHING NUM-
             BERS OF STUDENTS IN EDUCATION. . .)
```

An index term from the controlled language of the ERIC Thesaurus is input with field qualifier DE (descriptor); the asterisk (*) will limit the search to those records where the term is a major concept – this feature is available on only a few databases.

```
? ss united kingdom/id or great britain/id or england/if or
  uk/ti,de,id
    S2    1324  UNITED KINGDOM/ID
  S3    4601  GREAT BRITAIN/ID
  S4    2673  ENGLAND/IF
  S5    3498  UK/TI,DE,ID
  S6    9210  S2 OR S3 OR S4 OR S5
```

```
? s s1 and s6
          604  S1
         9210  S6
  S7       26  S1ANDS2
```

Geographical names are not controlled terms on ERIC; they are uncontrolled terms, or 'identifiers' (ID). 'UK' is entered as a 'natural language' term – all records will be retrieved where that term exists in the title, descriptor or identifier fields.

```
? t7/5/1
7/5/1
EJ285981    S0511533
  Reconciling the Irreconcilable: Declining Secondary School Rolls and
the Organization of the System.
  Dennison, W.F.
  Oxford Review of Education, v9 n2 p79-89   1983
  Language: English
  Document Type: JOURNAL ARTICLE (080); POSITION PAPER (120)
  Journal Announcement: CIJDEC83
  As secondary school enrollment declines in Great Britain in the 1980s,
local education authorities will face problems in deciding which schools
and/or programs to cut. School districts must recognize that, whether
they like it or not, parents will have an increasing impact on decision
making. (IS)
  Descriptors: Access to Education; Board of Education Role;
*Comparative Education; *Declining Enrolment; *Educational Demand;
*Educational Supply; Foreign Countries; Parent Role; School Closing;
Secondary Education; Selective Admission
  Identifiers: *Great Britain
```

'Declining enrolment' is in the descriptor field, and 'Great Britain' in the identifier field.

Although searches are generally well planned in advance, allowance is always made for modifying the search as a result of records retrieved – this is one great advantage of using an 'interactive' system. One common way of developing a search is to display the controlled language terms of relevant records retrieved, and then to input any of these which were overlooked or unknown previously.

2.2 Operations: proximity searching (full-text searching); (stringsearching not available on DIALOG); truncation

Commands and features introduced: proximity operators (N), (W), (F); FIND (F); truncation symbol (?)

It is useful to be able to search for a term in a particular field, as we have seen, but the ability to search for terms in a particular proximity to each other enhances searching considerably. On DIALOG, if two or more words are required to occur together in a record, e.g. Urban Planning, by inserting (W) between the terms the searcher can retrieve records containing those two terms, in that order, from any of the full-text searchable fields of the database – principally title, descriptor, identifier, abstract and corporate source fields. If an (N) is used between two terms, the system will retrieve the two terms together, but in any order. An (F) proximity operator is used if the requirement is that the two terms appear in the same field, but not necessarily together, and in any order. The FIND (F) command has an implied (W) proximity operator and searches the complete basic index.

EXAMPLE: Mideast File

```
   Set  Items  Description
   ----- ------- ----------------
? s saudi(w)arabia or iran              ←┘
              6553  SAUDI
              6380  ARABIA
              6090  SAUDI(W)ARABIA
              7874  IRAN
   S1        13300  SAUDI(W)ARABIA
                     OR IRAN
? s crime(2n)rate or criminals/
                      ti,de             ←┘
                98  CRIME
               189  RATE
                10  CRIME(2N)RATE
                79  CRIMINALS/TI,DE
   S2           84  CRIME(2N)RATE OR
                     CRIMINALS/TI,DE
? s s1 and s2                           ←┘
             13300  S1
                84  S2
   S3           10  S1ANDS2
? t3/6/1-2                              ←┘
 3/6/1
068733
  Amnesty to Prisoners Declared

 3/6/2
055373
  Saudi Arabia: Vigilance against Crime

? t3/5/2                                ←┘
 3/5/2
055373
  Saudi Arabia: Vigilance against Crime.
  Monday Morning vol. 14 iss 700 59-60p. december 23 1985
  Document Type: a
  Languages: English
```

The phrase SAUDI ARABIA is searched using the (W) proximity operator; the system will retrieve records with that phrase in any of the fields in the basic index. The operator (N) is used with the phrase CRIME RATE, as this could appear as RATE OF CRIME, RATE OF SERIOUS CRIME, as well as CRIME RATE. (2N) allows up to two words to appear between the selected terms. Both (N) and (W) can appear as (1N), (2N), (3N) etc. and (1W), (2W), (3W) etc.; e.g. UNITED(1W)EMIRATES to allow for United Arab Emirates; UNITED(3W)TEACHERS to allow for United Federation of College Teachers, United Federation of Teachers.

A commentary in December, 1985 on the low crime rate in Saudi Arabia. Under the Minister of the Interior............................
................etc.

Descriptors: Saudi Arabia-Society-Crime and criminals; Alien labour
Historical Period: 1980-1990
Section Headings: Saudi Arabia
?

'Saudi Arabia' would have been retrieved in either the title or descriptor fields; 'crime rate' in the abstract field. The search could be developed by using the descriptor 'crime and criminals' in combination with S1.

EXAMPLE: World Textile Abstracts

```
 Set  Items  Description
 ----  -------  ----------------
? s yorkshire(f)industry/ti,de
            8  YORKSHIRE/TI,DE
         5090  INDUSTRY/TI,DE
 S1         3  YORKSHIRE(F)INDUSTRY/TI,DE
? t1/6/1-3
 1/6/1
8207825  8207762
 The transformation of regional
systems: the Yorkshire woollen
industry, c.1780-c.1840

 1/6/2
8201209  8201468
 The Yorkshire wool dyeing and
finishing industry in 1981.

 1/6/3
 Cotton industry in Yorkshire
1780-1900
?
```

If the searcher wishes the terms to appear in the same field (e.g. title) but not necessarily in the close proximity as above, the letter (F) can be placed between the terms; if the two or more terms chosen appear in the same field of a record, in any order, that record will be retrieved. In this example, the searcher seeks to retrieve any records where the two terms YORKSHIRE and INDUSTRY appear in the same field, and searches only the title and descriptor fields.

A feature which is very important, particularly when searching natural language terms and phrases, is truncation – the ability to input the stem of a word, followed by the truncation symbol; the system will retrieve records where any term beginning with the word stem appears; e.g. S SCHOOL? will retrieve SCHOOL, SCHOOLS, SCHOOLING etc. On DIALOG the truncation symbol is the question mark (?).

EXAMPLE: Health Planning and Administration

```
? s length(2n)stay?; s bed? ?(2n)use? ←┘
        6565  LENGTH
        6621  STAY?
  S1    5100  LENGTH(2N)STAY?
       14300  BED? ?
       67739  USE?
  S2     123  BED? ?(2N)USE?
```

STAY? will retrieve STAY, STAYING, STAYED, within two words of LENGTH, in any field in the record. When a truncated term ends with ? ? (as in BED? ?), the system will retrieve terms with up to one extra letter only (e.g. BED, BEDS but not BEDDING); terms ending in ?? ? will retrieve terms with up to two extra letters only.

```
? t1/6/1 ←┘
 1/6/1
0399282  88026068  MED/88026068
  Length of stay for common surgical
procedures: variation among districts
?
```

2.3 Operations

searching using classification codes, subfiles etc.; (analysing search results not available on DIALOG)

When discussing the search in Chapter 6, reference was made to the fact that most databases have a feature whereby it is possible to search a subject area wider than that described by one term, or a few terms, by using a classification code, subfile, or other system or database feature.

EXAMPLE: Sociological Abstracts

```
? e sh=1900 ←┘
Ref     Items  Index-term
E1        157  SH=1844
E2       2357  SH=19
E3       8592  *SH=1900
E4       1790  SH=1900/38
E5       2418  SH=1900/39
E6..............etc
? se5; sglue(f)sniff?; s s1ands2 ←┘
  S1     2418  SH=1900/39
          368  GLUE
          154  SNIFF?
  S2       18  GLUE(F)SNIFF?
         2418  S1
           18  S2
  S3       10  S1ANDS2
```

Sociological Abstracts has section codes; code 1900 is 'The family and socialization'.

SH=section heading code

Searcher selects E5 – 'Adolescence and youth' (which is a subsection of code 1900), and combines this with a set on glue sniffing.

```
? t3/6/1                              ←┘
  3/6/1
B03803   64B3803-0
  A comparative examination of
two modes of intoxication – an
exploratory study of glue sniffing.
?
```

UNIT THREE

3.1 Operations: limiting a retrieved set of records by some criteria, e.g. language, date of publication; ranging

Commands and features introduced: LIMITALL (LALL); ranging operators

The DIALOG system uses the SELECT (S) command to narrow down a retrieved set of records (the command LIMIT (L) used to perform this function and can still be used, but it is preferable to use SELECT – it saves having to learn another command!). For example, a set could be limited to a particular range of accession numbers, to a range of dates, or to a particular language. On MEDLINE and certain other databases, the searcher can limit a set of records to those where a descriptor is a 'major' descriptor only.

EXAMPLE: MEDLINE

```
  S23   1522 "RELAXATION// MUSCLE"
? s s23/de*                           ←┘
  S24     448 23/DE*
?
```

In this example, the searcher has retrieved a large set of records on RELAXATION// MUSCLE and wishes to limit the set to those instances where this term is a major descriptor only – the /DE shows the field to be searched, the * indicates major descriptors only.

EXAMPLE: CAB Abstracts

```
          7022   CULTIVAT?/TI,DE
           557   EDIBLE/TI,DE
          9482   FUNG?? ?/TI,DE
  S1        14   CULTIVAT?(F)EDIBLE(F)FUNG?? ?/TI,DE
? s s1/eng                            ←┘
  S2        12 1/ENG
? t2/6/1                              ←┘
```

One very common requirement is to limit a set to those records where the original papers are in a particular language. The searcher first creates a set (NB Fung?? ? will retrieve both FUNGUS and FUNGI) and then uses the SELECT command to limit the set to English

```
  2/6/1
0331272   0C055-06215; 7U008-01525
  An easy technique of mushroom
cultivation
?
```

language papers only. The suffix /ENG can also be applied directly to a term, e.g. S MUSHROOM?/ ENG. On some databases this suffix does not apply; some databases limit by language by creating a set using the prefix LA= followed by the language or its abbreviation; this set is then combined with a set or sets on the subject of the search. The LIMITALL (LALL) command, followed by a qualifier, can be used at the beginning of a search, and each search statement will be limited by that qualifier.

It is possible to search a range of numbers, e.g. dates of publication, turnover of companies etc., either by using a colon (:), or by the operators >= greater than or equal to, <= less than or equal to, >greater than, <less than.

EXAMPLE: ERIC

```
  S7       353 (3OR6)AND(1OR2)
? s7 and py=1985:1989
           353 S7
        96106 PY=1985 : PY=1989
  S8          51 S7 AND PY=1985:1989
?
```

This search on ERIC is limited to those records published in the years 1985 to 1989; this could also have been input as PY>=1985.

3.2 Operations: saving a search on one database, changing to another database and conducting the same search on the new database; searching a number of databases at once ('multifile' searching); searching elements of records across databases

Commands and features introduced: SAVE; SAVE TEMP; EXECUTE STEPS (EXS); SAVE/SDI; RECALL; RELEASE; DIALOG OneSearch; TYPE (T) ... FROM EACH; MAP

An online enquiry is often not satisfied by searching just one database, and some databases, e.g. INSPEC, are split up into more than one file. Crossfile searching can take one of three forms:

(a) Conducting a search on one database, saving the search, changing to another database, and conducting the same search on the new database; this avoids the necessity of typing in or uploading the search more than once while online. The search can be saved permanently using the command SAVE, or temporarily for seven days using the command SAVE TEMP. To process the saved search on the new database, the command EXECUTE STEPS (EXS) is used.

EXAMPLE: Middle East Abstracts and Index/Mideast File

```
? ds
Set  Items  Description
S1   6654   SAUDI ARABIA OR IRAN
S2    234   CRIME OR CRIMINALS
S3     99   S1ANDS2

? save temp
Temp SearchSave "TD034" stored
      17may88 04:51:56 User000000
            $1.82    0.033 Hrs File248
            $0.00 4 Types in Format 6
            $0.00 4 Types
   $1.82  Estimated cost File248
   $0.33  DialnetE
   $2.15  Estimated cost this search
   $2.63  Estimated total session cost  0.045 Hrs
? b249; exs td034
      17may88 04:52:13 User000000
            $2.09    0.038 Hrs File248
            $0.00 4 Types in Format 6
            $0.00 4 Types
   $2.09  Estimated cost File248
   $0.38  DialnetE
   $2.47  Estimated cost this search
   $2.95  Estimated total session cost  0.050 Hrs

File 249:MIDEAST FILE - 1980-87/OCT
  (Copr. Learned Information 1987)
Set  Items  Description
----- -------- ----------------
      5500  SAUDI ARABIA
      7874  IRAN
S1   12345  SAUDI ARABIA OR IRAN
        98  CRIME
```

Searcher uses the command DISPLAY SETS (DS) to review the search so far on the initial database. The command SAVE TEMP is used to save the search temporarily; a number is allotted to the search, and a summary given of time and cost to date.

Searcher uses command BEGIN (B) followed by new database number, and 'stacks' the next command on the same line; the system will now change databases and immediately process the saved search on the new database.

If a search is to be stored more permanently than for a few days, the command SAVE is used. This feature is useful when a search is to

```
        91   CRIMINALS
S2     112   CRIME OR CRIMINALS
     12345   S1
       112   S2
S3      11   S1ANDS2
?
```

be regularly updated by the searcher, or when a particular subset of a database is used regularly in different searches (e.g. there are a number of terms in the ERIC Thesaurus describing children in the primary school age range; these terms could be ORd together and saved permanently, and combined with other subject sets when required).

Regular SDI (Selective Dissemination of Information) searches can be performed automatically by the system, for a small charge; for this, the SAVE/SDI command is used.

Saved searches can be deleted by RELEASEing them; e.g. RELEASE SB016. There is no need to delete searches saved temporarily using SAVE TEMP.

(b) Searching a number of databases at the same time, i.e. multifile searching. DIALOG introduced OneSearch in 1987, whereby a number of databases can be searched at the same time.

EXAMPLE: MEDLINE, EMBASE

```
? b 155,72,172,173                         ←┘
        10Oct88 10:00:14 User000000 Session D216.2
              $2.52   0.070 Hrs File154
              $0.15 3 Types in Format 5
              $0.00 3 Types in Format 6
              $0.15 6 Types
        $2.67 Estimated cost File154
        $0.70 DialnetE
        $3.37 Estimated cost this search
        $3.65 Estimated total session cost   0.077 Hrs

System:OS - DIALOG OneSearch
  File 155:MEDLINE   66-88/NOV

  FILE  72:EMBASE (EXCERPTA MEDICA) 82-88/ISS30
              (COPR. ESP BV/EM 1988)
  FILE 172:EMBASE (Excerpta Medica) 1980-81
              (Copr. ESP BV/EM 1984)
  File 173:EMBASE (Excerpta Medica) 1974-79
              (Copr. ESP BV/EM 1984)
```

Searcher selects the required files using the BEGIN (B) command as usual.

```
Set  Items   Description
----- -------  ----------------
? set detail on
DETAIL set on
? s nephrotic(n)syndrome(f)
   vaccin?/de

155: MEDLINE 66-88/NOV
     5624    NEPHROTIC/DE
   128385    SYNDROME/DE
    44519    VACCIN?/DE
       22    NEPHROTIC(N)SYNDROME(F)VACCIN?/DE
 72: EMBASE (EXCERPTA MEDICA) 82-88/ISS30
     1262    NEPHROTIC/DE
    38674    SYNDROME/DE   DC=0155219
    11984    VACCIN?/DE
       15    NEPHROTIC(N)SYNDROME(F)VACCIN?/DE
172:EMBASE (Excerpta Medica) 1980-81
      517    NEPHROTIC/DE
     9247    SYNDROME/DE   DC=0155219
     4040    VACCIN?/DE
        9    NEPHROTIC(N)SYNDROME(F)VACCIN?/DE
173:EMBASE (Excerpta Medica) 1974-79
     1423    NEPHROTIC/DE
    24606    SYNDROME/DE   DC=0155219
    11241    VACCIN?/DE
        9    NEPHROTIC(N)SYNDROME(F)VACCIN?/DE
TOTAL: FILES 155,72,172 and .........
     9190    NEPHROTIC/DE
   200912    SYNDROME/DE
    71784    VACCIN?/DE
S1     55    NEPHROTIC(N)SYNDROME(F)VACCIN?/DE
? t1/6/1-2 from each
 1/6/1     (Item 1 from file: 155)
05938217 86239217
  Decline of vaccine-induced anti-
pneumococcal antibody in children
with nephrotic syndrome.

 2/6/2     (Item 2 from file: 155)
05582920 85198920
  Live varicella vaccine: prevention
of nosocomial infection and
protection of high risk infants from
varicella infection.
```

The SET DETAIL on command instructs the system to give separate postings for each database, but you will see that a TOTAL is given at the end. If this detail is not required, just input the search as normal and the system will just give the TOTAL number of postings for the set.

When displaying records, the system will normally print all records from the first databases, then the next and so on. If the searcher wants some records from EACH database, the words FROM EACH must be input after the TYPE command. You will see from this example that the system does not eliminate duplicate records held by different databases.

```
 2/6/23    (Item 1 from file: 72)
07118702  EMBASE No. 88153050
  Peritonitis in children with nephrotic syndrome.

 2/6/24    (Item 2 from file: 72)
6255135   EMBASE No. 86250198
  Decline of vaccine-induced antipneumococcal antibody in children with
nephrotic syndrome.

 2/6/38    (Item 1 from file: 172)
. . . . . . . . . . . . . .
```

(c) Searching elements of records across databases

DIALOG has the facility of saving elements of records on one database for using on another database. In the example below, the searcher isolates a number of registry numbers on Chemname, a chemical dictionary, and then, by using the MAP command, stores all those registry numbers in a search statement which can then be processed on the main CA Search database.

EXAMPLE: Chemname, CA Search

```
? ds
Set  Items  Description
S1     227  DICHLOROFLUOROMETHYL?
S2      20  S1 AND THIO AND SULFAMIDE
S3       9  S2 AND DIMETHYL
S4       7  S3 AND PHENYL
? maprn s4

1 select statement(s)
serial£SA002

? b399
      02nov88 12:12:44 User000000 Session A17.2
              $3.38  0.019 Hrs File301
         $3.38  Estimated cost File301
         $0.19  DialnetE
         $3.57  Estimated cost this search
         $3.81  Estimated total session cost  0.026 Hrs

File 399:CA SEARCH 1967-1988 UD=10916
         (copr. 1988 by the Amer. Chem. Soc.)
```

The searcher gradually narrows down the search to seven records on the chemical dictionary database Chemname, and saves the registry numbers (RN) from those seven records using the MAP command, followed by the element being saved, i.e. RN.

The searcher then BEGINs file 399, the CA Search database, and uses the saved search as the search statement for the first set; this saves typing out all the registry numbers.

The results of this search statement can then be combined with other sets to refine the search.

```
Set    Items   Description
----   -----   -----------
? exs sa002
          60   RN=731-27-1
         522   RN=1085-98-9
           2   RN=1087-94-1
           2   RN=12698-56-5
           4   RN=17648-71-4
           2   RN=27831-81-8
           2   RN=27831-82-9
           2   RN=27831-83-0
           0   RN=56590-61-5
           3   RN=79235-99-7
           0   RN=90416-56-1
  S1     555   RN=731-27-1 + RN=1085-98-9 + RN=1087-94-1
                + RN=12698-56-5 + RN=17648-71-4 + RN=27831-81-8
                + RN=27831-82-9 + RN=27831-83-0 + RN=56590-61-5
                + RN=79235-99-7 + RN=90416-56-1
? s s1 and wood(f)preserv?
  S2        24 S1 AND WOOD(F)PRESERV?

? t2/6/1
  2/6/1
104134986   CA: 104(16)134986a   JOURNAL
  Laboratory evaluation of algicidal biocides for use on constructional
materials. 3. Use of the vermiculite bed technique to evaluate toxic
washes, surface coatings and surface treatments
  JOURNAL: Int. Biodeterior. DATE: 1985   VOLUME: 21   NUMBER: 4
PAGES: 285-293
?
```

3.3 Operations: printing 'offline'; sorting records; downloading records; transferring records to an electronic mail facility

Commands and features introduced: PRINT (PR); SORT; use of format 4 for downloading; PRINT (PR) . . . via Dialmail

After a set of relevant records has been retrieved, it can often be more economical, particularly if large numbers of records are required, to have them printed 'offline' by the online hosts and mailed to the searcher or end-user. The high-speed printing of search results generally takes place in the evening of the day of the search, and mailing follows immediately. The longest wait, even across continents, is about six days, but it is often quicker than this; inland this can be as little as one or two days. Other alternatives to printing online, as well as printing offline, are downloading into a local microcomputer or mainframe, or transferring the records to DIALOG's electronic mail facility, Dialmail. The searcher decides which method is preferable, depending on a number of variables, the principal ones being the speed of the terminal and printing equipment, how urgently the records are required, how many records there are, what format is required (e.g. are abstracts required, on full-text databases is the whole text required?), and what the financial implications of the different methods are.

If it is decided to print offline, the command PRINT (PR) is used, followed by the set number, format, and range of items (or ALL if whole set is required) – as in the TYPE command. Many databases also have the facility to sort records, and this is often incorporated in the offline PRINT command.

EXAMPLE: Pais International

```
  S36   19  33AND35
? pr36/5/all                                    ←┘
P004: PRINT  36/5/ALL   est. cost
                        of $7.60
? logoff                                        ←┘
etc.....etc.....
```

Searcher prints the whole set offline. The system repeats the command to show that it has been accepted; if a mistake has been made, the searcher can enter PR- to cancel the last command. PRINT commands can be cancelled up to two hours after they have been entered.

EXAMPLE: ERIC

```
  S17   36  S16 AND PY=1985:1989
? pr17/5/all/au                                ←┘
P012: PRINT 17/5/ALL/AU (items 1-36) est. cost $5.04
?
```

EXAMPLE: British Education Index

```
  S11   20  9OR10
? pr11/5/all via dialmail                       ←┘
P013: PRINT 11/5/ALL VIA DIALMAIL (items 1-20) est. cost of $5.00
?
```

The example from ERIC shows an offline print which includes the request to sort the records by AUthor.

The example from British Education Index shows a PRINT command transferring records to Dialmail; these records would be available for printing online from Dialmail the following morning.

For downloading records, format 4 can be used, in which each field is labelled with a tag.

System 2

European Space Agency Information Retrieval Service (ESA-IRS)

UNIT ONE

1.1 Operations: logging-on to the system; choosing a database (file)

Commands and features introduced: logging-on information; BEGIN (B)

The Information Retrieval Service (IRS) of the European Space Agency (ESA) is based in Frascati, Italy, and currently gives access to over 100 databases. IRS has centres in several countries, and agents or contacts in others, to give customer support to their service; in the United Kingdom this support is provided by IRS-DIALTECH (see Appendix 1).

ESA-IRS can be accessed via the various national post, telegraph and telephone services, and commercial data transmission networks. In the United Kingdom, users contact the nearest 'node' of British Telecom's Packet SwitchStream (PSS) network, and then make the link with the IRS computer in Frascati. The example below shows a log-on via the Manchester (UK) node of PSS, with a terminal working at 1,200 baud (120 characters per second (cps)).

For the purpose of clarity, the characters input by the searcher in the examples below are underlined; this is not the case when actually working online.

The searcher first dials the node of the network (in many cases the terminal or modem will be programmed to do this automatically), and after identifying the type of terminal being used, and the speed of transmission, will receive a response similar to the following from the node:

EXAMPLE:

```
MAN A002-6164340405
NESAIRS000000        ←┘
ADD?
A219201156           ←
```

Response from the MANchester node of PSS. The Network User Identifier (NUI) is entered – a number unique to the user. In this case ESA-IRS lets searchers use their own Identifier.

←┘ = return

The network asks for the ADDress – to which online host does the searcher wish to be connected?

```
234219201156+COM
Please enter your ESA-QUEST password
$$$$$$$$ Connection accepted in file032
        Port=8A5-E ; Quest-language selected
```

The ADDress is repeated by way of confirming the connection. The next response is from ESA-IRS, asking for the password.

```
--  File 51, McCarthy is now available with
    BEGIN PROFILE and SELECT MCC
------------------------------------------------
--  New File now online: METALS DATA
    For details see ?File125
------------------------------------------------
```

At this stage, the searcher will be given any system news of immediate importance, and then given the question mark (?), which is the searcher's prompt to input something.

```
? b75                ←┘
------------21Apr88  10:16:37  User00000--
   0.32 AU 0.39 Minutes in File 32
   0.32 AU approx Total
File 75:GLASS:1970-88,02
SET  ITEMS  DESCRIPTION (+ =OR;* =AND;- =NOT)
---  -----  ------------------------------------
?
```

The searcher selects the database (file) required by entering its number or name, preceded by the command BEGIN, or its abbreviation (B). In this case, the searcher could have entered B GLASSFILE.

Costs are calculated using Accounting Units (AU), which are set each year for each European currency.

1.2 Operations: entering search statements and creating sets of records; using Boolean operators; displaying records

Commands and features introduced: SELECT (S); COMBINE (C); Boolean operators AND and OR; 'stacking' commands; TYPE (T); DISPLAY (D); PAGE (P)

The general principles and methods of searching have been discussed in Chapters 5 and 6. After the initial analysis of the subject of the search, the identification of the concepts involved and the selection of appropriate terms to describe those concepts on this database, the terms are input using the SELECT (S) command.

EXAMPLE: HSELINE

```
SET   ITEMS   DESCRIPTION (+ = OR;* = AND;- = NOT)
----- ---------- -------------------------------------------------------

? s isocyanates; s asthma;
     s asthmatic
  1     296     ISOCYANATES
  2     412     ASTHMA
  3     123     ASTHMATIC
```

SET, ITEMS and DESCRIPTION are the headings for the subsequent search results, giving the SET number, the number of ITEMS or records retrieved for the DESCRIPTION (i.e. the terms or phrases input by the searcher). Terms can be 'stacked' on one line, as long as each command is separated by a semicolon (;), as in the example; the system will process each command in turn.

The system will search the basic index for these three terms, find how many records (ITEMS) there are for each, and display this information. (NB The ASTHMA concept could be input more simply using truncation (see 2.2 below).)

```
? c1and(2or3)
  4       27     1AND(2OR3)
?
```

Upon receiving the ? prompt, the searcher inputs the next statement using the logical operators AND and OR, thereby requiring a set that gives only those records that are included in BOTH set 1 and EITHER set 2 OR set 3. The COMBINE (C) command is used.

The details of the records retrieved in set 4 can be displayed online by the use of the TYPE (T) or DISPLAY (D) commands. There are a number of different formats available and the searcher can choose whichever is most appropriate in the circumstances; some of the formats vary from one database to another, but the common formats available are:

Format name	*Record content*
T (Technical)	ESA-QUEST accession numbers
S (Scan)	File name, title
B (Browse)	File name, title, keywords, classification codes, publication date, language
BA (Browse, with Abstract)	Format B, with abstract
R (Reference)	File name, title, author, corporate source, bibliographic details
A (All)	Full record
X	All fields plus field and subfield tags and special markers (used with DOWNLOAD command)

The searcher would normally consult the appropriate database details when planning a search to verify which formats were available. A TYPE (T) command usually consists of these elements:

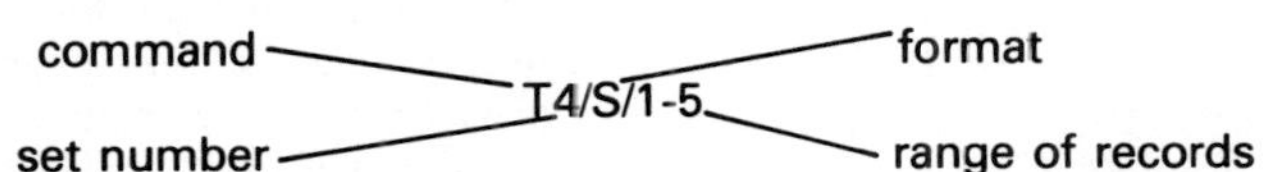

TYPE (T) gives a continuous output, DISPLAY (D) gives one screen at a time to facilitate searching on VDU terminals; the command PAGE (P) brings up the next screen of a display.

EXAMPLE: HSELINE

```
? t4/S/1-4

      TYPE 4/S/1-4
   HSELINE
ISOCYANATES AND RESPIRATORY DISEASE : CURRENT STATUS
```

The searcher will often at this stage browse through the titles to make sure the records retrieved are relevant. The command T4/S/1-4 asks the system to type out the titles (format S) of the first four (1-4) records of set 4.

HSELINE
SMALL AIRWAY HYPERACTIVITY AMONG LIFELONG NON-ATOPIC NON-SMOKERS EXPOSED TO ISOCYANATES

(NB Records in sets are in reverse-chronological order, so that the first records displayed are the latest entered into the database.)

HSELINE
ISOCYANATE ASTHMA IN A CAST IRON FOUNDRY

HSELINE
OUTCOME OF ASTHMA INDUCED BY ISOCYANATES

? t4/a/1 ←

TYPE 4/A/1
201 503 HSELINE 88000499
ISOCYANATES AND RESPIRATORY DISEASE : CURRENT STATUS
Musk, A.W.; Peters, J.M. and others.
American Journal of Industrial Medicine. 1988, vol.13 no.3
Page: 331-349.

Reviews the known respiratory effects of isocyanates. There is good evidence to indicate that isocyanates: cause chemical bronchitis/pneumonitis; are potent pulmonary sensitizers capable of causing 'isocyanate asthma'; cause nonspecific airways disease, including chronic bronchitis; can induce a general asthmatic state; and can cause hypersensitivity pneumonitis. Similar dose-response relationships are seen for both acute and chronic effects. There are plants operating in which exposures are well controlled and in which no respiratory effects can be detected. Suggestions are provided for preplacement assessment and periodic surveillance for workers exposed to these compounds. 114 refs.
?

The searcher asks for the first record to be TYPEd online in full; this includes the abstract; this would be simultaneously printed on a printer, or saved in electronic form for later printing, so that the client can have a printed copy of the record.

The options open to the searcher at this stage are numerous – one or more of them may be: to browse through the remainder of the set; to print out all the records in the set; to develop the search further and display resulting records; to conduct a similar search on another database; to end the searching session.

1.3 Operations: reviewing a search; ending the search and searching session (logging-off)

Commands and features introduced: DISPLAY SETS (DS); LOGOFF; LOGOFFHOLD; LOGOFFBUT

The searcher wishing to change to another database would normally use the BEGIN (B) command, followed by the name or number of the required database; this would erase all previous sets and enable the searcher to begin at set 1 again in the new database. In many cases, before changing databases, the searcher would SAVE the search already conducted (see 3.2).

There are many occasions on which the searcher requires to see a display of the search to date – particularly when the search statements have scrolled off a VDU screen! To review a search, enter DISPLAY SETS (DS).

EXAMPLE: HSELINE

```
? ds                                   ←┘
SET  ITEMS  DESCRIPTION
 1    296   ISOCYANATES
 2    412   ASTHMA
 3    123   ASTHMATIC
 4     27   1*(2+3)
```

The command DISPLAY SETS (DS) on its own will give the whole search; specific sets, or a range of sets, can be specified, e.g. DS 2; DS 6-16.

To end a searching session and disconnect from the host computer, the searcher would type the LOGOFF command; no further input is required by the searcher.

EXAMPLE: CAB Abstracts

```
? logoff                               ←┘
-------------06Feb89  18:20:17  User00000--
    1.15 AU 6.93 Minutes in File 124
    6.89 AU 20 Online Prints
    3.50 AU Session Charge
   11.54 AU approx Total
ESA-QUEST session terminated
         at 18:20:21

CLR PAD (00) 00:00:07:36 238 23
```

The command LOGOFFHOLD will disconnect the searcher from the system, but will save the search on the last database for a maximum of 20 minutes – giving the searcher time for a coffee, or two! If the searcher reconnects within that time limit, the search can be continued. LOGOFFBUT ends the searching session, but allows the searcher to start with another password without disconnecting. After disconnection from the host computer, a message from the network shows how long the network was used (7 mins. 36 secs.) and how many 'segments' of data were received (288) and how many were sent (23). A 'segment' holds up to 64 characters, half a 'packet'.

UNIT TWO

2.1 Operations: displaying the index file; using both controlled and natural language terms; searching specific fields

Commands and features introduced: EXPAND (E); searching for author with prefix AU=; limiting search statements to specific fields using a suffix, e.g. /CT, /TI

The ability to display terms from the index file, where all directly searchable terms are listed, is useful for finding out the occurrence of both controlled and natural language terms; and also for finding out the precise format of a term – for example, that of an author's name. For this operation the EXPAND (E) command is used. If no particular field (e.g. AU= for the author field) is asked for by the searcher, the EXPAND command will display the basic index only.

EXAMPLE: Food Science and Technology Abstracts

The searcher EXPANDs the term HYDROXYPROLINE. An alphabetical listing is given, each with a reference number, the number of records (ITEMS) containing that term, the term itself, and the number

```
Set  Items  Description
----- -------  ----------------
? e hydroxyproline                                ←┘
     EXPAND HYDROXYPROLINE

REF  ITEMS  INDEX-TERM                            T RT
E1      11  HYDROXYPROLIN
E2       7  HYDROXYPROLINBESTIMMUNG
E3*    482  HYDROXYPROLINE                          2
E4       2  HYDROXYPROLINE CONTENT OF CONNECTIVE TISSUE
E5       1  HYDROXYPROLINE DETN. HPLC-COLUMN SWITCHING
E6       8  HYDROXYPROLINE DETN. IN MEAT
E7      11  HYDROXYPROLINE DETN. IN MEAT PRODUCTS
E8       2  HYDROXYPROLINE DETN. IN TAIWAN MEAT PRODUCTS
E9       2  HYDROXYPROLINE DETN. IN TAIWAN MEAT, STAND..
E10.....
...Pages.Lines: More=  12.8
```

of related terms (RT) – this is available on those databases with an online thesaurus only; normally 19 terms are listed. An asterisk (*) indicates the item input by the searcher. The searcher can SELECT a term or terms directly from the list, e.g. SE3, or SE3,E6,E8 or SE3-E6,E8,E10-E12; a set will then be established, as in the example.

```
? se6-e9
  1       14 E6-E9
             E3: HYDROXYPROLINE
?
```

EXAMPLE: CAB Abstracts

```
? e freemartins
                        EXPAND FREEMARTINS
REF   ITEMS   INDEX-TERM                  T RT
E1        3   FREEMARTINISMULUI
E2        2   FREEMARTINISMUS
E3 *    134   FREEMARTINS                   1
E4        2   FREEMONT
.........
...Pages.Lines: More= 12.8
? ee3
REF   ITEMS   INDEX-TERM                  T RT
R1 *    134   FREEMARTINS                   1
R2      220   INTERSEXUALITY                5

?
```

Where a database has an online thesaurus, it is possible to display any related terms (RT) by EXPANDing the E reference number of the appropriate term, e.g. E E3.

To search in a field which is not in the basic index, a field prefix is necessary, e.g. S AU=BLOGGS, J. However, it is important, particularly when searching authors' names, to EXPAND the name first, to find the exact format used, especially the format of the initials. The searcher input the initials without a space, but the EXPAND command shows the correct format, and the searcher is able to select from the display.

EXAMPLE: CAB Abstracts

```
? e au=hashim, m.m.
                        EXPAND AU=HASHIM, M.M.
REF   ITEMS   INDEX-TERM                  T RT
E1        1   AU=HASHIM, L. O.
E2        4   AU=HASHIM, M.
E3            AU=HASHIM, M.M.
E4        1   AU=HASHIM, M. M.
E5        2   AU=HASHIM, M. N.
E6        2   AU=HASHIM, N.
E7        2   AU=HASHIM, N. H.
.........
E19      45   AU=HASHIMOTO, A.
...Pages.Lines: More= 12.8
? se4
  1        1 E4
             E3: AU=HASHIM, M.M.
```

The great majority of bibliographic databases use a controlled language for indexing records and these terms are held in one field in the record; on ESA-IRS they are called 'controlled terms', and are directly searchable. In addition, most words taken from other fields within the record, e.g. title, abstract, are also directly searchable as natural language terms. Some databases, such as the Health and Safety Executive database HSELINE, do not have a controlled language. The searcher will normally find appropriate terms when planning the search either from manual sources or from EXPANDing terms online.

EXAMPLE: Food Science and Technology Abstracts

```
? s meat by-products, use of
  1     10 MEAT BY-PRODUCTS, USE OF
? s pharmaceutical
  2    857 PHARMACEUTICAL
? c1and2
  3      3 1AND2
? t3/a/1
         TYPE 3/A/1
88-02-s0030 FSTA 88009940 URE
  Maximizing by-product utilization
  Berry, B.W.; Field, R.A.; Reynolds, A.E.
  United States of America, American Meat
Science Association 39th Reciprocal Meat
Conference
  Meat Sci. Res. Lab., Beltsville,
Maryland 20705, USA
  Proceedings, Annual Reciprocal
Meat Conference of the American
Meat Science Association
  No. 39, 9-12, 1987  In ENGLISH
  Category Code : S (MEAT,
POULTRY AND GAME)

  Utilization of by-products of the slaughter
and meat-processing industries is discussed
with reference to: the extent of use of various
edible by-products from beef, pork, and lamb
carcasses; inedible by-products; pharmaceutical
by-products..........
  Controlled Terms: By-products / meat by-
products, use of / Meat / use of meat by-
products
?
```

This multi-word controlled term is entered without a field qualifier; if a single term is entered, and only those records where the term is in the controlled language field are required, the qualifier /CT would need to be added, e.g. MEAT/CT.

Many databases also have a field for 'uncontrolled terms', which are extra indexing terms relating to a particular record, but are not from the controlled language; the qualifier is /UT. More than one field may be specified in the search statement, e.g. SMEAT/TI,CT,UT.

Although searches are generally well planned in advance, allowance is always made for modifying the search as a result of records retrieved – this is one great advantage of using an 'interactive' system. One common way of developing a search is to display the controlled language terms of relevant records retrieved, and then to input any of these which were overlooked or unknown previously; in the above example, USE OF MEAT BY-PRODUCTS is also used as a controlled term, as well as the one input in the first search statement.

2.2 Operations: proximity searching (full-text searching); (stringsearching not available on ESA-IRS); truncation

Commands and features introduced: proximity operators (W), (F), (P), (S); truncation symbol (?)

It is useful to be able to search for a term in a particular field, as we have seen, but the ability to search for terms in a particular proximity to each other enhances searching considerably. On ESA-IRS, if two or more words are required to occur together in a record, e.g. URBAN PLANNING, by inserting (W) between the terms the searcher can retrieve records containing those two terms, in that order, from any of the full-text searchable fields of the database – principally the title, controlled term, uncontrolled term and abstract fields. An (F) operator is used if the requirement is that the two terms appear in the same field, but not necessarily together, and in any order. The (S) operator will search terms in the same sentence, but in any order; and the (P) operator will find a fixed number of words in between terms, in the order in which the terms are input.

EXAMPLE: Acompline

```
? s activity(f)holidays; s special(w)interest(f)holidays ←┘
  1      34 ACTIVITY(F)HOLIDAYS
  2       1 SPECIAL(W)INTEREST(F)HOLIDAYS
? s learning(f)holidays; c1-3/or ←┘
  3       1 LEARNING(F)HOLIDAYS
  4      35 1-3/OR
? t4/s/1-2 ←┘
              TYPE 4/S/1-2
     Acompline
TIME-OFF ARRANGEMENTS
```

The words ACTIVITY and HOLIDAYS are required to appear in the same field, in any order. The phrase SPECIAL INTEREST is searched with the (W) operator – the two terms must appear together in the order input; the word HOLIDAYS

Acompline
PORTSMOUTH'S TOURISM
DEVELOPMENT STRATEGY
? t4/a/2

can appear anywhere in the same field. Search statement 4 shows a short way of ORing together a number of sets. The operator (W) can appear as (1W), (2W), (3W) etc. to allow 'up to' that number of words to appear between the terms selected, e.g. SPECIAL(1W)HOLIDAYS would retrieve both SPECIAL HOLIDAYS and SPECIAL INTEREST HOLIDAYS.

TYPE 4/A/2
87-NZ-34014 Acompline 87038324
PORTSMOUTH'S TOURISM
DEVELOPMENT STRATEGY
CS: PORTSMOUTH CITY
COUNCIL
Plann Exch Local Econ Dev Inf Serv Initiative, Mar 1987 (A306) 2pp
Res.Lib.Ident.: 011351

Portsmouth City Council is seeking to develop tourism as a source of new jobs to compensate for those lost by the closure of the Naval dockyard. Its marketing and other activities are designed to attract domestic tourists taking short breaks or second holidays, heritage conscious foreign visitors from the United States and elsewhere, and small or medium sized conferences. The city has an unrivalled collection of international maritime attractions including the Mary Rose, Victory, HMS Warrior, the Royal Naval Museum and the Gosport Submarine Museum.

Geo-Location: PORTSMOUTH; UNITED KINGDOM; UNITED STATES
Uncontrolled Terms: United Kingdom, local government
Controlled Terms: CONFERENCE / INTERNATIONAL / COLLECTION / LOCAL GOVERNMENT / MARKET RESEARCH / HOLIDAY / DOMESTIC / FOREIGN / TOURIST / MARITIME / TOURISM / DESIGN / URBAN / EMPLOYMENT
?

The searcher TYPEs out the second record in full; this record has been retrieved because the terms ACTIVITIES and HOLIDAYS have been found in the same field, i.e. the abstract field – not really in the correct context, however! It may be necessary to re-input the phrase as ACTIVITY(W)HOLIDAYS to make it more precise.

A feature which is very important, particularly when searching natural language terms and phrases, is truncation – the ability to input the stem of a word, followed by the truncation symbol; the system will retrieve records where any term beginning with the word stem appears; e.g. S INTEREST? will retrieve INTEREST, INTERESTED, INTERESTING, INTERESTS etc. On ESA-IRS the truncation symbol is the question mark (?).

EXAMPLE: HSELINE

```
? s uranium; s employ?; s worker? ?          ↵
  1       586 URANIUM
  2      5834 EMPLOY?
  3      7940 WORKER? ?
? c1and(2or3)                                ↵
  4        49 1AND(2OR3)
? s hazard?; s danger?; s expos?             ↵
  5     10083 HAZARD?
  6      2251 DANGER?
  7     10168 EXPOS?
? c5-7/or; c4and8                            ↵
  8     20384 5-7/OR
  9        28 4AND8
? t9/s/1-2                                   ↵
              TYPE 9/S/1-2
          HSELINE
  RADIATION DOSES AND CAUSE-SPECIFIC MORTALITY AMONG
WORKERS AT A NUCLEAR MATERIALS FABRICATION PLANT

          HSELINE
  RELATIVE RISK MODELS FOR ASSESSING THE JOINT EFFECT OF
MULTIPLE FACTORS
? t9/a/1                                     ↵
              TYPE 9/A/1
-201 421 HSELINE 88000461
  RADIATION DOSES AND CAUSE-SPECIFIC MORTALITY AMONG
WORKERS AT A NUCLEAR MATERIALS FABRICATION PLANT
  Checkoway, H.; Pearce, N. and others.
  American Journal of Epidemiology, Feb. 1988, vol.127, no.2, Page:
255-266

  A historical cohort mortality study conducted among 6,781 white male
employees from a nuclear weapons materials fabrication plant for the
years 1947-1979. Exposures of greatest concern are alpha and gamma
radiation emanating primarily from insoluble uranium compounds ......
?
```

2.3 Operations: searching using classification codes, subfiles etc.; analysing search results

Commands and features introduced: ZOOM

When discussing searching in Chapter 6, reference was made to the fact that most databases have a feature whereby it is possible to search a subject area wider than that described by one term, or a few terms, by using a classification code, subfile, or other system or database feature.

EXAMPLE: Glassfile

```
? e cc=aa                                    ←┘

REF    ITEMS   INDEX-TERM
E1         1   AU=5KRAMOV G.T.
E2         1   AU=763-766, 2 FIG.
E3 *    3110   CC=AA
E4       791   CC=AB
E5      2002   CC=BA
E6      3387   CC=BB
E7      1448   CC=BC
..........etc......
```

Some of the class codes on Glassfile are as follows:

A Generalities on glass.
- AA Vitreous state. Structure.
- AB Physics and chemistry of vitreous materials.

B Glass properties and measure methods.
- BA Glass properties in general.
- BB Controls and tests. Chemical analysis. Standardization.
- BC Physical properties of glass.
- BD ....etc.......

As there are likely to be numerous records on the composition of glass, the searcher narrows down the search to those records which are in the general classification group of 'Physics and chemistry of vitreous materials'.

```
? se4; s composition(s)verre?/ti,ct; s composition(s)glass?/ti,ct   ←┘
   1       791   CC=AB
   2       515   COMPOSITION(S)VERRE?/TI,CT
   3       189   COMPOSITION(S)GLASS?/TI,CT
? c1and(2or3)                                ←┘
   4        10   1AND(2OR3)
? s la=anglais; c4and5                       ←┘
   5     25259   LA=ANGLAIS
   6         4   4AND5
? t6/s/1-2                                   ←┘
                 TYPE 6/S/1-2
   GLAS
   Temperature de transformation et comportement a la devitrification
de verres dans le domaine de composition Na20.2Si02-Ba0.2Si02 (en
anglais) Glass transition temperature and devitrification behaviour of
glasses in the Na20.2Si02-Ba0.2Si02 composition range.

   GLAS
   Reactions entre Si02 et des fontes de composition Na20.3Si02 - en
anglais- (Reactions between Si02 and Na20.3Si02 glass metals)
?
```

As Glassfile is a French-produced database, both English and French terms are entered to ensure maximum retrieval; also records are limited to English language papers only.

An aid developed by ESA-IRS for developing 'interactive' searching is the ZOOM command. This analyses a retrieved set of records and lists the frequency with which index terms have been used, and helps the searcher in identifying the most relevant words or phrases used in the set: these words and phrases can then be entered as search terms to develop the search.

EXAMPLE: HSELINE

ZOOM without qualification will analyse index terms from the last set. (To analyse a previous set, add the set number, e.g. ZOOM 2.)

```
? s hazard?(f)uranium              ←┘
  4      18 HAZARD?(F)URANIUM
? zoom                             ←┘
                    Text Analysis Results
Frq   Words/Phrases
----- ------------------------------------------
  4   HAZARDS
  2   EXPOSURE
  2   RADIATION
  2   URANIUM
  1   ACCESS
  1   CHEMICAL HAZARDS
  1   COAL MINING
  1   COOLANT ACCIDENTS
. . . . . . . . . . .
. . . Pages.Line: More 2.2
?
```

UNIT THREE

3.1 Operations: limiting a retrieved set of records by some criteria, e.g. language, date of publication; ranging

Commands and features introduced: LIMIT (L), LIMITALL (LALL)

The ESA-IRS system uses the LIMIT (L) command to narrow down a retrieved set of records. For example, a set could be limited to a particular range of accession numbers, to a range of dates, or to a particular language.

EXAMPLE: INSPEC

```
? ds                                ←┘
SET  ITEMS  DESCRIPTION
  1    722  LANGUAGE
              TRANSLATION
  2   6239  COMPUTER
              APPLICATIONS
```

One very common requirement is to limit a set to those records where the original papers are in a particular language. The searcher has input a search, and entered DISPLAY SETS

```
  3     205  HUMANITIES DATA
                   PROCESSING
  4     258  MACHINE TRANS-
                   LATION
  5     299  (1+4)*(2+3)
? 5/eng
  6     169  S/ENG
? t6/s/1-5

        TYPE 6/S/1-5
       INSPEC
GPSG and german word order

       INSPEC
Second Conference on Applied Language Processing
......etc
```

(DS) to review the search to date. On this database it is possible to use the LIMIT (L) command, followed by the set number and the three-letter abbreviation for the chosen language.

On some databases this suffix does not apply; to limit by language a set is created by using the prefix LA= followed by the language or its abbreviation; this set is then combined with a set or sets on the subject of the search. It is advisable to EXPAND LA= first to be sure of the form the language takes.

EXAMPLE: Acompline

```
? lall/87-89
      LIMIT ALL/87-89
? s local government finance
  1    900  LOCAL GOVERN-
                MENT FINANCE
? s poll(w)tax; s community(w)
    charge
  2    102  POLL(W)TAX
  3.....etc.....
```

A range of dates can be included as part of a LIMIT ALL (LALL) command; a huge subject like LOCAL GOVERNMENT FINANCE on Acompline is limited to those records published in the last three years only.

3.2 Operations: saving a search on a database, changing to another database and conducting the same search on the new database; searching a number of databases at once ('multifile' searching); (searching elements of records across databases not available on ESA-IRS)

Commands and features introduced: END/SAVE; .EXECUTE STEPS (.EXS); .RECALL; .RELEASE; END/SDI; QUEST-CLUSTER (QCT)

An online enquiry is often not satisfied by searching just one database, and some databases, e.g. CAB Abstracts, are split up into more than one file. Crossfile searching can take one of two forms:

(a) Conducting a search on one database, saving the search, changing to another database, and conducting the same search on the new database; this avoids the necessity of typing in or uploading the search more than once while online. To process the saved search on the new database, the command .EXECUTE STEPS (.EXS) is used.

EXAMPLE: Acompline/CAB Abstracts

Searcher uses the command DISPLAY SETS (DS) to review the search so far on the initial database.

```
? ds
SET  ITEMS  DESCRIPTION
  1     34  ACTIVITY(F)HOLIDAYS
  2      1  SPECIAL(W)INTEREST(F)HOLIDAYS
  3      1  LEARNING(F)HOLIDAYS
  4     35  1-3/OR
```

The command END/SAVE is used to save the search; a number is allotted to the search, and a summary given of the time and cost to date.

```
? end/save
SEARCH SERIAL£:2UOD
-----------------03May88   17:43:44   User00000--
     1.99 AU 1.78 Minutes in File 35
     1.99 AU approx Total
? b124;.exs 2uod
-----------------03May88   17:43:50   User00000--
     2.01 AU 1.96 Minutes in File 35
     2.01 AU approx Total
File 124:CAB : 1986-1988,09

SET  ITEMS  DESCRIPTION (+ = OR;* = AND;- = NOT)
---- -----  ---------------------------------------
  1    317  ACTIVITY(F)HOLIDAYS
  2      9  SPECIAL(W)INTEREST(F)HOLIDAYS
  3      7  LEARNING(F)HOLIDAYS
  4    326  1-3/OR
```

The searcher uses the command BEGIN (B) followed by the new database number, and 'stacks' the next command on the same line; the system will now change databases and immediately process the saved search on the new database.

```
? t4/s/1-2
                 TYPE 4/S/1-2
          CAB
3R010-00729 Rural Recreation and
  Tourism Abs
Activity holidays – adventure in
retirement
```

Regular SDI (Selective Dissemination of Information) searches can be performed automatically by the system, for a small charge; for this, the END/SDI command is used. Saved searches can be listed by using

```
        CAB
3R007-01849 Rural Recreation and
   Tourism Abs
Activity holidays and
activities on holiday
?
```

the command .RECALL, and deleted by the command .RELEASE, followed by the saved search number.

(b) Searching a number of databases at the same time, i.e. multifile searching. ESA-IRS offer the feature QUEST-CLUSTER (QCT), whereby up to eight databases can be searched at the same time. The searcher enters QCT, followed by the numbers of the databases required, then enters B 255 to begin the search. ESA-IRS have some pre-defined groups of databases, e.g. FOODSCIENCE (file 251), which includes Food Science and Technology Abstracts, VITIS and PACKABS.

EXAMPLE: FOODSCIENCE

```
? b251
------------12Jul88 12:38:59 User00000--
    0.11 AU 0.13 Minutes in File 32
    0.11 AU approx Total
File 251: FOODSCIENCE
SET   ITEMS   DESCRIPTION (+ =OR;* = AND;- = NOT)
----- ---------- -------------------------------------------------------
```

The searcher chooses the pre-defined group of databases called FOODSCIENCE. The system gives a set number and items as usual, having searched all three databases.

```
? s meat(f)pharmaceutic?
    1     41   MEAT(F)PHARMACEUTIC?
? t1/s/1-4
                TYPE 1/S/1-4
              FSTA
   New compositions rich in ele-
ments and their manufacturing
process
              FSTA
   Diet therapy of celiac disease and dermatitis herpetiformis
              PACKABS
   Deep-drawing-, filling- and closing machines in a comparison of their
performance
   Tiefzieh-, Full- und Verschliessmaschinen im Leistungsvergleich
              PACKABS
   Spotlight on plastics packages
   Schlaglicht auf Kunststoffverpackungen
?
```

When displaying the titles, it can be seen that some are from the FSTA database, and some from PACKABS; they are displayed in reverse-chronological order as normal.

EXAMPLE: INSPEC, CAB Abstracts

```
? qct 8,16,124                                    ←┘
TOPICS IDENTIFIED
? b255                                            ←┘
-------------17Nov88  15:53:40  User 00000--
     0.42 AU 0.51 Minutes in File 32
     0.42 AU approx Total
File 255: QUEST CLUSTER SEARCH
SET   ITEMS   DESCRIPTION (+ = OR;* = AND;- = NOT)
-----  ---------  ------------------------------------------------
Base   8:INSPEC:1969-88,24
Base 16: CAB: 1970-1985, 12
  (SEE ALSO FILE 132)
Base 124: CAB: 1986-1988,09
  (SEE ALSO FILE 132)
? s son(s)lumiere                                 ←┘
  1        5      SON(S)LUMIERE
? t1/s/1-2                                        ←┘
                  TYPE 1/S/1-2
          CAB
  Audio-visual media in countryside interpretation

          INSPEC
  The impact of electronics on lighting
?
```

3.3 Operations: printing 'offline'; (sorting records not available on ESA-IRS); downloading records; (transferring records to an electronic mail facility not available on ESA-IRS)

Commands and features introduced: PRINT (PR); DOWNLOAD (DL), FORMAT X

After a set of relevant records has been retrieved, it can often be more economical, particularly if large numbers of records are required, to have them printed 'offline' by the online host and mailed to the searcher or end-user. The high-speed printing of search results generally takes place in the evening of the day of the search, and mailing follows immediately. The longest wait, even across continents, is about six days, but it is often quicker than this; inland this can be as little as one or two days. Another alternative to printing online, as well as printing offline, is downloading into a local microcomputer or mainframe. The searcher decides which method is preferable, depending on a number of variables, the principal ones being the speed of the terminal and printing equipment, how urgently the records are required, how many records there are, what format is required (e.g. are abstracts required, on full-text databases is the whole text required?), and what the financial implications of the different methods are.

If it is decided to print offline, the command PRINT (PR) is used, followed by the set number, format and range of records – as in the TYPE command. If a mistake is made, the searcher can enter PR- to cancel the last command.

EXAMPLE: Acompline

```
    18      91      17NOT16
? pr18/a/1-20
Printed 18/A/1-20
        6.84 AU approx print cost
?
```

The searcher prints the first 20 records of the set offline. The system repeats the command to show that it has been accepted; if a mistake has been made, the searcher can enter PR- to cancel the last command.

If downloading to store the records electronically, the command DOWNLOAD (DL) would be used, e.g. DL 18/X/1-50, where X is the special format for downloading, as it includes fields and subfields, tags and special markers.

System 3
BLAISE-LINE

UNIT ONE

1.1 Operations: logging-on to the system; choosing a database (file)

Commands and features introduced: logging-on information; FILE

The British Library's BLAISE-LINE service gives access in the United Kingdom to about 20 databases, including the British National Bibliography (BNB) database, and LCMARC. BLAISE (British Library Automated Information Service) is accessed via British Telecom's Packet SwitchStream (PSS), the national data network, with 'nodes' throughout the country, and from outside the United Kingdom via national post, telegraph and telephone services (PTTs), and commercial data transmission networks. BLAISE-LINE is also available via JANET (the Joint Academic Network), which provides networking facilities to universities, polytechnics, research councils etc. throughout the United Kingdom. When using PSS, searchers contact the nearest node of the network, and then make the link with the BLAISE-LINE computer in Harlow, Essex. The example below shows a log-on via the Manchester (UK) node of PSS, with a terminal working at 1,200 baud (120 characters per second (cps)).

For the purpose of clarity, the characters input by the searcher in the examples below are underlined; this is not the case when actually working online.

The searcher first dials the node of the network (in many cases the terminal or modem will be programmed to do this automatically), and after identifying the type of terminal being used, and the speed of transmission, will receive a response similar to the following from the node:

EXAMPLE:

```
MAN A002-6164340213
NNAAAAA111BBB        ←┘
ADD?
A227900102           ←┘

PLEASE ENTER USERID/PASSWORD
XXXXXXXXXXXXXXXXX    ←┘
BL TIME 16:19:09 DATE 25 APR 88 LINE BL1LUB

PROG?

HELLO FROM BLAISE-LINE

YOU ARE NOW CONNECTED TO THE LCCMARC FILE

SEARCH 1?
USER:
file bnb             ←┘

PROG:
YOU ARE NOW CONNECTED TO THE BNBCMARC FILE

SEARCH 1?
USER:
```

Response from the MANchester node of PSS. The Network User Identifier (NUI) is entered – a number unique to the user.

←┘ = return.

The network asks for the ADDress – to which online host does the searcher wish to be connected?

The ADDress is repeated by way of confirming the connection. The next response is from BLAISE-LINE asking for the USER IDentification number and PASSWORD, which can be entered together or separately.

PROGram is the prompt for the system to relay information. The searcher does not enter anything until receiving the USER prompt; this is the searcher's prompt to input something.

The searcher is automatically connected to the 'greeting file'–the LCCMARC database (the current Library of Congress MARC database).

If another database is required, the command FILE is used, followed by the name of the database. FILE BNB will give the current BNBMARC database.

SEARCH 1? means enter a search statement or a command.

1.2 Operations: entering search statements and creating sets of records; using Boolean operators; displaying records

Commands and features introduced: PRINT (PRT); Boolean operators AND and OR; 'stacking' commands; FIND (FD)

The general principles and methods of searching have been discussed in Chapters 5 and 6. After the initial analysis of the subject of the search, the identification of the concepts involved and the selection of appropriate terms to describe those concepts on this database, the terms are input; there is not normally any need to use a command to enter terms.

EXAMPLE: BNBCMARC

```
SEARCH 1?
USER:
libraries or information            ↵

PROG:
TERM (LIBRARIES) APPEARS IN (34) CONTEXTS
TERM (INFORMATION) APPEARS IN (8) CONTEXTS
SEARCH 1 FOUND 4330 ITEM(S).

SEARCH 2?
USER:
1 and Lancashire                    ←

PROG:
TERM (LANCASHIRE) APPEARS IN (12) CONTEXTS
SEARCH 2 FOUND 13 ITEM(S).

SEARCH 3?
USER:
prt br 1-3                          ↵

PROG:
```

The searcher asks for any occurrences of the terms LIBRARIES or INFORMATION in the index file, and combines the terms with logical operator OR. All the fields in the index file are searchable, so the term chosen often appears in more than one 'field' or 'context'. In search 1 there were 4,330 records with either LIBRARIES or INFORMATION in them. The second search statement combines the results of the first statement with another term – LANCASHIRE, which results in 13 records containing LANCASHIRE AND either INFORMATION OR LIBRARIES. Commands can be 'stacked' on one line, if they are enclosed in inverted commas (" "), with a search statement being preceded by the command FIND (FD). For example, the searcher could input: "file bnb" "fd libraries or information". ↵ The system would change to the BNBCMARC database and process the first search statement.

If there had been no records found in search 2, the message *NO ITEMS FOUND would have been received, and SEARCH 2 would have appeared again – this heading only changes when a set of records is established.

A Boolean statement can also be entered using < >, for example: <LIBRARIES OR INFORMATION> AND LANCASHIRE; the part of the statement in brackets is processed first.

The command PRINT (PRT) is used to display records. All PRINT commands are charged for online or offline, except for PRINT BROWSE (PRT BR), so it is advisable to use this instead of PRT TI to browse through titles; it gives the contents of the title and other fields with 'subject' information, and is helpful in developing the search. PRT BR 1-3 will give the first three records in the set.

```
*1
TI  – Clayton in history  the story of Clayton-le-Woods to
      1880  by George L. Bolton
DC  – 942.7  67  19
SJT – Lancashire. Clayton-le-
      Woods, to 1880
GH  – Clayton-le-Woods (Lancashire)
      History
```

TI = Title; DC = Dewey class no.
SJT = Subject summary
GH = Geographic LC subject heading
SH = Subject heading

```
*2
TI  – Pendle industrial information handbook
DC  – 914.27  64504858  19
SJT – Lancashire. Pendle (District)  Visitors Guides  For industrial
        Development
GH  – Pendle (Lancashire)  Description and travel  Guide-books
GH  – Pendle (Lancashire)  Industries

*3
TI  – The Library service to prisons in Lancashire
DC  – 027.6  65  094276  19
SJT – Lancashire. Prisons. Libraries
SH  – Prison Libraries  England  Lancashire

SEARCH 3?
USER:
prt fu 3

PROG:

3

RCN – 0902228439
CB  – b8325807
```

As well as PRINT BROWSE, there are other pre-defined PRINT commands, namely PRINT (PRT), PRINT FULL (PRT FU) and PRINT DETAILED (PRT DL). PRINT (PRT) – standard – will give the basic bibliographic details – ISBN, author, title, publisher; PRINT FULL will give these details plus DC, SJT, ED (edition), PH (col-

```
DC  - 027.6  65  094276  19
TI  - The Library service to prisons in Lancashire
PU  - Preston  The Lancashire Library  1982
PH  - [31]p  30cm  pbk
PI  - Unpriced
NO4 - Bibliography: p28

SEARCH 3?
USER:
```

lation), PI (price) and CIP status, NO (note), RCN (record control number), and PU (publisher).

PRINT DETAILED will give all the fields for a record. If a PRINT command requests many records, after every 25 lines the system will ask the following question: CONTINUE PRINTING? (YES/NO), to which the searcher answers Y or N.

Records will be displayed in reverse-chronological order.

The options open to the searcher at this stage are numerous – one or more of them may be: to browse through the remainder of the set; to print out more or all the records in the set; to develop further the search and display the resulting records; to conduct a similar search on another database; to end the searching session.

1.3 Operations: reviewing a search; ending the search and searching session (logging-off)

Commands and features introduced: RECAP; STOP (or LOGOFF, OFF or BYE)

The searcher wishing to change to another database would use the FILE command, followed by the name of the required database; this would erase all previous sets and enable the searcher to begin at Search 1 again on the new database. In many cases, before changing databases, the searcher would SAVE the search already conducted (see 3.2).

There are many occasions on which the searcher requires to see a display of the search to date – particularly when the search statements have scrolled off a VDU screen! To review a search, enter RECAP.

EXAMPLE: BNBCMARC

```
SEARCH 3?
USER:
recap ↵

PROG:
```

RECAP without any qualification will list all the search statements; if particular statements are required, the command is followed by the appropriate search number or numbers, e.g. RECAP 2; RECAP 3,5-8,12.

```
SEARCH FORMULATION BEGINNING AT SEARCH 1 :
  (LIBRARIES OR INFORMATION) --                4330 ITEMS FOUND

SEARCH FORMULATION BEGINNING AT SEARCH 2 :
  (SEARCH 1 AND LANCASHIRE) --                   13 ITEMS FOUND

SEARCH 3?
USER:
```

To end a searching session and disconnect from the host computer, the searcher would type the STOP (or LOGOFF, OFF or BYE) command, followed by Y (YES); no further input is required by the searcher.

EXAMPLE: BNBCMARC

```
SEARCH 3?
USER:
stop y                          ←┘

PROG:
***Session summary for userid XXXXX, 28th Feb 89

Session started at 12:45:24
File   Connect      ---Online Prints--        Estimated
       Time/Hrs   MARC Browse Other             cost
BNB   0.0286        0       4       7           2.18

Session ended at 12:47:17.
********************************
Total session time: 00:01:53 = 0.0313 hours
Estimated total cost   2.23

GOOD-BYE!

PLEASE ENTER /LOGIN

CLR DTE (00) 00:00:01:56  64  32
```

The command STOP Y (STOP YES) is entered (or alternatively LOGOFF Y, OFF Y, or BYE Y). The Y (YES) answer can be entered separately but there is no advantage in this. By sending the message PLEASE ENTER /LOGIN, the system gives the searcher the opportunity to re-enter BLAISE-LINE if required; otherwise the searcher is dropped from PSS after a short while; or alternatively the searcher may enter (CNTR P) CLR to disconnect from PSS. On disconnection from the PSS network, a message shows how long the network was used for (1 min. 56 secs.) and how many 'segments' of data were received (64) and how many were sent (32). A 'segment' holds up to 64 characters, half a 'packet'.

UNIT TWO

2.1 Operations: displaying the index file; using both controlled and natural language terms; searching specific fields

Commands and features introduced: NEIGHBOR (NBR); searching for author with qualifier (AU); limiting search statements to specific fields using qualifiers (e.g. DC, SH); SELECT (SEL)

The ability to display terms from the index file, where all directly searchable terms are listed, is useful for finding out the occurrence of both controlled and natural language terms; and also for finding out the precise format of a term – for example, that of an author's name. For this operation, the NEIGHBOR (NBR) command is used. If no particular field (e.g. (AU) for the author field) is asked for by the searcher, the NEIGHBOR command will give an alphabetical display of all terms in the index file adjacent to the chosen term.

EXAMPLE: LCCMARC

```
SEARCH 1?
USER:
nbr happenings
PROG:
```

The searcher NEIGHBORs the term HAPPENINGS without a qualifier, and a display is given of all terms from the index file adjacent to the term; this includes controlled indexing terms (subject headings (SH)), natural language terms (text words (TW)), publishers (PU), authors etc.

```
SELECT  NO.OF ITEMS  TERM
   1        22       HAPPENING (TW)
   2         3       HAPPENING ART (SH)
   3        14       HAPPENINGS (TW)
   4        53       HAPPENS (TW)
   5         1       HAPPES (TW)
   6         1       HAPPI (TW)
   7         1       HAPPIBOOK (PU)
   8         1       HAPPIE (TW)
   9        15       HAPPIER (TW)
  10         3       HAPPIEST (TW)
UP N, DOWN N, OR SELECT?
```

It is possible to SELECT (SEL) directly from the NEIGHBOR display.

USER:
sel 3 ↵

PROG:
SEARCH 1 FOUND 3 ITEM(S).

SEARCH 2?
USER:
prt br 1 ↵

PROG:

*1
TI – Le th:e:atre de la mort Tadeus Kantor textes r:eunis et pr:esent:es par Denis Bablet
DC – 792 .09438 19
SH – Experimental theatre Poland Krakow
SH – Happening (Art)
GA – e-pl---

SEARCH 2?
USER:

EXAMPLE: LC77
SEARCH 1?
USER:
happening art or performance art ↵

PROG:
SEARCH 1 FOUND 37 ITEM(S)

Qualifiers can be entered at the beginning of a search statement, and that qualifier will then apply to all subsequent terms in the statement, unless another qualifier is entered after one or more of the terms.

SEARCH 2?
USER:
(tw) happening and art or happening and arts ↵

PROG:
SEARCH 2 FOUND 20 ITEM(S)

SEARCH 3?
USER:
1 OR 2 ↵

Multi-word controlled terms (e.g. PERFORMANCE ART) do not require a qualifier, but it is advisable to qualify single controlled terms, if natural language terms are not required as well – e.g. PERFORMANCE (SH); without a qualifier, the system will retrieve all occurrences of the term.

PROG:
SEARCH 3 FOUND 42 ITEM(S)

SEARCH 4?
USER:
prt br 1 ↵

```
PROG:

*1
TI  –  Illegal America  Franklin Furnace, NYC, February 10-March
       6,
         1982  Vito Acconci . . . [et al] curator, Jeanette
       Ingberman
DC  –  700 .973  07401471  19
SH  –  Dissident art  United States  Exhibitions
SH  –  Conceptual art  United States  Exhibitions
SH  –  Performance art  United States  Exhibitions
SH  –  Art, Modern 20th century  United States  Exhibitions
SH  –  Politics in art  United States Exhibitions
GA  –  n-us---

SEARCH 4?
USER:
```

EXAMPLE: LCCMARC

```
SEARCH 1?
USER:
nbr west j d (au)                    ↵

PROG:

SELECT   NO.OF ITEMS   TERM
    1         8        WEST J
    2         2        WEST JA
    3         6        WEST JB
    4         3        WEST JD
    5         2        WEST JERSEY CHAPTER
    6         1        WEST JERSEY HEALTH SYSTEM
    7         2        WEST JO
    8         1        WEST JP
    9         1        WEST JW
   10         1        WEST K
UP N, DOWN N, OR SELECT?

USER:
sel 4                                ↵

PROG:
SEARCH 1 FOUND 3 ITEM(S)

SEARCH 2?
USER:
```

To display an alphabetical listing of terms in a particular field, the searcher enters a qualifier after the NEIGHBOR command. It is important, particularly when searching authors' names, to NEIGHBOR the name first, to find the exact format used, especially the format of the initials – if this searcher had input WEST J D, nothing would have been retrieved, as there is no space between initials.

The searcher can SELECT (SEL) a term or terms directly from the NEIGHBOR display.

The searcher can ask for a display of terms above (UP) or below (DOWN) the last display.

2.2 Operations: (proximity searching not available on BLAISE-LINE); stringsearching; truncation

Commands and features introduced: TS; SENS; SKIP; truncation symbol (:); variable character symbol (//)

It is useful to be able to search for a particular 'string' or 'strings' of characters within one or more fields of a set of records; this feature is called 'stringsearching'. There are four parts to a stringsearch statement, two of which are optional:

1	2	3	4
TS (abbreviation for Title Search)	(e.g.) 1 (the number of the set to be searched)	(e.g.)(DC) (the field to be searched)	(the string of characters being sought)

Numbers 2 and 3 are optional – the system will automatically default to the last search statement unless the searcher specifies otherwise; depending on the database, the system will automatically default to a particular field (e.g. title field on MARC). The set to be stringsearched should be of a manageable size – no more than 200–300 records normally; the system scans the OLDEST records first; with a large set of records, it is possible to SKIP the older records and scan only the more up-to-date records.

EXAMPLE: BNBMARC50/70

```
SEARCH 1?
USER:
philips
PROG:
TERM ( PHILIPS ) APPEARS IN (4) CONTEXTS
SEARCH 1 FOUND 219 ITEM(S)

SEARCH 2?
USER:
ts (dc) 338:
```

From the 219 records, the searcher wishes to find those with the Dewey Decimal Number beginning with 338. The command TS is entered, the set number is omitted as the system will default to the last set, the field abbreviation is entered in brackets, and lastly the Dewey 'string' is entered, followed by the truncation symbol (:) – the system will retrieve any of the 219 records with the Dewey number beginning with 338 (for truncation, see below). If a

PROG:

truncation symbol is entered before the string also, the system will retrieve the string anywhere in the field, e.g. TS (TI) :ANTON:
TS originally stood for 'title search', but it is used for stringsearching any fields on the record which can be searched, including some unindexed fields.

(112) ITEMS SEARCHED : (0) ITEM(S) FOUND SO FAR. CONTINUE?
(YES/NO)

USER:
y

PROG:
SEARCH 2 FOUND 1 ITEM(S).

SEARCH 3?
USER:
prt br

PROG:

Beginning with the earliest records, the system gives a 'slice' of CPU time to the calculation, and then reports back with the number of records searched and the number located with the required 'string'; to continue, the searcher enters Y.

If the set to be stringsearched is very large, the searcher can SKIP the older records, e.g. with a set of 2,345, the searcher might enter: TS (TI) SKIP 2000 :SHIFT WORK:

*1
TI – Growth of an enterprise the life of Anton Philips by P.J. Bouman [translated from the Dutch]
DC – 338.7 61 62130924 18
OD – 338.7 61 62130924 18
HP – Philips Anton
HC – Philips Gloeilampen fabrieken

SEARCH 3?
USER:

When SENS is used instead of TS, two or more items can be stringsearched in the same SENtence. There are numerous refinements to the stringsearch feature (see the BLAISE-LINE user manual).

A feature which is very important, particularly when searching natural language terms and phrases, is truncation – the ability to input the stem of a word, followed by the truncation symbol; the system will retrieve records where any term beginning with the word stem appears; e.g. INTEREST: will retrieve INTEREST, INTERESTED, INTERESTS etc. On BLAISE-LINE the truncation symbol is the colon (:).

EXAMPLE: BNBCMARC

```
SEARCH 1?
USER:
woman or women                    ↵
PROG:
TERM (WOMAN) APPEARS IN (8) CONTEXTS
TERM (WOMEN) APPEARS IN (10) CONTEXTS
SEARCH 1 FOUND 6090 ITEM(S)

SEARCH 2?
USER:
1 and 910: (dc) or 1 and explor: or 1 and travel:    ↵
PROG:
TERM (910:) APPEARS IN (165) CONTEXTS
TERM (EXPLOR:) APPEARS IN (60) CONTEXTS
TERM (TRAVEL:) APPEARS IN (98) CONTEXTS
SEARCH 2 FOUND 67 ITEM(S)

SEARCH 3?
USER:
prt br 1                          ↵
PROG:
*1
TI  – Spinsters abroad  Victorian lady explorers  Dea Birkett
DC  – 910  .88042  19
OD  – 910  .4  18
SJT – Travel by women, history
SH  – Voyages and travels
SH  – Travellers, Women  History
SEARCH 3?
USER:
```

Truncation is particularly useful on the MARC databases for Dewey classification numbers; in this case 910: would retrieve any Dewey number beginning with 910; so very wide subject areas may be covered by just one input. EXPLOR: would retrieve EXPLORE, EXPLORING, EXPLORER, EXPLORERS etc.; TRAVEL: would retrieve TRAVEL, TRAVELS, TRAVELLERS, TRAVELLING etc. If only one extra character is required at the end of a word (e.g. the plural of a word) the variable character symbol (//) can be used.

2.3 Operations: searching using classification codes, subfiles etc.; (analysing search results not available on BLAISE-LINE)

When discussing the search in Chapter 6, reference was made to the fact that most databases have a feature whereby it is possible to search a subject area wider than that described by one term or a few terms, by using a classification code, subfile, or other system or database feature. On the MARC databases this is achieved by searching the Dewey Decimal Classification numbers. These can be input in their complete form, or in truncated form, using the qualifier (DC). The example above under 'truncation' shows one way this can be input: 910: (General geography. Travel) is a very general number, but one could be more specific: 910.8: (Travel by specific kinds of persons). Some frequently used truncations have been stored by the system, and these can be recalled when needed, using the qualifier (DT); some of these stored truncations are: 02 Libraries; 2 Religion; 309 Social situation.

UNIT THREE

3.1 Operations: limiting a retrieved set of records by some criteria, e.g. language, date of publication; ranging

Commands and features introduced: GREATER THAN...., LESS THAN...., FROM.... TO.....

The BLAISE-LINE system uses three methods for limiting by criteria such as language, type of publication, date of publication etc., namely stringsearching, direct searching and ranging.

Stringsearching (see 2.2) enables the searcher to find any 'string' of characters in a particular field. The information code field on the MARC databases contains a wealth of information.

EXAMPLE: BNBCMARC

```
SEARCH 1?
USER:
940.3: (dc)                ←┘

PROG:
TERM (940.3:) APPEARS IN (35) CONTEXTS
SEARCH 1 FOUND 36 ITEM(S)

SEARCH 2?
USER:
ts (ic) :1977:             ←┘

PROG:
SEARCH 2 FOUND 3 ITEM(S)

SEARCH 3?
USER:
```

The information code field can hold several different types of information, including entry date, form of publication etc. In this example, the searcher stringsearches the information code field of a set of records for the publication date 1977. This could have been input as a direct search in the following way:
940.3: (dc) and 1977 (yr) ←┘

Many of the codes in the information code field have been converted to search terms in the inversion process, so it is possible to use these in a direct search with the qualifier (IC), e.g. CHILD (IC)—for children's works.

EXAMPLE: LCCMARC

PROG:
SEARCH 3 FOUND 30 ITEM(S)

SEARCH 4?
USER:
3 and greater than 1983 (yr) ←

PROG:
SEARCH 4 FOUND 19 ITEM(S)

SEARCH 5?
USER:

Ranging can be used with dates in the following forms: GREATER THAN ---- (after the date input); LESS THAN ---- (before the date input); FROM ---- TO ---- (between two inclusive dates).

3.2 Operations: saving a search on one database, changing to another database and conducting the same search on the new database; (searching a number of databases at once ('multifile' searching) available in 1989 on BLAISE-LINE); (searching elements of records across databases not available on BLAISE-LINE)

Commands and features introduced: SAVE; SAVESEARCH; STORESEARCH; OFFSEARCH

An online enquiry is often not satisfied by searching just one database, and some databases, e.g. BNBMARC, LCMARC, are split up into more than one database. On BLAISE-LINE it is possible to conduct a search on one database, save the search, change to another database and conduct the same search on the new database; this avoids the necessity of typing in or uploading the search more than once while online.

On BLAISE-LINE, either SAVESEARCH or SAVE can be used to save the initial search. SAVESEARCH is entered at the beginning of the search, and will save all search statements, even those with no records in them. SAVE is entered at the end of a search, but does not retain any search statements with no records in them. In both cases, the required records must be in the last search statement, as this is the only one which is displayed when the search is processed later. STORESEARCH is used for storing searches which are run automatically as an SDI (Selective Dissemination of Information) service. OFFSEARCH is used to search databases in batch mode offline.

EXAMPLE: LCCMARC

SEARCH 1?
USER:
savesearch ↵

SAVESEARCH is entered at the beginning of a search, and all search statements will be saved, even when no records are retrieved.

PROG:
ENTER SEARCH –

STS SEARCH 1?
USER:
performance art or happening art ↵

PROG:
SEARCH 1 FOUND 33 ITEM(S)

When all search statements have been entered, searcher inputs FINISHED, and is asked to enter a name for the saved search. (NB The required records must be in the LAST search statement, as this is the only one displayed when the search is run later.)

STS SEARCH 2?
USER:
finished ↵

PROG:
SEARCHNAME?

USER:
happening ↵

PROG:
SEARCH SET FROM SEARCH 1 SAVED AS 'HAPPENING'.
SAVESEARCH COMMAND COMPLETED.

SEARCH 2?
USER:
file lc77 ↵

The searcher changes to another database, and inputs the saved search's name, followed by the qualifier (SN).

PROG:
YOU ARE NOW CONNECTED TO THE LCMARC77/83 FILE.

SEARCH 1?
USER:
happening (sn) ↵

PROG:
SEARCH 1 FOUND 12 ITEM(S)

SEARCH 2?
USER:

There is only ever one search statement displayed – the last in the search.

SAVE works in a similar way, with two important differences: the command SAVE is input at the END of the search; and it will not include any search statements with no records.

3.3 Operations: printing 'offline'; sorting records; downloading records; (transferring records to an electronic mail facility not available on BLAISE-LINE)

Commands and features introduced: PRINT OFFLINE

After a set of relevant records has been retrieved, it can often be more economical, particularly if large numbers of records are required, to have them printed 'offline' by the online host and mailed to the searcher or end-user. The high-speed printing of search results generally takes place the evening of the day of the search, and mailing follows immediately. The longest wait, even across continents, is about six days, but it is often quicker than this; inland this can be as little as one or two days. Another alternative to printing online, as well as printing offline, is downloading into a local microcomputer or mainframe. The searcher decides which method is preferable, depending on a number of variables, the principal ones being the speed of the terminal and printing equipment, how urgently the records are required, how many records there are, what format is required, and what the financial implications of the different methods are.

If it is decided to print offline, the command PRINT (PRT) is used in the normal way, but the word OFFLINE is added at the end of the command. Some databases have the facility to sort records, and the sort command is entered as part of the offline print command.

EXAMPLE: BNBCMARC
SEARCH 7?
USER:
prt include dc offline ↵

The searcher prints all the records of the set offline.

PROG:
REQUESTER'S NAME, OR SAME

USER:
same ↵

If SAME is input in answer to this question, the offline print will be sent to the name and address stored on the system.

PROG:
TITLE FOR PRINTOUT, OR NONE-

USER:
sort = auti ↵

The SORT command is entered, if required, during the offline print sequence; the different SORT formats can be obtained by reference to the BLAISE-LINE user manual.

PROG:
TITLE FOR PRINTOUT, OR NONE-

USER:
films ↵

PROG:
OK? (Y/N/CANCEL/ADDRESS)

USER:
y ↵

PROG:
OFF-LINE PRINT COMPLETED

SEARCH 7?
USER:

AUTI sorts by author, and then by title within the author sequence.

This title will be printed at the head of the offline print output. If the offprints need to be sent to a different address from that stored on the host's computer, this can be entered after the title.

System 4
National Library of Medicine (BLAISE-LINK)

UNIT ONE

1.1 Operations: logging-on to the system; choosing a database (file)

Commands and features introduced: logging-on information; FILE

The British Library's BLAISE-LINK service enables users in the United Kingdom to link into the National Library of Medicine's ELHILL system in Bethesda, Maryland. BLAISE (British Library Automated Information Service) provides the link and support services, e.g. help desk, documentation. NLM's system currently offers about 20 databases on medical and related subjects. BLAISE-LINK is accessed in the United Kingdom via British Telecom's Packet SwitchStream (PSS), the national data network, with 'nodes' throughout the country. When using PSS, searchers contact the nearest node of the network, and then make the link with the NLM computer in Maryland. The example below shows a log-on via the Manchester (UK) node of PSS, with a terminal working at 1,200 baud (120 characters per second (cps)).

For the purpose of clarity, the characters input by the searcher in the examples below are underlined; this is not the case when actually working online.

The searcher first dials the node of the network (in many cases the terminal or modem will be programmed to do this automatically), and after identifying the type of terminal being used, and the speed of transmission, will receive a response similar to the following from the node:

EXAMPLE:

MAN A002-6164340213 NNAAAAA111BBB ↵ ADD? A931103010002000 ↵	Response from the MANchester node of PSS. The Network User Identifier (NUI) is entered – a number unique to the user. ↵ = return.
PLEASE ENTER /LOGIN /login ↵	
PLEASE ENTER USERID/PASSWORD OR LOGON XXXXXXXXXXXXXXXX ↵	The network asks for the ADDress – to which online host does the searcher wish to be connected?
NLM TIME 9:17:27 DATE 88:127 LINE 633 GM£030	The ADDress is repeated by way of confirming the connection. The next response is from NLM, asking the searcher to enter /LOGIN, and then the USER IDentification number and PASSWORD; these can be entered together, or singly.
WELCOME TO THE NATIONAL LIBRARY OF MEDICINE'S ELHILL RETRIEVAL SYSTEM YOU ARE NOW CONNECTED TO THE MEDLINE (1986 FORWARD) FILE	
SS1 /C? USER: file b83 ↵	The searcher does not enter anything until receiving the USER prompt; this is the searcher's prompt to input something. The searcher is automatically connected to the 'greeting file' – the current MEDLINE database.
PROG: YOU ARE NOW CONNECTED TO THE BACK83 (1983 – 85) FILE	
SS 1 /C? USER:	If another database is needed, the command FILE is used, followed by the name of the database. FILE B83 will give the MEDLINE Backfile covering the years 1983–5. PROGram is the prompt for the system to relay information. SS 1 /C? means enter search statement 1 or a command.

1.2 Operations: entering search statements and creating sets of records; using Boolean operators; displaying records

Commands and features introduced: PRINT (PRT); Boolean operators AND and OR; 'stacking' commands; FIND (FD)

The general principles and methods of searching have been discussed in Chapters 5 and 6. After the initial analysis of the subject of the search, the identification of the concepts involved and the selection of appropriate terms to describe those concepts on this database, the terms are input; there is not normally any need to use a command to enter terms.

EXAMPLE: MEDLINE (1986−)

```
SS 1 /C?
USER:
meningioma                    ←

PROG:
SS (1) PSTG (716)

SS 2 /C?
USER:
sacrum or sacral (tw)         ←

PROG:
SS (2) PSTG (358)

SS 3 /C?
USER:
1 and 2                       ←

PROG:
SS (3) PSTG (1)
```

The searcher asks for any occurrences of the term MENINGIOMA; this is a term from the Medical Subject Headings, so does not require any qualification. The system responds with the message that in search statement 1 (SS 1) there are 716 'postings' (PSTG), or records. The searcher next uses the logical operator OR to find occurrences of the term SACRUM (taken from Medical Subject Headings) or SACRAL (which is a natural language term and needs to be qualified by (TW) – a 'text-word').

The logical operator AND is used to combine the first two search statements; search statement 3 retrieves a record which contains both MENINGIOMA and either SACRUM or SACRAL.

Commands can be 'stacked' by including double quote marks between them: e.g.

FILE MEDLINE""FD MENINGIOMA will change to the MEDLINE database and then retrieve a set of records on MENINGIOMA.

To display a set of retrieved records, the searcher uses the PRINT (PRT) command. There are three

SS 4 /C?
USER:
prt ti ←

PROG:

'standard' print commands: PRINT (PRT), which gives authors, title and source information; PRINT FULL (PRT FU), which gives the above details plus language, main headings, subheadings, name of substance (NM), and CAS Registry Number (RN), where available; and PRINT DETAILED (PRT DTL) which gives all fields available for a record. The searcher can also tailor a PRINT command by choosing the fields to display – in this case the title field is chosen to assess the relevance of the record.

1
TI – Haemangiopericytic meningioma of the sacral canal: a case report.

SS 4 /C?
USER:
prt fu ←

The searcher decides that it is relevant, and enters the PRINT FULL (PRT FU) command.

PROG:

1
UI – 88154926
AU – Bridges LR
AU – Roche S
AU – Nashef L
AU – Rose FC
TI – Haemangiopericytic meningioma of the sacral canal: a case report
LA – Eng
MH – Adult
MH – Case Report
MH – Combined Modality Therapy
MH – Human
MH – Male
MH – Meningeal Neoplasms/*PATHOLOGY/SURGERY
MH – Meningioma/*PATHOLOGY/SURGERY
MH – Sacrum/*PATHOLOGY
MH – Spinal Neoplasms/*PATHOLOGY/SURGERY
SO – J Neurol Neurosurg Psychiatry 1988 Feb; 51(2):288-90

MH = main headings from Medical Subject Headings; displaying these may help in developing the search. Some of the main headings have subheadings (e.g. Sacrum/*PATHOLOGY, where PATHOLOGY is the subheading; subheadings can be used directly in a search statement). The terms that are asterisked cover major subjects in the paper, and the record will be found under these headings in the printed *Index medicus*.

SS 4 /C?
USER:

To PRINT selectively from a set with more than one record, the following options can be used:
PRT 6 (the six most recent records)
PRT -6 (the sixth record)
PRT 3-6 (the given range of records)
PRT 3, 6, 7-9, 10 (these individual records – the comma is optional).
Records are displayed in reverse-chronological order.

The options open to the searcher at this stage are numerous – one or more of them may be: to browse through the remainder of the set; to print out more or all the records in the set; to develop the search further and display the resulting records; to conduct a similar search on another database; to end the searching session.

1.3 Operations: reviewing a search; ending the search and searching session (logging-off)

Commands and features introduced: RECAP; DIAGRAM; STOP

The searcher wishing to change to another database would use the FILE command, followed by the name of the required database; this would erase all previous sets and enable the searcher to begin at search 1 again on the new database. In many cases, before changing databases, the searcher would SAVE the search already conducted (see 3.2).

There are many occasions on which the searcher requires to see a display of the search to date – particularly when the search statements have scrolled off a VDU screen! To review a search, enter RECAP.

EXAMPLE: MEDLINE

```
SS 4 /C?
USER:
recap                                    ←
PROG:
SEARCH FORMULATION BEGINNING AT SS 1:
  (MENINGIOMA (MN) ) --                       716 POSTINGS
```

RECAP without any qualification will list all the search statements; if particular statements are required, the command is followed by the appropriate search statement number or numbers:

e.g. RECAP 2
RECAP 3,5-8, 12

```
SEARCH FORMULATION BEGINNING AT SS 2:
  (SACRUM (MN)   OR SACRAL (TW)   ) -- 358 POSTINGS

SEARCH FORMULATION BEGINNING AT SS 3:
  (SS 1 AND SS 2  )                   --   1 POSTING

SS 4 /C?
USER:
```

The command DIAGRAM will give a more detailed analysis of the search statements established.

To end a searching session and disconnect from the host computer, the searcher would type the command STOP followed by Y (YES); no further input is required by the searcher.

EXAMPLE:

```
SS 7 /C?
USER:
stop y
```

The command STOP Y (STOP YES) is entered. The Y (YES) answer can be entered separately, but there is no advantage in this.

```
TIME 00:06:00        NLM TIME 16:25:09
. . .
PROG:
GOOD-BYE!
*** END OF SESSION ***

CLR DTE (00)   00:00:04:36  89  17
```

On disconnection from the PSS network, a message shows how long the network was used for (4 mins. 36 secs.) and how many 'segments' of data were received (89) and how many were sent (17). A 'segment' holds up to 64 characters, half a 'packet'.

UNIT TWO

2.1 Operations: displaying the index file; using both controlled and natural language terms; searching specific fields

Commands and features introduced: NEIGHBOR (NBR); searching for author with qualifier (AU); limiting search statements to specific fields using qualifiers (e.g. TW, MH); SELECT (SEL)

The ability to display terms from the index file, where all directly searchable terms are listed, is useful for finding out the occurrence of both controlled and natural language terms; and also for finding out the precise format of a term – for example, that of an author's name. For this operation, the NEIGHBOR (NBR) command is used. If no particular field (e.g. (AU) for the author field) is asked for by the searcher, the NEIGHBOR command will give an alphabetical display of all terms in the index file adjacent to the chosen term.

EXAMPLE: MEDLINE (1986-)

```
SS 1 /C?
USER:
nbr carpal tunnel  ←┘

PROG:
```

The NEIGHBOR (NBR) command will give a short listing of alphabetically related terms close to the term input. (TW) signifies a 'text-word' – a natural language term; (MH) is a main heading – an index term taken from the controlled language – Medical Subject Headings (MeSH).

```
SELECT £   POSTINGS   TERM
   1         421      CARPAL (TW)
   2         295      CARPAL BONES (MH)
   3         248      CARPAL TUNNEL SYNDROME (MH)
   4           1      CARPALIA (TW)
   5           6      CARPALS (TW)
UP N OR DOWN N OR ENTER A SELECT COMMAND
```

The question UP N OR DOWN N enables the searcher to display terms either above or below the initial list. To select from the list, the command SELECT (SEL) is used, followed by the appropriate number or numbers on the display.

```
USER:
sel 3  ←┘

PROG:
SS (1) PSTG (248)

SS 2 /C?
USER:
```

EXAMPLE: TOXLIT

```
SS 1/C?
USER:
nbr pettigrew a.b. (au)  ←┘
```

To display an alphabetical listing of terms in a particular field, the searcher enters a qualifier after the NEIGHBOR command. It is important, particularly when searching

PROG:

SELECT £	POSTINGS	TERM
1	3	PETTICAN P
2	4	PETTIFOR JM
3	2	PETTIGREW AB
4	2	PETTIGREW C
5	1	PETTIGREW CA JR

UP N OR DOWN N OR ENTER A SELECT COMMAND

authors' names, to NEIGHBOR the name first, to find the exact format used, especially the format of the initials – if this searcher had input PETTIGREW A.B., nothing would have been retrieved, as the initials have been input as AB.

The searcher can SELECT (SEL) a term or terms directly from the NEIGHBOR display.

USER:
sel 3 ↵

PROG:
SS (1) PSTG (2)

SS 2 /C?
USER:
prt ti, au ↵

PROG:

1
TI – Serum and urine levels of cephapirin in dogs, and its relation to antibacterial effect
AU – Hashim MM
AU – Pettigrew AB

2
TI – Serum levels of cephapirin following intraruminal and intra-abomasal administration in goats
AU – Hashim MM
AU – Pettigrew AB

SS 2 /C?
USER:

EXAMPLE: MEDLINE
SS 1 /C?
USER:
myocardial infarction ↵

When inputting a MeSH heading, it is not necessary to add a qualifier, for the system will automatically recognize the term as a MeSH head-

```
PROG:
SS (1) PSTG (1348)

SS 2 /C?
USER:
coronary disease                    ↵

PROG:
SS (2) PSTG (1873)

SS 3 /C?
USER:
1 or 2                              ↵

PROG:
SS (3) PSTG (2984)

SS 4 /C?
USER:
(tw) australia                      ↵

PROG:
SS (4) PSTG (401)

SS 5 /C?
USER:
3 and 4                             ↵

PROG:
SS (5) PSTG (2)

SS 6 /C?
USER:
prt 1                               ↵

PROG:

1
UI  - 88120723
TI  - Coronary thrombolysis and myocardial salvage by tissue
      plasminogen activator given up to 4 hours after onset of
      myocardial infarction. National Heart Foundation of
      Australia Coronary Thrombolysis Group.
SO  - Lancet 1988 Jan 30;1(8579):203-8.

SS 6 /C?
USER:
```

ing; to search natural language terms, the qualifier (TW) is used. Both MYOCARDIAL INFARCTION and CORONARY DISEASE are taken from the MeSH headings, and therefore require no qualification. AUSTRALIA is searched here as a natural language term, so the qualifier (TW) is used. (AUSTRALIA is also a MeSH heading, and can be used with the EXPLODE command – see 2.3 below – to increase the number of records retrieved.)

2.2 Operations: (proximity searching (full-text searching) not available on BLAISE-LINK); stringsearching; truncation

Commands and features introduced: TS; SENS; SKIP; truncation symbol (:); variable character symbol (//)

It is useful to be able to search for a particular 'string' or 'strings' of characters within one or more fields of a set of records; this feature is called 'stringsearching'. There are four parts to a stringsearch statement, two of which are optional:

1	2	3	4
TS	(e.g.) 1	(e.g.)(LA)	(e.g.) ENG
(abbreviation for Title Search)	(the number of the set to be searched)	(the field to be searched)	(the string of characters being sought)

Numbers 2 and 3 are optional – the system will automatically default to the last search statement unless the searcher specifies otherwise; depending on the database, the system will automatically default to a particular field (e.g. title field on MEDLINE). The set to be stringsearched should be of a manageable size – no more than 200–300 records normally; the system scans the OLDEST records first; with a large set of records, it is possible to SKIP the older records and scan only the more up-to-date records.

EXAMPLE: MEDLINE (1985-)

```
SS 1 /C?
USER:
carpal tunnel syndrome          ←┘

PROG:
SS (1) PSTG (248)

SS 2 /C?
USER:
ts (la) eng                     ←┘
```

From the 248 records, the searcher wishes to find those where the original paper is in English. The command TS is entered, the set number is omitted as the system will default to the last set, the field abbreviation is entered in brackets, and lastly the language 'string' is entered; there are always just three characters in the language field on MEDLINE. TS originally stood for 'title search', but it is used for stringsearching any fields on the record which can be searched, including some unindexed fields.

(80) SCHD (60) QUAL; CONT? (Y/N)

USER:
y ↵

PROG:
(193) SCHD (132) QUAL; CONT? (Y/N)

USER:
y ↵

PROG:
SS (2) PSTG (156)

SS 3 ?C?
USER:

Beginning with the earliest records, the system gives a 'slice' of CPU time to the calculation, and then reports back with the number of records searched and the number located with the required 'string'; to continue, the searcher enters Y.

If the set to be stringsearched is very large, the searcher can SKIP the older records, e.g. with a set of 2,345, the searcher might enter: TS (TI) SKIP 2000 :SHIFT WORK:

The intermediate message received means
(80) SEARCHED (60) QUALIFY, i.e. 60 of the first 80 records stringsearched have the required 'string'.

EXAMPLE: MEDLINE (1983–5 file)

SS 1 /C?
USER:
exp encephalomyelitis ↵

PROG:
MM (ENCEPHALOMYELITIS) (2)
1 C10.228.228.291
2 C10.228.440
NUMBER, NONE, OR EXPAND-

USER:
1, 2 ↵

PROG:
SS (1) PSTG (172)

SS 2 /C?
USER:
ts (ti) :myalgic: or :myalgic: (ab) ↵

PROG:
(80) SCHD (2) QUAL; CONT? (Y/N)

USER:
y ↵

When searching for a 'string' of characters within a larger field, truncation symbols (the colon) are needed before and after the 'string' of characters, e.g. :MYALGIC:

PROG:
(164) SCHD (10) QUAL; CONT? (Y/N)

USER:
y ↵

PROG:
SS (2) PSTG (10)

SS 3 /C?
USER:

When SENS is used instead of TS, two or more terms can be stringsearched in the same SENtence. There are numerous refinements to the stringsearch feature (see the BLAISE-LINK user manual).

A feature which is very important, particularly when searching natural language terms and phrases, is truncation – the ability to input the stem of a word, followed by the truncation symbol; the system will retrieve records where any term beginning with the word stem appears; e.g. INTEREST: will retrieve INTEREST, INTERESTED, INTERESTS etc. On BLAISE-LINK the truncation symbol is the colon (:).

EXAMPLE: TOXLINE

SS 1 /C?
USER:
zinc or copper ↵

PROG:
SS (1) PSTG (8793)

SS 2 /C?
USER:
1 and air and all pollut: ↵

PROG:
SS (2) PSTG (326)

SS 3 /C?
USER:

Truncation is particularly useful when searching natural language terms; TOXLINE as a whole does not have controlled language terms.

It is advisable in most cases to precede the truncated term by the word ALL to avoid a multi-meaning message, i.e. a list of all the terms beginning with the truncated term. POLLUT: would retrieve POLLUTANT, POLLUTION, POLLUTED, POLLUTING etc.

If only one extra character is required (e.g. the plural of a word), the variable character symbol (#) can be used; e.g. ALL WOM#N; ALL CAT# to retrieve CAT or CATS but not CATIONIC etc.

2.3 Operations: searching using classification codes, subfiles etc.; (analysing search results not available on BLAISE-LINK)

Commands and features introduced: EXPLODE (EXP)

When discussing the search in Chapter 6, reference was made to the fact that most databases have a feature whereby it is possible to search a subject area wider than that described by one term, or a few terms, by using a classification code, subfile, or other system or database feature. On the MEDLINE database on NLM this is achieved by using the Medical Subject Headings – Tree Structures, an example of which is given in Fig. 6. The Tree Structures are arranged hierarchically, the more specific term being indented under the more general term; for example:

PEPTIC ULCER
  DUODENAL ULCER
    CURLING'S ULCER*

By using the EXPLODE (EXP) feature followed by the general term, the searcher will obtain a set of records where the general term, and any of the more specific terms indented under it, have been used as index terms. On MEDLINE, papers are indexed as specifically as possible, i.e. a paper on Duodenal Ulcer would be indexed under Duodenal Ulcer and not necessarily Peptic Ulcer as well. The EXPLODE feature automatically ORs together records containing either the general term or any term indented under it in the hierarchy.

EXAMPLE: MEDLINE

EXP GALLBLADDER DISEASES will retrieve not only papers indexed by GALLBLADDER DISEASES, but also those indexed by more specific terms in the MeSH Tree Structures.

```
SS 1 /C?
USER:
exp gallbladder diseases or exp gallbladder neoplasms
PROG:
MM (GALLBLADDER NEOPLASMS)  (2)
                1  C4.588.274.120.401
                2  C6.130.564.522
NUMBER, NONE, OR EXPAND
```

Similarly EXP GALLBLADDER NEOPLASMS will retrieve records indexed by the more specific terms

USER:
<u>1, 2</u> ↵

PROG:
SS (1) PSTG (2173)

SS 2 /C?
USER:

indented under this term in the MeSH Tree Structures, as well as those indexed under the term GALL-BLADDER NEOPLASMS itself.

Where the term occurs more than once in the Tree Structures, the searcher is given a multi-meaning message, asking which contexts are required. Further details about the contexts can be obtained by EXPANDing.

Some general, frequently used EXPLODEd subjects are stored in the system, and can be retrieved by just one input, followed by the qualifier (PX). These 'pre-explosions' can be found listed in the BLAISE-LINK user manual; two examples are HEART DISEASE, and LIPIDS.

UNIT THREE

3.1 Operations: limiting a retrieved set of records by some criteria, e.g. language, date of publication; ranging

Commands and features introduced: GREATER THAN...., LESS THAN...., FROM.... TO.....

The BLAISE-LINK system uses three methods for limiting by criteria such as language, type of publication, date of publication etc., namely stringsearching, direct searching and ranging.

Stringsearching enables the searcher to find any 'string' of characters in a particular field, and 2.2 above gives an example of searching for papers in the ENGLISH language using stringsearching. The language can also be searched directly, as in the example below; this can sometimes result in a number of time-overflow messages, to which the searcher answers (Y)ES to continue.

EXAMPLE: MEDLINE

SS 1 /C?
USER:
<u>cystic fibrosis and eng (la)</u> ↵

PROG:
SS (1) PSTG (346)

SS 2 /C?
USER:

The MEDLINE database uses checktags as part of its indexing system; these are very highly posted terms such as HUMAN, REVIEW, CHILD, ANIMAL etc. These can be searched directly to limit a search statement, e.g. TERATOGENS AND HUMAN; this may result in a number of time-overflow messages. Alternatively, these checktags may be searched using the stringsearch feature in the main heading (MH) field; e.g. TS (MH) HUMAN.

EXAMPLE: MEDLINE

```
USER:
1 and 2 or 1 and 3        ←┘

SS (4) PSTG (522)

SS 5 /C?
USER:
4 and review              ←┘

PROG:
SS (5) PSTG (79)

SS 6 /C?
USER:
ts (la) eng               ←┘

PROG:
SS (6) PSTG (74)

SS 7 /C?
USER:
```

The searcher uses the checktag REVIEW to limit the records already retrieved; the set of records is further reduced by stringsearching the language field for ENGlish language papers only.

It is possible to limit a set of records to a particular range of dates; this feature is called 'ranging'. Three expressions can be used: LESS THAN . . ., GREATER THAN . . ., and FROM . . . TO . . .; the date of entry may be used by inputting year/month/day, e.g. 841231, or the year of publication, e.g. 84. These expressions are used in conjunction with a term or terms or search statement number, e.g. 3 AND GREATER THAN 850101 (any records from search statement 3 entered after 1 January 1985); CYSTIC FIBROSIS AND LESS THAN 861231 (any records indexed with term CYSTIC FIBROSIS and entered on the database before 31 December 1986); 2 AND FROM 870101 TO 871231 (any records in search statement 2 entered during 1987). Publication date may be ranged by using the last two digits of the year, e.g. 4 AND GREATER THAN 85 (any records in search statement 4 published after 1985).

3.2 Operations: saving a search on one database, changing to another database and conducting the same search on the new database; (searching a number of databases at once ('multifile' searching) available in 1989 on BLAISE-LINK); (searching elements of records across databases not available on BLAISE-LINK)

Commands and features introduced: SAVE; SAVESEARCH; STORESEARCH; OFFSEARCH

An online enquiry is often not satisfied by searching just one database, and some databases, e.g. MEDLINE, TOXLINE, are split up into more than one database. On BLAISE-LINK it is possible to conduct a search on one database, save the search, change to another database and conduct the same search on the new database; this avoids the necessity of typing in or uploading the search more than once while online.

On BLAISE-LINK, either SAVESEARCH or SAVE can be used to save the initial search. SAVESEARCH is entered at the beginning of the search, and will save all search statements, even those with no records in them. SAVE is entered at the end of a search, but does not retain any search statements with no records in them. In both cases, the required records must be in the last search statement, as this is the only one which is displayed when the search is processed later. STORESEARCH is used for storing searches which are run automatically as an SDI (Selective Dissemination of Information) service. OFFSEARCH is used to search databases in batch mode offline.

EXAMPLE: MEDLINE/Back86

SS 1 /C?
USER:
<u>savesearch</u> ←

The SAVESEARCH command is input at the beginning of the search; all subsequent search statements will be saved, including any which retrieve no records.

PROG:
ENTER SEARCH-

STS SS 1 /C?
USER:
<u>(tw) ectatic and all vessel:</u> ←

PROG:
SS (1) PSTG (3)

STS SS 2 /C?
USER:
ts (la) eng ←┘

PROG:
SS (2) PSTG (3)

STS SS 3 /C?
USER:
finished ←┘

When all the search statements have been input, the command FINISHED is entered, and a name for the SAVEd search. All the required records should be in the LAST search statement, as this is the only one which will appear when the search is processed.

PROG:
SEARCHNAME?

USER:
ectatic ←┘

PROG:
SEARCH SET FROM SS 1 FORWARD SAVED AS 'ECTATIC'
SAVESEARCH COMPLETED.

SS 3 /C?
USER:
file b86 ←┘

Searcher changes to another database; the saved search name is entered, followed by the qualifier (SN).

PROG:
YOU ARE NOW CONNECTED TO THE BACK86 (1986 - 87) FILE

SS 1 /C?
USER:
ectatic (sn) ←┘

PROG:
SS (1) PSTG (9)

SS 2 /C?
USER:
prt ti 1-2 ←┘

PROG:

1
TI – Treatment of port-wine stains: analysis

2
TI – Unexpected vascular response to epinephrine in port wine stains.

SS 2 /C?
USER:

EXAMPLE: MEDLINE/Back83

SS 1 /C?
USER:
exp sleep deprivation ↵

Searcher inputs the search, and uses the command SAVE at the end to save the search; please note that the SAVE command will not include any search statements which have retrieved no records – SAVESEARCH at the beginning of the search must be used to include these. The records required must all be in the final search statement of the search, as this is the only one printed out when the search is processed later.

PROG:
MM (SLEEP DEPRIVATION) (2)
1 F2.830.855.671
2 G11.561.826.587
NUMBER, NONE, OR EXPAND-

USER:
1, 2 ↵

PROG:
SS (1) PSTG (229)

SS 2 /C?
USER:
exp health personnel ↵

PROG:
SS (2) PSTG (12214)

SS 3 /C?
USER:
1 and 2 ↵

PROG:
SS (3) PSTG (4)

SS 4 /C?
USER:
save sleep ↵

The searcher gives the SAVEd search a name, which is used when the search is processed on another database.

PROG:
SEARCH SET FROM SS 1 FORWARD SAVED AS 'SLEEP'

SS 4 /C?
USER:
prt. . . . . . .etc. ↵

SS 4 /C?
USER:
file b83 ↵

PROG:
YOU ARE NOW CONNECTED TO THE BACK83 (1983 – 85) FILE

SS 1 /C?
USER:
sleep (sn) ↵

The searcher inputs the SAVEd search's name, followed by the qualifier (SN), and the system processes the search, and gives the results in the first search statement.

PROG:
SS (1) PSTG (6)

SS 2 /C?
USER:
prt. . . . . . .etc. ↵

3.3 Operations: printing 'offline'; sorting records; downloading records; (transferring records to an electronic mail facility not available on BLAISE-LINK)

Commands and features introduced: PRINT OFFLINE

After a set of relevant records has been retrieved, it can often be more economical, particularly if large numbers of records are required, to have them printed 'offline' by the online host and mailed to the searcher or end-user. The high-speed printing of search results generally takes place the evening of the day of the search, and mailing follows immediately. The longest wait, even across continents, is about six days, but it is often quicker than this; inland this can be as little as one or two days. Another alternative to printing online, as well as printing offline, is downloading into a local microcomputer or mainframe. The searcher decides which method is preferable, depending on a number of variables, the principal ones being the speed of the terminal and printing equipment, how urgently the records are required, how many records there are, what format is required, and what the financial implications of the different methods are.

If it is decided to print offline, the command PRINT (PRT) is used in the normal way, but the word OFFLINE is added at the end of the command.

EXAMPLE: MEDLINE
SS 8 /C?
USER:
prt include ab offline ↵

The searcher prints all the records of the set offline.

PROG:
REQUESTER'S NAME, OR SAME

If SAME is input in answer to this question, the offline print will be

USER:
same ↵

PROG:
SEARCH TITLE, NONE-

USER:
meningioma ↵

PROG:
OK? (Y/N/C/ADDRESS)

USER:
y ↵

PROG:
OFF-LINE PRINT COMPLETED

SS 8 /C?
USER:

sent to the name and address stored on the system.

If records need to be SORTed enter SORT= followed by two-letter abbreviation (e.g. SORT=AU) at any stage in the offline print question and answer sequence.

This title will be printed at the head of the offline print output. (C= cancel.) If the offprints need to be sent to a different address from that stored on the host's computer, this can be entered after the title.

There are no special commands for downloading.

System 5

ORBIT

UNIT ONE

1.1 Operations: logging-on to the system; choosing a database (file)

Commands and features introduced: logging-on information; FILE

The ORBIT system, based in McLean, Virginia, currently offers about 90 databases; it is accessed by direct dial, or via one of the commercial data transmission networks such as Tymnet or Telenet, or via its own network Orbitnet. From outside the United States, the system may be accessed via national post, telegraph and telephone services (PTTs), to link into one of the networks mentioned above. In the United Kingdom, users contact the nearest 'node' of British Telecom's Packet SwitchStream (PSS) network, and then make the link with ORBIT's computer via either British Telecom's International Packet SwitchStream (IPSS), or by Orbitnet. When using PSS, searchers contact the nearest node of the network, and then make the link with the ORBIT computer in McLean. The example below shows a log-on via the Manchester (UK) node of PSS, with a terminal working at 1,200 baud (120 characters per second (cps)).

For the purpose of clarity, the characters input by the searcher in the examples below are underlined; this is not the case when actually working online.

The searcher first dials the node of the network (in many cases the terminal or modem will be programmed to do this automatically), and after identifying the type of terminal being used, and the speed of transmission, will receive a response similar to the following from the node:

EXAMPLE:

```
MAN A002-6164340403
NORBIT1,GO1                              ←┘
ADD?
A215700147                               ←┘

234215700147 + GO1-COM

PLEASE ENTER /LOGIN
/login                                   ←┘

PLEASE ENTER USERID
XXXXXXXXXXXXXXXX                         ←┘

WELCOME TO ORBIT SEARCH SERVICE, A DIVISION OF PERGAMON
ORBIT INFOLINE. (11/24/88  11.23 A.M.  EASTERN TIME)
ENTER SECURITY CODE:
XXXXXX                                   ←┘

PROG:
****
ORBIT LONDON USER DAY
  *  9TH DECEMBER 1988 -- TYPE NEWSDOC N117 FOR DETAILS!

NEW TELECOMMUNICATIONS
  *  ORBITNET REDUCES YOUR COSTS AND INCREASES THE SPEED
     AND QUALITY OF TELECOMMUNICATIONS TO ORBIT FOR
     EUROPEAN USERS . . . . . .

YOU ARE NOW CONNECTED TO THE ORBIT DATABASE
FOR A TUTORIAL, ENTER A QUESTION MARK. OTHERWISE, ENTER
A COMMAND.

USER:
file rapra                               ←┘

PROG:
ELAPSED TIME ON ORBIT: 0.02 HRS
YOU ARE NOW CONNECTED TO THE RAPRA DATABASE.
COVERS 1972 TO DATE (8822/UP)

   ALL DOCUMENTS CITED ON RAPRA ARE AVAILABLE FROM RAPRA
   TECHNOLOGY. ENTER EXPLAIN ORDER RAPRA FOR DETAILS.

SS 1 /C?
USER:
```

Response from the MANchester node of PSS. The Network User Identifier (NUI) is entered – a number unique to the user. In this case, ORBIT lets users use its own Identifier.

←┘ = return.

The network asks for the ADDress – to which online host does the searcher wish to be connected?

The ADDress is repeated by way of confirming the connection. The next response is from ORBIT, asking the searcher to enter /LOGIN, and then the USER IDentification number. Following this, a security code is entered; the system then responds with any system news of immediate importance.

The searcher does not enter anything further until receiving the USER prompt; this is the searcher's prompt to input something.

The searcher is automatically connected to the ORBIT database. Normally, another database is needed, so the command FILE is used, followed by the name of the database. FILE RAPRA gives access to the Rapra database covering the years 1972–88.

PROGram is the prompt for the system to relay information.

SS 1 /C? means enter search statement 1 or a command.

1.2 Operations: entering search statements and creating sets of records; using Boolean operators; displaying records

Commands and features introduced: PRINT (PRT); Boolean operators AND and OR; 'stacking' commands; FIND (FD)

The general principles and methods of searching have been discussed in Chapters 5 and 6. After the initial analysis of the subject of the search, the identification of the concepts involved and the selection of appropriate terms to describe those concepts on this database, the terms are input; there is not normally any need to use a command to enter terms.

EXAMPLE: Rapra (1972–88)

The searcher asks for any occurrences of the term COMBUSTION.

```
SS 1 /C?
USER:
combustion ↵
```

The system responds with the message that in search statement 1 there are 1,356 'postings' (PSTG), or records. The searcher next uses the logical operator OR to find occurrences of the terms MODIFIED OR MODIFICATION; SS 2 retrieves 358 records where EITHER MODIFIED OR MODIFICATION has been used as a term.

```
PROG:
SS 1 PSTG (1356)

SS 2 /C?
USER:
modified or modification ↵

PROG:
SS 2 PSTG (358)
```

SS 3 /C?
USER:
1 and 2 ←

PROG:
SS 3 PSTG (83)

The logical operator AND is used to combine the first two search statements; search statement 3 includes records which contain both COMBUSTION and either MODIFIED or MODIFICATION.

This resulting set can be combined with another term, using the search statement number, to narrow down the set further; search statement 4 gives 36 records with COMBUSTION and FOAM and either MODIFIED or MODIFICATION.

SS 4 /C?
USER:
3 and foam ←

PROG:
SS 4 PSTG (36)

SS 5 /C?
USER:
prt ti 1 ←

PROG:

To display a set of retrieved records, the searcher uses the PRINT (PRT) command. There are 'standard' print commands: PRINT (PRT), which gives author(s), title and source information; PRINT FULL (PRT FU), which gives all the fields available for a record; PRINT TRIAL, which displays subject terms. The searcher can also tailor a PRINT command by choosing the fields to display – in this case the title field of the first record is chosen to assess the relevance of the record. Indiv-idual records can be chosen by use of the hyphen, e.g. PRINT 5-8, or PRINT -3 (the third record of the set). Records are displayed in reverse-chronological order.

Commands can be 'stacked' on one line by separating commands by the semi-colon (;), e.g. FILE RAPRA; NBR STIROL. The commands will be processed in order.

FIND (FD) command can be used to select a term when 'stacking' commands, or to avoid answering a system message.

-1-
TI – FIRE RULES MEAN MORE BUSINESS FOR FOAM AND FABRIC
MAKERS

SS 5 /C?
USER:
prt fu ←

The searcher decides that a record is relevant, and enters the PRINT FULL (PRT FU) command.

```
PROG:

-1-
AN   - 344561
ABN  - 0002014L
IS   - 8802
TI   - FIRE RULES MEAN MORE BUSINESS FOR FOAM AND FABRIC
          MAKERS
AU   - Rawsthorn A
SO   - Financial Times No.30437,14th Jan.1988,p.7
LO   - UK
DT   - J
IT   - COMBUSTION MODIFICATION; FLAMMABILITY; COMMER-
       CIAL INFORMATION; COMPANY; COMPANIES; FABRIC; FLAME
       RETARDANT; FLAMMABILITY; FURNITURE; MARKET;
       PLASTIC; REGULATION; RESILIENCE; SALES; TECHNICAL;
       THERMOPLASTIC; UPHOLSTERY
ST   - REGULATIONS, flammability, UK, cellular materials, furniture;
       FURNITURE, flammability, regulations; FLAMMABILITY,
       regulations, furniture; UK, regulations, flammability.
CC   - EA; OC; UH; KT
CL   - 1832-43C6-6124-968
AB   - The announcement of the revised fire regulations which cover
       the fire resistance of upholstered furniture has created
       opportunities for the British foam and fabric industries. For the
       foam industry these rules offer a chance to increase sales of the
       combustion-modified high resilience foams developed over the
       last few years. Similarly, fabric manufacturers should be able to
       take advantage of demand for flame retardant fabrics. These
       opportunities are discussed in detail.

SS 5 /C?
USER:
```

AN = Accession number
ABN = Abstract number
IS = Issue number; AU = Author

SO = Source; LO = Location
DT = Document type (Journal)
IT = Index terms; ST = Subject terms; CC = Category codes
CL = Classification codes
AB = Abstract

To PRINT selectively from a set with more than one record, the following options can be used:
PRT 6 (the six most recent records)
PRT -6 (the sixth record)
PRT 3-6 (the given range of records)
PRT 3, 6, 7-9, 10 (these individual records – the comma is optional).

The options open to the searcher at this stage are numerous – one or more of them may be: to browse through the remainder of the set;

to print out more or all the records in the set; to develop the search further and display the resulting records; to conduct a similar search on another database; to end the searching session.

1.3 Operations: reviewing a search; ending the search and searching session (logging-off)

Commands and features introduced: HISTORY (HIS or HIST); STOP (or LOGOFF)

The searcher wishing to change to another database would use the FILE command, followed by the name of the required database; this would erase all previous sets and enable the searcher to begin at Search Statement 1 again on the new database. In many cases, before changing databases, the searcher would SAVE the search already conducted (see 3.2).

There are many occasions on which the searcher requires to see a display of the search to date – particularly when the search statements have scrolled off a VDU screen! To review a search, enter HISTORY (HIS, HIST).

EXAMPLE: Rapra Abstracts

```
SS 5 /C?
USER:
his
```

HIS without any qualification will list all the search statements; if particular statements are required, the command is followed by the appropriate search statement number or numbers:
e.g. HIS 2
HIS 3,5-8,12

```
PROG:
SS 1: COMBUSTION (1356)
SS 2: MODIFIED OR MODIFICATION
      (358)
SS 3: 1 AND 2 (83)
SS 4: 3 AND FOAM (36)

SS 5 /C?
USER:
```

To end a searching session and disconnect from the host computer, the searcher would type the command STOP followed by Y (YES); no further input is required by the searcher.

EXAMPLE:

SS 7 /C?
USER:
stop y ←┘

The command STOP Y (STOP YES) is entered. The Y (YES) answer can be entered separately, but there is no advantage in this. As an alternative, LOGOFF Y could be used.

PROG:
TERMINAL SESSION FINISHED 11/24/88 11.39 A.M. (EASTERN TIME)
ELAPSED TIME ON RAPRA: 0.12 HRS
ELAPSED TIME THIS TERMINAL SESSION: 0.14 HOURS
ORBIT SEARCH SESSION COMPLETED. THANKS FOR USING ORBIT!

CLR DTE (00) 00:00:08:02 261 25

On disconnection from the PSS network, a message shows how long the network was used for (8 mins. 2 secs.) and how many 'segments' of data were received (261) and how many were sent (25). A 'segment' holds up to 64 characters, half a 'packet'.

UNIT TWO

2.1 Operations: displaying the index file; using both controlled and natural language terms; searching specific fields

Commands and features introduced: NEIGHBOR (NBR); searching for author with qualifier /AU; limiting search statements to specific fields using qualifiers (e.g. IT, TI); SELECT (SEL)

The ability to display terms from the index file, where all directly searchable terms are listed, is useful for finding out the occurrence of both controlled and natural language terms; and also for finding out the precise format of a term – for example, that of an author's name. For this operation, the NEIGHBOR (NBR) command is used. If no particular field (e.g. /AU for the author field) is demanded by the searcher, the NEIGHBOR command will give an alphabetical display of all terms in the index file adjacent to the chosen term.

EXAMPLE: Rapra Abstracts

```
SS 1 /C?
USER:
nbr aramid fibre        <--'

PROG:

SELECT£  POSTINGS  TERM
      1         1  ARAMID ARROW/TN
      2         3  ARAMID COPOLYMER/IT
      3      1141  ARAMID FIBRE/IT
      4         2  ARAMID FIBRE-REINFORCED PLASTIC/IT
      5         3  ARAMID FIBRES/MH
UP N OR DOWN N?
```

The NEIGHBOR (NBR) command will give a short listing of alphabetically related terms close to the term input; NEIGHBORing this term is particularly useful for showing how FIBRE is spelt on this database; on an American database it would have been FIBER.

The question UP N OR DOWN N? enables the searcher to display terms either above or below the initial list. To select from the list, the command SELECT (SEL) is used, followed by the appropriate number or numbers on the display.

```
USER:
sel 3-5                 <--'

PROG:
SS 1 PSTG (1144)

SS 2 /C?
USER:
```

EXAMPLE: Rapra Abstracts

```
SS 1 /C?
USER:
nbr nomex 111/tn        <--'

PROG:

SELECT£  POSTINGS  TERM
      1       180  NOMEX
      2         1  NOMEX FLEXCORE
      3         3  NOMEX III
      4         1  NOMEX M
      5         3  NOMEX 410
UP N OR DOWN N?
```

To display an alphabetical listing of terms in a particular field, the searcher enters a qualifier after the NEIGHBOR command. It is important, particularly when searching authors' names, to NEIGHBOR the name first, to find the exact format used, especially the format of the initials.

In this example, the searcher uses the qualifier /TN (for trade names).

The searcher can SELECT (SEL) a term or terms directly from the NEIGHBOR display.

```
USER:
sel 3                                  ←┘

PROG:
SS 1 PSTG (3)

SS 2 /C?
USER:
prt.......                             ←┘
```

EXAMPLE: Forest

The searcher is only certain of the first initial. The display indicates that the third name is probably the required one, and it is possible to SELect directly from the display.

```
SS 1 /C?
USER:
nbr englund b/au                       ←┘

PROG:
SELECT£   POSTINGS   TERM
      1          5   ENGLERTH G H/AU
      2          1   ENGLESSON T/AU
      3          1   ENGLUND B O/AU
      4          1   ENGLUND J S/AU
      5          1   ENGSTROM L/AU
UP N OR DOWN N?

USER:
sel 3                                  ←┘

PROG:
SS 1 PSTG (1)

SS 2 /C?
USER:
prt                                    ←┘

PROG:
-1-
AN   - NO1388
TI   - WOOD-FRAME FOUNDATIONS FOR LOW RISE
       BUILDINGS - A FEASIBLE ALTERNATIVE
AU   - ENGLUND B O
SO   - etc.........
```

The great majority of bibliographic databases use a controlled language for indexing records, and these terms are held in one field in the record; on ORBIT they are called 'index terms', and are directly searchable. In addition, most words taken from other fields within the record, e.g. title, abstract, are also directly searchable as natural language terms. The searcher will normally find appropriate terms when planning the search either from manual sources or from NEIGHBORing terms online, as above.

EXAMPLE: Rapra Abstracts

```
SS 1 /C?
USER:
kevlar/it,tn or nomex/tn

PROG:
SS 1 PSTG (753)

SS 2 /C?
USER:
1 and skis

SS 2 PSTG (3)

SS 3 /C?
USER:
prt ti 1

PROG:
-1-
TI   - COMPOSITES IN CHAMPIONSHIP SKIS

SS 3 /C?
USER:
```

KEVLAR is a controlled term on this database; the searcher qualifies the term by asking for only those records where the term is either an index term (IT), or a trade name (TN). Nomex is not a controlled term, and in this case is qualified by TN. More records could have been found on both these by searching the terms without any qualifiers – then the whole basic index would have been searched, including controlled terms, uncontrolled terms, trade names etc.

Although searches are generally well planned in advance, allowance is always made for modifying the search as a result of records retrieved – this is one great advantage of using an 'interactive' system. One common way of developing a search is to display the controlled language terms of relevant records retrieved, and then to input any of these which were overlooked or unknown previously; this can be done automatically on ORBIT (see 2.3).

2.2 Operations: proximity searching (full-text searching); stringsearching; truncation

Commands and features introduced: proximity operators (W), (S), (F); TS; truncation symbol (:); variable character symbol (#)

It is useful to be able to search for a term in a particular field, as we have seen, but the ability to search for terms in a particular proximity to each other enhances searching considerably. On ORBIT, if two or more words are required to occur together in a record, e.g. Urban Planning, by inserting (W) between the terms the searcher can retrieve records containing those two terms together, in that order, from any of the full-text searchable fields of the database – principally title, index term, supplementary term and abstract fields. An (F) proximity operator is used if the requirement is that the two terms appear in the same field, but not necessarily together, and in any order; the (S) operator is used when the terms are required to occur in the same sentence.

EXAMPLE: Rapra Abstracts

SS 1 /C?
USER:
combustion (w) modified

PROG:
SS 1 PSTG (18)

SS 2 /C?
USER:
combustion (f) modified

PROG:
SS 2 PSTG (35)

SS 3 /C?
USER:

The phrase COMBUSTION MODIFIED is searched first using the (W) proximity operator; the system retrieves records with that phrase in any of the fields in the basic index. (W) can appear as (1W) – up to one word between the two terms input, (2W) etc.

If the searcher wishes the terms to appear in the same field (e.g. title) but not necessarily in the close proximity as above, the letter (F) can be placed between the terms; if the two or more terms chosen appear in the same field in the record, in any order, that record will be retrieved.

It is useful to be able to search for a particular 'string' or 'strings' of characters within one or more fields of a set of records; this feature is called 'stringsearching'. With the introduction of proximity searching on ORBIT, stringsearching is not as important as in the past, but it remains a powerful searching tool. There are four parts to a stringsearch statement, two of which are optional:

1	2	3	4
TS	(e.g.) 1	(e.g.) /TI	(e.g.) :MYALGIC:
(abbreviation for Title Search)	(the number of the set to be searched)	(the field to be searched)	(the string of characters being sought)

Numbers 2 and 3 are optional – the system will automatically default to the last search statement unless the searcher specifies otherwise; depending on the database, the system will automatically default to a particular field. The set to be stringsearched should be of a manageable size – no more than 200–300 records normally; the system scans the OLDEST records first.

A feature which is very important, particularly when searching natural language terms and phrases, is truncation – the ability to input the stem of a word, followed by the truncation symbol; the system will retrieve records where any term beginning with the word stem appears; e.g. INTEREST: will retrieve INTEREST, INTERESTED, INTERESTS etc. On ORBIT, the truncation symbol is the colon (:). If only one extra character is required (e.g. an 's' for the plural of words), the variable character symbol (//) can be used.

EXAMPLE: Rapra Abstracts

```
SS 1 /C?
USER:
all expand:/ti and all polystyrene /// ti    ←┘

PROG:
SS 1 PSTG (164)

SS 2 /C?
USER:
prt ti 1-4    ←┘

PROG:


-1-
TI   - EXPANDABLE POLYSTYRENE
```

Truncation is particularly useful when searching natural language terms. In this case, the searcher is looking for the terms in the titles only.

It is advisable in most cases to precede the truncated term by the word ALL to avoid a multi-meaning message, i.e. a list of all the terms beginning with the truncated term.

EXPAND: would retrieve EXPANDS, EXPANDED, EXPANDABLE, EXPANDING etc.

-2-
TI – PRODUCTION LINE FOR THE MANUFACTURE OF MOULDINGS MADE FROM EXPANDABLE POLYSTYRENE

-3-
TI – EPSICON EXPANDED POLYSTYRENE PERMANENT FOAM-WORK

-4-
TI – BASF EXPANDS POLYSTYRENE PLANT IN SOUTH KOREA

SS 2 /C?
USER:

If only one extra character is required (e.g. the plural of a word), the variable character symbol (#) can be used; in the example, POLYSTYRENE# would retrieve POLYSTYRENE or POLYSTYRENES, but not POLYSTYRENESULPHONIC. (NB Record number 4 shows that terms are not always in the required context!)

2.3 Operations: searching using classification codes, subfiles etc.; analysing search results

Commands and features introduced: GET

When discussing the search in Chapter 6, reference was made to the fact that most databases have a feature whereby it is possible to search a subject area wider than that described by one term, or a few terms, by using a classification code, subfile, or other system or database feature.

EXAMPLE: World Patent Index

USER:
nbr a61j-017/00/ic

The International Patent Classification (IPC) is one of the classification schemes searchable on World Patent Index. A61J-017/00 is the code for babies' dummies. The use of this code overcomes the problem of listing all the terms which might be involved, e.g. DUMMY, DUMMIES, TEATS, TEETHING RINGS, PACIFYING NIPPLES etc.

```
PROG:
SELECT   POSTINGS   TERM
       1          1   A61J-015/06/IC
       2         72   A61J-017/IC
       3         72   A61J-017/00/IC
       4         14   A61J-019/IC
       5         12   A61J-019/00/IC
UP N OR DOWN N?
```

USER:
sel 3 ↵

PROG:
SS 1 PSTG (72)

SS 2 /C?
USER:
all fill: or all load: ↵

PROG:
SS 2 PSTG (274275)

SS 3 /C?
USER:
1 and 2 ↵

PROG:
SS 3 PSTG (11)

SS 4 /C?
USER:
prt ti 1-3 ↵

PROG:

-1-
TI – Suction test for baby – has elastic body fastened by flange with U=shaped radial cross=section to brim of rigid holder

-2-
TI – Baby's dummy with silicone rubber teat – filled with softer . . . etc

An aid for developing 'interactive' searching on ORBIT is the GET command. This analyses a retrieved set of records and lists the frequency with which index terms, and other fields, have been used, and helps the searcher in identifying the most relevant terms used in a set; these terms can then be entered automatically as search terms on the same or another database.

EXAMPLE: Lisa

SS 1 /C?
USER:
online or on(w)line or on-line ←┘

PROG:
SS 1 PSTG (8061)

SS 2 /C?
USER:
information (f) retrieval or ir ←┘

PROG:
SS 2 PSTG (5276)

SS 3 /C?
USER:
1 and 2 ←┘

PROG:
SS 3 PSTG (2055)

SS 4 /C?
USER:
get it rank gt 100 ←┘

Having conducted a wide search on online information retrieval, the searcher wishes to analyse the resulting set for the index terms (IT) that have been used at least one hundred times in the 2,055 records (GT 100), and to rank them by the number of occurrences (RANK). Some of these index terms could then be used as part of the search if appropriate.

PROG:
THERE ARE 2431 UNIQUE VALUES
OCCURRENCES TERM
686 COMPUTERISED SUBJECT INDEXING – INFORMATION STORAGE AND RETRIEVAL SYSTEMS BY SUBJECT SPECIFICATION: 0

If the word TOSEL is included in the GET command, each term will be given a SELECT number, allowing sets to be created directly from the GET display.

231	INFORMATION SERVICES
174	USA
173	COORDINATE SUBJECT INDEXING: DATA BASES
147	UK
145	ON-LINE INFORMATION RETRIEVAL
136	COMPUTERISED
125	MAGNETIC TAPE
117	USE OF INFORMATION SERVICES

SS 4 /C?
USER:

UNIT THREE

3.1 Operations: limiting a retrieved set of records by some criteria, e.g. language, date of publication; ranging

The ORBIT system uses three methods for limiting by criteria such as language, type of publication, date of publication etc., namely stringsearching, direct searching and ranging.

Stringsearching enables the searcher to find any 'string' of characters in a particular field (see 2.2 above). The language of a paper can be searched directly, as in the example below; this can sometimes result in a number of time-overflow messages.

EXAMPLE: Iconda

SS 1 /C?
USER:
maintenance (s) plan:/ti,it,st ←

The searcher asks for records which contain the terms MAINTENANCE and PLAN: in the same sentence (PLAN: would retrieve PLANS, PLANNED, PLANNING etc.) – there are actually 114 different entries in the basic index for terms beginning with PLAN; this produces a multi-meaning message.

PROG:
MM (PLAN:) (114)
ALL OR NONE?

USER:
all ←

PROG:
SS 1 PSTG (70)

SS 2 /C?
USER:
1 and english/la ←

On most databases it is possible to limit a search statement by the language of the original paper. Direct searching in this way can also be used for limiting by date of publication, date of entry to the database etc.

PROG:
SS 2 PSTG (56)

SS 3 /C?
USER:

It is possible to limit a set of records to a particular range of dates; this feature is called 'ranging'.

EXAMPLE: SAE Abstracts

SS 8 PSTG (60)

SS 9 /C?
USER:
8 and 86-89 ←┘

The searcher limits the records in search statement 8 to those entered into the database in the years 1986–9.

PROG:
SS 9 PSTG (34)

SS 10 /C?
USER:
prt include it 1-5 ←┘

PROG:
etc. . . . .

3.2 Operations: saving a search on one database, changing to another database and conducting the same search on the new database; (searching a number of databases at once ('multifile' searching) not available on ORBIT); searching elements of records across databases

Commands and features introduced: SAVE; RECALL

An online enquiry is often not satisfied by searching just one database, and some databases, e.g. NTIS, CA Search, World Patent Index, are split up into more than one database. On ORBIT it is possible to conduct a search on one database, save the search, change to another database and conduct the same search on the new database; this avoids the necessity of typing in or uploading the search more than once while online.

On ORBIT, the SAVE command is used to save the initial search. It is entered at the end of the search, and will save all search statements, even those with no records in them.

EXAMPLE: WPIL/WPI

SS 4 /C?
USER:
save dummy ←┘

PROG:
SAVE DUMMY COMPLETED

The searcher saves the search on the current World Patent Index (WPIL) database; then moves to the retrospective WPI database. The command RECALL is used, followed by the name of the SAVEd search, to process the search on the new database.

SS 4 /C?
USER:
file wpi ↵

PROG:
ELAPSED TIME ON WPIL: 0.15 HRS
YOU ARE NOW CONNECTED TO THE WPI DATABASE
COVERS BASIC 1963 – 80: UPDATED TO 8851/UPEQ

PROXIMITY SEARCHABLE

SS 1 /C?
USER:
recall dummy ↵

PROG:
PROCESSING
SS 1: A61J-017/00/IC (51)
SS 2: ALL FILL: OR ALL LOAD: (183281)
SS 3: 1 AND 2 (3)

SS 4 /C?
USER:
prt ti ↵

PROG:

-1-
TI – Fluid filled teething ring......etc......

ORBIT has the facility of saving elements of records on one database for using on another database. In the example below, the searcher creates a set for PERSPEX on the chemical dictionary database Chemdex; from this it is possible to SELeCT the registry numbers (RN); and then on the main CAS82 database, SELeCT one or more of the registry numbers automatically.

EXAMPLE: Chemdex/CAS82

SS 1 /C?
USER:
perspex ↵

PROG:
SS 1 PSTG (1)

SS 2 /C?
USER:
prt fu ↵ Printing out the record is optional; there is one main registry number,

PROG:
-1-
RN – 9011-14-7 (See also 9011-73-8, 37206-27-2, etc. . . . .)

but 17 other related numbers which might be useful in a crossfile search.

SS 2 /C?
USER:
prt sel rn ↵

Searcher enters PRINT SELECT and all the registry numbers are printed out, with a SELECT number.

PROG:
SELECT£ TERM
1 9011-14-7/RN
2 9011-73-8/RN
etc. . .

SS 2 /C?
USER:
file cas82 ↵

Searcher requests the CAS82 database, and SELects just the first registry number; all 18 numbers could have been SELected by inputting SEL 1-18.

PROG:
ELAPSED TIME ON CHEMDEX: 0.05 HRS
YOU ARE NOW CONNECTED TO THE CAS82 DATABASE
. . .etc. . .

SS 1 /C?
USER:
sel 1 ↵

PROG:
SS 1 PSTG (1793)

SS 2 /C?
USER:

3.3 Operations: printing 'offline'; sorting records; downloading records; transferring records to an electronic mail facility

Commands and features introduced: PRINT OFFLINE STORAD (PRTOFF); PRINT ELECTRONIC (PRTELEC)

After a set of relevant records has been retrieved, it can often be more economical, particularly if large numbers of records are required, to have them printed 'offline' by the online host and mailed to the searcher or end-user. The high-speed printing of search results generally takes place the evening of the day of the search, and mailing follows immediately. The longest wait, even across continents, is about six days, but it is often quicker than this; inland this can be as little as one or two days. Another alternative to printing online, as well as printing offline, is downloading into a local microcomputer or mainframe computer, or transferring the required records to ORBIT's electronic prints facility. The searcher decides which method is preferable, depending on a number of variables, the principal ones being the speed of the terminal and printing equipment, how urgently the records are required, how many records there are, what format is required (e.g. are abstracts required; on full-text databases is the whole text required?), and what the financial implications of the different methods are.

If it is decided to print offline, the command PRINT (PRT) is used in the normal way, with the word OFFLINE added to the end. When first signing on to ORBIT, a user would store name and address in the system using the STORAD command; when printing offline this command is added to the end of the PRINT command, so ORBIT can send the results to the address as stored.

EXAMPLE: Iconda

SS 7 /C?
USER:
5 and 6 ↵

SS 7 PSTG (63)

SS 8 /C?
USER:
prt fu offline storad ↵

Searcher prints the results of the last search statement offline; to print earlier search statements, the search statement number would have to be added, as in a normal print command; e.g. PRT FU SS 4 OFFLINE STORAD.

PROG:
REQUESTER?

USER:
J. Bloggs ↵

The REQUESTER's name, with the title, will be included in the heading information on the offline print.

PROG:
TITLE?

USER:
Maintenance Management ↵

PROG:
63 CITATIONS REQUESTED.
OK? (Y/N/C)

The opportunity is given to answer Yes, No, or Cancel to the offline print command.

USER:
y ←┘

The SORT command can be included in an offline print command, e.g. PRTOFF SORT AU.

PROG:
YOUR OFF-LINE PRINT NUMBER IS P3111637
OFF-LINE PRINT COMPLETED

There are no special commands for downloading records.

SS 8 /C?
USER:
stop y....... ←┘

Prints can be ready after only two hours, if the PRINT ELECTRONIC command is used to transfer offprints to ORBIT's electronic mail facility.

System 6

Pergamon Financial Data Services

UNIT ONE

1.1 Operations: logging-on to the system; choosing a database (file)

Commands and features introduced: logging-on information; FILE

Pergamon Financial Data Services (PFDS), formerly Pergamon Infoline, currently gives access to about 40 databases, and the computer is based in Oxford, England. In the United Kingdom, users contact the nearest 'node' of British Telecom's Packet SwitchStream (PSS) network, and then make the link with the PFDS computer. From outside the United Kingdom, the system may be accessed via national post, telegraph and telephone services (PTTs) and international data transmission networks. The example below shows a log-on via the Manchester (UK) node of PSS, with a terminal working at 1,200 baud (120 characters per second (cps)).

For the purpose of clarity, the characters input by the searcher in the examples below are underlined; this is not the case when actually working online.

The searcher first dials the node of the network (in many cases the terminal or modem will be programmed to do this automatically), and after identifying the type of terminal being used, and the speed of transmission, will receive a response similar to the following from the node:

EXAMPLE:

```
MAN A002-6164340239
N000000000000          ←┘
ADD?
A284400162             ←┘

234284400162 + COM
```

Response from the MANchester node of PSS. The Network User Identifier (NUI) is entered – a number unique to the user. ←┘ = return.

The network asks for the ADDress – to which online host does the searcher wish to be connected?

```
Welcome to Pergamon Financial Data Services

Username: XXXXXX       ←┘
XXXXXX
Password: AAAAAA       ←┘
```

The ADDress is repeated by way of confirming the connection. The next response is from PFDS, asking for the Username and Password.

```
*****************************************************
*  NEW DATABASE - EUROPE'S LARGEST COMPANIES       *
*  (File ELC). Half hour free connect time during January.  *
*  Type ?NEWS and then ELC for more details.       *
*****************************************************

          HELP DESK 01 993-7333
  15 DEC 1988 9:04 (LONDON TIME)

Infoline Version 4.0

Please enter a file name or MENU

/ uktm                 ←┘

       UK TRADE MARKS Version 1

The Database includes Crown Copyright material

          Crown Copyright 1988.

New prices come into effect 1st January 1989.
Type ?PRICE for more details.

Updated on 14th December for week ending 18th November (UP = 8843)

Enter your request
/
```

At this stage, the searcher will be given any system news of immediate importance, will be asked to enter a file (database) name, and then will be asked to 'Enter your request'; the searcher's prompt to input something is the (/). The MENU option gives access to other services not using the Infoline commands, e.g. the gateway to ESA-IRS, menu searching of JordanWatch.

1.2 Operations: entering search statements and creating sets of records; using Boolean operators; displaying records

Commands and features introduced: SELECT (S); COMBINE (C); Boolean operators AND and OR; 'stacking' commands; TYPE (T); DISPLAY (D)

The general principles and methods of searching have been discussed in Chapters 5 and 6. After the initial analysis of the subject of the search, the identification of the concepts involved and the selection of appropriate terms to describe those concepts on this database, the terms are input using the SELECT (S) command.

EXAMPLE: Management and Marketing Abstracts

```
/ s management                              ↵
Set 1: 18386 management
/ s objectives or objective                 ↵
Set 2:  1744 objectives
Set 3:   872 objective
Set 4:  1983 objectives or objective
/ c 1 and 4                                 ↵
Set 5:  1058 1 and 4
/ s senior management                       ↵
Set 6:   238 senior management
/ c 5 and 6                                 ↵
Set 7:    20 5 and 6
/
```

The searcher uses the SELECT (S) command to find all the occurrences of the term MANAGEMENT on the database; a space is required between the command and the term. The resulting set of records is given a set number. The logical operator OR is used in the second search statement; individual sets are given for each term, and then a further set OR-ing the two together. The searcher then uses the COMBINE (C) command to find only those records where both MANAGEMENT AND either OBJECTIVES OR OBJECTIVE have been used as terms. This is further refined by combining the index term SENIOR MANAGEMENT with set 5. Commands can be 'stacked' on one line, by separating them with a semi-colon, e.g. s management; s objectives.

The details of the records retrieved in set 7 can be displayed online by the use of the TYPE (T) or DISPLAY (D) commands. There are a number of different formats available and the searcher can choose whichever is most appropriate in the circumstances; the formats vary from one database to another, so reference would need to be made to the database details supplied by PFDS; generally, the higher the format number, the more information is given from the record.

A TYPE (T) command usually consists of these elements:

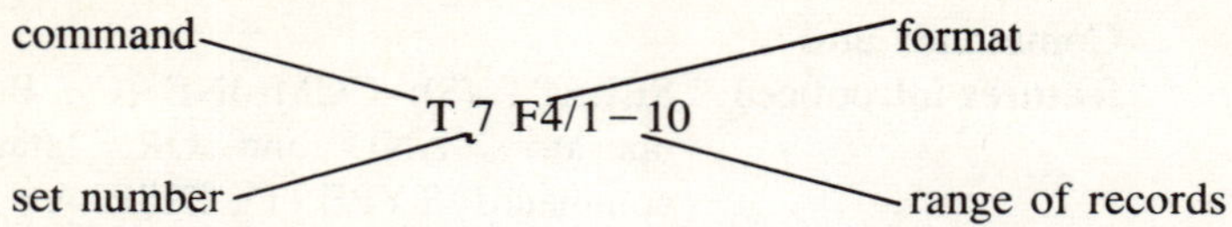

EXAMPLE: Management and Marketing Abstracts

/ t f2/1-2

Item 1
ACN : 04-89-01171 JA: 8904 UP: 8904 <PIN: 8 46939>
TTL : THE IMPORTANCE OF SETTING IS OBJECTIVES
REF : J. Inf. Syst. Manage. vol. 6, no. 1, Winter 1988, pp 61-64
ISSN: 0739-9014 LC: EN DT: J PY: 1988

Item 2
ACN : 04-89-00888 JA: 8903 UP: 8902 <PIN: 8546596>
TTL : HIGH REALITY BUSINESS SIMULATIONS FOR MANAGERS
REF : Train. Manage. Dev. Methods vol. 2, no. 2, 1988, pp 6, 75-6, 84.
ISSN: 0951-3507 LC: EN DT: J PY: 1988

The searcher chooses format 2 initially; this gives the main bibliographical details, and helps the searcher to see whether the records are relevant or not. Format 4 would give more information, including an abstract.

(NB Records are in reverse-chronological order, so that the first records displayed are the latest entered into the database.)

The options open to the searcher at this stage are numerous – one or more of them may be: to browse through the remainder of the set; to print out all the records in the set; to develop the search further and display resulting records; to conduct a similar search on another database; to end the searching session.

1.3 Operations: reviewing a search; ending the search and searching session (logging-off)

Commands and features introduced: LIST (LS); LOGOUT (or LOGOFF, STOP or END)

The searcher wishing to change to another database would normally use the FILE command, followed by the name of the required database; this would erase all previous sets and enable the searcher to begin at set 1 again on the new database. In many cases, before changing databases, the searcher would SAVE the search already conducted (see 3.2).

There are many occasions on which the searcher requires to see a display of the search to date – particularly when the search statements have scrolled off a VDU screen! To review a search, enter LIST (LS).

EXAMPLE: Management and Marketing Abstracts

```
/ ls                                     ←┘

  Set   Items   Command
Set 1: 18386    management
Set 2: 1744     objectives
Set 3: 872      objective
Set 4: 1983     objectives or objective
Set 5: 1058     1 and 4
Set 6: 238      senior management
Set 7: 20       5 and 6
/
```

The command LIST (LS) on its own will give the whole search; specific sets, or a range of sets, can be specified, e.g. LS 2; LS 3-6.

To end a searching session and disconnect from the host computer, the searcher would type the LOGOUT command (or LOGOFF, STOP or END); no further input is required by the searcher.

EXAMPLE: Management and Marketing Abstracts

```
/ logout                                   ←┘

User   000000       08-APR-1989          Session number  9451
File   MMA          Start time 08:44:05  End time 08:52:50
Purchase  Format  Quantity  Rate   Cost (UK pounds)  Order number
Hours               0.1396  75.00  10.47
Display      2          2    0.22   0.44
File total cost (estimated)        10.91

  000000  logged out at  8-APR-1989 08:52:58
CLR DTE   (4B)  00:00:08:59  202  66
```

After disconnection from the host computer, a message from the network shows how long the network was used (8 mins. 59 secs.) and how many 'segments' of data were received (202) and how many were sent (66). A 'segment' holds up to 64 characters, half a 'packet'.

UNIT TWO

2.1 Operations: displaying the index file; using both controlled and natural language terms; searching specific fields

Commands and features introduced: EXPAND (E or EX or NBR); searching for author with prefix AU=; limiting search statements to specific fields, e.g. CT, TI

The ability to display terms from the index file, where all directly searchable terms are listed, is useful for finding out the occurrence of both controlled and natural language terms; and also for finding out the precise format of a term – for example, that of an author's name. For this operation the EXPAND (E) command is used, or NEIGHBOR (NBR). If no particular field (e.g. AU= for the author field) is asked for by the searcher, the EXPAND command will default to a particular field, depending on the database (e.g. the trade mark field on the UK Trade Marks database).

EXAMPLE: UK Trade Marks

The searcher EXPANDs the term BRITANNIA, and on this database the system defaults to the trade mark field; an alphabetical listing is given, each with a reference letter, the number of items (records) containing that term, and the term itself.

```
/ e britannia                              ←┘

        Items     Terms
A           1   TM = BRITAMINS
B           1   TM = BRITAMPEN
C           1   TM = BRITAINE
D           1   TM = BRITANNA
E          68** TM = BRITANNIA
F           1   TM = BRITANNIA AND EVE
```

G 3 TM = BRITANNIA AUCTIONS BRITANNIA EXCHANGE
H 1 TM = BRITANNIA B
I 1 TM = BRITANNIA BATTERIES LIMITED B B
More terms are available
Choose letters to combine
/ e ↵

To continue the display, type in 'more'.

Set 1: 68 TM = BRITANNIA
Continue, choose letters or enter a command
/ c 1 and gs = picture ↵

Set 2: 1 1 and gs = picture

/ t f4/1 ↵

**indicates the item input by the searcher. The searcher can choose a term or terms directly from the list by using the reference letters, as in the example; a range of letters can be chosen, e.g. f, h-i. A set will then be established, as in the example.

Item 1
APPLICATION NUMBER : 1227203 UPDATE CODE : 8715 <PIN: 31907278>
TRADE MARK : BRITANNIA AUCTIONS BRITANNIA EXCHANGE
TRADE MARK TYPE : 3, Composite
APPLICATION STAGE : 1, New Application Lapsed
APPLICATION DATE : 840927
REGISTER PART : A
SCHEDULE : 4
CLASS OF GOODS : 420; Furniture, articles of wood, cork, etc.
PROPRIETOR : BRITANNIA EXCHANGE LIMITED AND BRITANNIA AUCTIONS LIMITED
PROPRIETOR ADDRESS : . . . etc

When searching authors' names, it is advisable to EXPAND the name first, to find the exact format used, especially the format of the initials; this would take the form E AU=BLOGGS, J.

The great majority of bibliographic databases use a controlled language for indexing records and these terms are held in one field in the record; on PFDS they are called 'descriptors', and are directly searchable. In addition, most words taken from other fields within the record, e.g. title, abstract, are also directly searchable as natural language terms. The searcher will normally find appropriate terms when planning the search either from manual sources or from EXPANDing terms online.

EXAMPLE: Management and Marketing Abstracts

```
/ s ct=management by objectives      ←┘ MANAGEMENT BY OBJECT-
                                        IVES is a controlled term, and this
Set  1:  161   ct=management by objectives
/ s ct=management buy-out            ←┘ is prefixed by the abbreviation CT=.
                                        Similarly, MANAGEMENT BUY-
Set  2:  98    ct=management buy-out
/ c 1 and 2                          ←┘ OUT is a controlled term. Other
                                        fields can be searched in a similar
Set  3:   4    1 and 2                  way, e.g. title terms – S TT=MBO.
/ t f3/1                             ←┘

Item 1
  ACN : 04-87-00758  JA: 8702  UP: 8702     PIN 7346756
  TTL : MANAGEMENT BUY-OUTS (MBO) AND BUY-INS (MBI)
  AUT : Meinertzhagen R R
  REF : Modern Management vol. 1, no. 1, Winter 1986, pp 18-19
        LC: EN   DT: J  PY:1986
  CLA : 4320
  DES : MH: Corporate planning
        CT: ABSORB; ADVISOR; BANK; CAPITAL; COMPANY;
        EXECUTIVE; HIGH; MANAGEMENT; MANAGEMENT BUY-
        OUT; MANAGEMENT BY OBJECTIVES; PROFESSIONAL;
        PROPORTION; SELL; SUBSIDIARY; TAKEOVER; TEAMS
  LOC : GL: EUROPE; UNITED KINGDOM
        GC: EU;EZUKM
/
```

Although searches are generally well planned in advance, allowance is always made for modifying the search as a result of records retrieved – this is one great advantage of using an 'interactive' system. One common way of developing a search is to display the controlled language terms of relevant records retrieved, and then to input any of these which were overlooked or unknown previously.

2.2 Operations: proximity searching (full-text searching); stringsearching; truncation

Commands and features introduced: WITHIN (WN); WITH (W); SCAN (SC or STRS); truncation symbol (*)

It is useful to be able to search for a term in a particular field, as we have seen, but the ability to search for terms in a particular proximity to each other enhances searching considerably. On PFDS, if two or more words are required to occur together in a record, e.g. Urban Planning, by preceding the words by WN 2, the searcher can retrieve records containing those terms adjacent to each other, in that order.

EXAMPLE: Management and Marketing Abstracts

```
/ s wn 2 senior,management

Set  1:  259
/
```

The searcher is looking for records where the two terms SENIOR and MANAGEMENT are adjacent to each other, in that order. WITH (W) can also be used – depending on the database, this searches for terms in the same field or sentence.

It is useful to be able to search for a particular 'string' or 'strings' of characters within one or more fields of a set of records; this feature is called 'stringsearching'; PFDS uses the SCAN (SC) command. There are four parts to a SCAN command:

1	2	3	4
SCAN or SC or STRS	(e.g.) 7 (number of set to be searched; defaults to last set if not specified)	(e.g.) TI (the field(s) to be searched)	(e.g.) EQUIPMENT (string of characters being sought)

EXAMPLE: Management and Marketing Abstracts

```
Set  8:  78  6 and 7
/ sc ct management by objectives

Set  9:  3   sc 8 ct management by objectives
/
```

A set of records is established first; then the searcher SCans the controlled term field for the string of characters MANAGEMENT BY OBJECTIVES.

A feature which is very important, particularly when searching natural language terms and phrases, is truncation – the ability to input the stem of a word, followed by the truncation symbol; the system will retrieve records where any term beginning with the word stem appears; e.g. INTEREST* will retrieve INTEREST, INTERESTED, INTERESTS etc. On PFDS, the truncation symbol is the asterisk (*).

EXAMPLE: Planning Exchange

```
/ s planning and law                    ↵

Set  1:  3933  planning
Set  2:  969   law
Set  3:  310   planning and law
/ s europe*                             ↵

Set  4:  365   europe*
/ c 3 and 4                             ↵

Set  5:  18    3 and 4
/ t f2/1                                ↵

Item 1
  ACN : AN: E2271      UP: 8712    <PIN: 52271>
  TTL : TI : European Environmental Yearbook 1987
  AUT : CS : DocTer International UK
        AD: London
  REF :
        CI : 815 PAGES   PY:  1987
        PU: DocTer International UK
        PP: London
```

By truncating the term EUROPE*, the searcher is asking the system to retrieve any records where the word stem EUROPE is present, i.e. it will retrieve EUROPE, EUROPEAN, EUROPE'S etc.

2.3 Operations: searching using classification codes, subfiles etc.; analysing search results

Commands and features introduced: GET

When discussing the search in Chapter 6, reference was made to the fact that most databases have a feature whereby it is possible to search a subject area wider than that described by one term, or a few terms, by using a classification code, subfile, or other system or database feature. On the UK Trade Marks database, for instance, classification codes can be used.

EXAMPLE: UK Trade Marks

```
/ s heritage                            ↵

Set  1:  110   TM = HERITAGE
/ e cl = 416                            ↵
```

Class number 416 covers paper, paper articles, stationery etc. This is EXPANDed first; it could have been searched directly by inputting S CL=416. When COMBINEd with the previous set, it reduces considerably the number of trade marks under HERITAGE.

```
        Items    Terms
A      12043   CL=412
B        817   CL=413
C       5544   CL=414
D       1131   CL=415
E      30187** CL=416
F       9786   CL=417
G       5012   CL=418
H      11312   CL=419
I      10553   CL=420
More terms are available
Choose letters to combine
/ e                                  ↵
Set  2:  30187  cl=416(EX)  E
Continue, choose letters or enter a command
/ c 1 and 2                          ↵
Set  3:  10       1 and 2
/ t f4/1                             ↵
Item 1
APPLICATION NUMBER : 1299623  UPDATE CODE : 8708  <PIN:
                     33790198>
TRADE MARK         : gdp HERITAGE
TRADE MARK TYPE    : 4 , Stylised Word
APPLICATION STAGE  : 1 , New Application
APPLICATION DATE   : 870203
REGISTER PART      : A
SCHEDULE           : 4
CLASS OF GOODS     : 416; Paper and paper articles, stationery,
                     office requisites, etc.
PROPRIETOR         : etc............etc............
/
```

An aid for developing 'interactive' searching is the GET command. This analyses a retrieved set of records and lists the terms from the analysed field in rank order. If the index term field is analysed in this way, the most commonly used index terms in the set can be listed, and used to develop the search.

UNIT THREE

3.1 Operations: limiting a retrieved set of records by some criteria, e.g. language, date of publication; ranging

Commands and features introduced: GREATER THAN (GT)

The PFDS system uses three methods for limiting by criteria such as language, type of publication, date of publication etc., namely stringsearching, direct searching and ranging.

Stringsearching enables the searcher to find any 'string' of characters in a particular field (see 2.2 above). The language of a paper can be searched directly by using the field qualifier (see 2.1 above).

Certain numeric fields can be 'ranged', and then combined with another set; e.g. S PY=GT 86 (searcher selects publication year (PY) after (GT) 1986).

3.2 Operations: saving a search on one database, changing to another database and conducting the same search on the new database; (searching a number of databases at once ('multifile' searching) not available on PFDS); searching elements of records across databases

Commands and features introduced: PROFILE SAVE (P SAVE); PROFILE RUN (P RUN); SDI

An online enquiry is often not satisfied by searching just one database, and some databases are split up into more than one database. On PFDS it is possible to conduct a search on one database, save the search, change to another database and conduct the same search on the new database; this avoids the necessity of typing in or uploading the search more than once while online.

On PFDS, the PROFILE SAVE (P SAVE) command is used to save the initial search. It is entered at the end of the search, and will save all search statements, even those with no records in them.

EXAMPLE: Management and Marketing Abstracts

```
/ ls 5-7                         ←┘

Set 5: 1058  1 and 4
Set 6: 238   senior management
Set 7: 20    5 and 6
/ p save                         ←┘
"SAVE"
Saved with 7 lines of text
/
```

Searcher enters the temporary save PROFILE SAVE. This search can then be recalled on another database, or on the same database, by using the command PROFILE RUN

(P RUN). It is important when saving profiles to run on another database that any terms used in the search are compatible with the terms used on the other database.

PFDS has the facility of saving elements of records on one database for using on another database. In the example below, the searcher creates a set for a company on one database, and then changes to another database and searches that database too without having to re-enter the search.

EXAMPLE: JSS/Jordans

Jordans Shareholder Service and JordanWatch are compatible databases for crossfile searching.

This example shows an imaginary search, beginning with a shareholder (SH), who has shares in just one company. The GET command is used to SAVE the company registration number (RN); and the change is made to the JordanWatch database, where the GET command is used again to create a set for the company in which BLOGGS J has shares.

```
Set  1:  1  SH=Bloggs J. ESQ
/ t f4/1                                   ←┘

Item 1
Ref : 00012345  Holdings as at 31 Oct 88  Filed 14 Jan 89  Issued 23,432
RN : 98765432  ...etc...
/ get rn save=bloggs                       ←┘

1 unique terms saved as bloggs
/ file jordans                             ←┘

      JORDANWATCH VERSION 2

Select option

1 – JordanWatch Company Information
2 – Order / Monitoring
3 – InfoLine Searching
4 – Logoff

Enter option number
/ 3                                        ←┘
You are now in the InfoLine Search System
Please enter a Command, type MENU to return
/ get use=bloggs prefix="rn="              ←┘

Set  1:  1  RN=98765432
/ t f4/1                                   ←┘

Item 1
etc.........
```

3.3 Operations: printing 'offline'; sorting records; downloading records; (transferring records to an electronic mail facility not available on PFDS)

Commands and features introduced: PRINT (PR)

After a set of relevant records has been retrieved, it can often be more economical, particularly if large numbers of records are required, to have them printed 'offline' by the online host and mailed to the searcher or end-user. The high-speed printing of search results generally takes place the evening of the day of the search, and mailing follows immediately. The longest wait, even across continents, is about six days, but it is often quicker than this; inland this can be as little as one or two days. Another alternative to printing online, as well as printing offline, is downloading into a local microcomputer or mainframe computer. The searcher decides which method is preferable, depending on a number of variables, the principal ones being the speed of the terminal and printing equipment, how urgently the records are required, how many records there are, what format is required (e.g. are abstracts required; on full-text databases is the whole text required?), and what the financial implications of the different methods are.

If it is decided to print offline, the command PRINT (PR) is used, followed by the elements used in the TYPE command, i.e. set number, format and number of records required, or ALL.

EXAMPLE:

```
Set  11:  65  9 and 10
/ pr f4/all

SET 11 printed with 65 out of 65
          items
/
```

← The last set is presumed if no set number is entered; the searcher could have input a range of records, e.g. PR F4/1-25.

It is possible to SORT records online, e.g. SORT 11 CN (sorting on company name); after this, the offline print command can be entered.

Records can be downloaded using the DOWN command, followed by the format and range of records.

The command FLOPPY allows records to be written on to a floppy disc, which is then sent by mail to the user.

System 7

Data-Star

UNIT ONE

1.1 Operations: logging-on to the system; choosing a database (file)

Commands and features introduced: logging-on information

Data-Star, based in Switzerland, currently gives access to over 100 databases. In the United Kingdom, users contact the nearest 'node' of British Telecom's Packet SwitchStream (PSS) network, and then make the link with Data-Star via the International Packet SwitchStream (IPSS). From outside the United Kingdom, the system may be accessed via national post, telegraph and telephone services (PTTs) and international data transmission networks. The example below shows a log-on via the Manchester (UK) node of PSS, with a terminal working at 1,200 baud (120 characters per second (cps)).

For the purpose of clarity, the characters input by the searcher in the examples below are underlined; this is not the case when actually working online.

The searcher first dials the node of the network (in many cases the terminal or modem will be programmed to do this automatically), and after identifying the type of terminal being used, and the speed of transmission, will receive a response similar to the following from the node:

EXAMPLE:

```
MAN A002-6164340239
N000000000000                    ↵
ADD?
A9228464110115                   ↵
```

Response from the MANchester node of PSS. The Network User Identifier (NUI) is entered – a number unique to the user.

↵ = return.

The network asks for the ADDress – to which online host does the searcher wish to be connected?

```
228464110115+COM

D A T A - S T A R , PLEASE ENTER YOUR USERID : XXXXXX ↵

ENTER YES IF BROADCAST MSG IS DESIRED_: ↵

ENTER DATA BASE NAME_: dhss
                             ↵
*SIGN-ON   11.56.03      01.12.88
D-S/DHSS/OCT.1983 - 06.NOV.1988   SESSION 249
COPYRIGHT BY BRITISH CROWN COPYRIGHT, 1984
```

The ADDress is repeated by way of confirming the connection. The next response is from Data-Star, asking for USER IDentification.

Any system news will be given at this stage.

```
D-S - SEARCH MODE - ENTER QUERY

  1_:
```

The searcher is requested to enter a database name, and then is put into the SEARCH MODE – the searcher can immediately begin inputting terms, after receiving the set number and the searcher's cue to input something (_:).

1.2 Operations: entering search statements and creating sets of records; using Boolean operators; displaying records

Commands and features introduced: SELECT (S); COMBINE (C); Boolean operators AND and OR; 'stacking' commands; ..PRINT (..P); ..SEARCH (..S)

The general principles and methods of searching have been discussed in Chapters 5 and 6. After the initial analysis of the subject of the search, the identification of the concepts involved and the selection of appropriate terms to describe those concepts on this database, the terms are input; if the searcher is in SEARCH MODE, there is no necessity to enter a command when inputting terms. If not in SEARCH MODE, it is necessary to enter ..SEARCH (..S) to enter SEARCH MODE, and then begin searching.

EXAMPLE: DHSS

```
D-S - SEARCH MODE - ENTER QUERY
  1_: alcoholism or alcoholics

  RESULT      493

  2_: statistics

  RESULT     2132

  3_: 1 and 2

  RESULT       25

  4_:
```

After receiving the cue (_:) in SEARCH MODE, the searcher inputs the first search statement, asking for records which include the words ALCOHOLISM or ALCOHOLICS. The system replies with the number of records containing EITHER of the terms. Search statement 2 is entered in a similar way, and then the results of the two search statements are ANDed together, to create a third set of records which contain STATISTICS and either ALCOHOLISM or ALCOHOLICS. The system will search the basic index for these three terms, as no particular field of the records has been asked for. The ALCOHOL concept could be input more simply using truncation (see 2.2).

The details of the records retrieved in set 3 can be displayed online by the use of the ..PRINT (..P) command. There are three main formats available and the searcher can choose whichever is most appropriate in the circumstances: ALL – all paragraphs; BIBL – the main bibliographic paragraphs; or a selection of paragraphs, e.g. AU, TI, SO, AB. A ..PRINT (..P) command usually consists of the following elements (the system will default to the latest set if no set number is given):

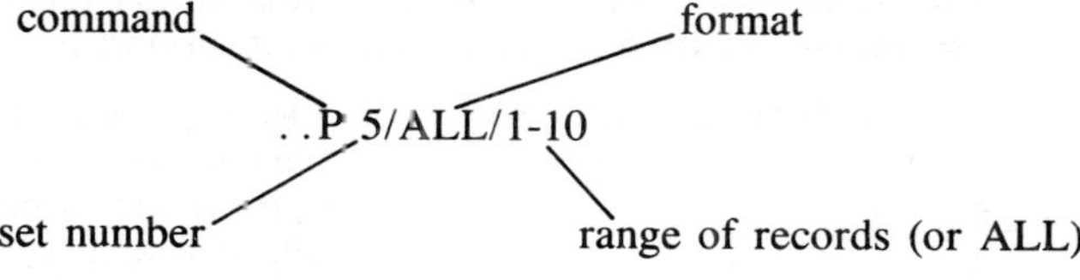

EXAMPLE: DHSS

4_: . . p ti/1-4 ↵

The searcher will often at this stage browse through the titles to make sure the records retrieved are relevant. The command . . PRINT (. . P) asks the system to display the first four records of the retrieved set. Records are displayed in reverse-chronological order, i.e. the first records displayed are those input into the database most recently.

1
TI Occupational mortality among bartenders and waiters

2
TI Decline in alcohol-related problems in Sweden greatest among young people

3
TI Alcohol-related problems amongst selected hospital patients and the cost incurred in their care

4
TI Alcohol : the major public health issue of our time

END OF DOCUMENTS

_: . . p all/4 ↵

Having browsed through the first four titles, the searcher asks for the fourth record to be displayed in full, with ALL the fields in the record being displayed. The system

4
AN 071849 8705
TI Alcohol : the major public health issue of our time
AU BARRY-N.
SO Social-Work-Today, Birmingham, 1987, Jan 12, vol 18, no 19, p10-11, Bliss (QNU)
YR 87.
PT Journal Article
LG EN.
DE Alcoholism; Alcohol-use; Alcoholism-control; Addiction; YYQ.
AB A report entitled 'Alcohol – our favourite drug' edited by Dr Bruce Ritson is reviewed. Based on experiences at the alcohol problems clinic in Edinburgh, the report charts some of the personal and social effects of alcohol abuse on the individual and his family, quoting statistics where relevant. The example of Albyn House of Aberdeen is used to illustrate a possible way of helping drunken offenders. However, it relies on public funds for its continued existence and there is little government support for such centres.

END OF DOCUMENT

_: . . s ↵

D-S - SEARCH MODE - ENTER QUERY
4_:

then gives the (_:) cue, enabling the searcher to carry on in PRINT MODE; to return to SEARCH MODE, the searcher must input ..SEARCH (..S).

The options open to the searcher at this stage are numerous – one or more of them may be: to browse through the remainder of the set; to print out all the records in the set; to develop the search further and display resulting records; to conduct a similar search on another database; to end the searching session.

1.3 Operations: reviewing a search; ending the search and searching session (logging-off)

Commands and features introduced: ..DISPLAY (..D); ..CHANGE (..C); ..OFF

The searcher wishing to change to another database would use the ..CHANGE (..C) command, followed by the four-letter acronym for the required database; this would erase all previous sets and enable the searcher to begin at set 1 again on the new database. In many cases, before changing databases, the searcher would ..SAVE (..SV) the search already conducted (see 3.2).

There are many occasions on which the searcher requires to see a display of the search to date – particularly when the search statements have scrolled off a VDU screen! To review a search, enter ..DISPLAY (..D).

EXAMPLE: DHSS

4_: ..d all ←

The command ..D on its own will give the last set only; ..D ALL will give the whole search; individual sets or ranges of sets can be displayed, e.g. ..D 3, or ..D 4,6-12,15.

```
QN    DOCS SEARCH TERMS
 1     493 ALCOHOLISM OR ALCOHOLICS
 2    2132 STATISTICS
 3      25 1 AND 2
END OF DISPLAY
```

D-S - SEARCH MODE - ENTER QUERY
4_:

To end a searching session and disconnect from the host computer, the searcher would type the . .OFF command; no further input is required by the searcher.

EXAMPLE: DHSS

```
4_: ..off                                ←┘

*CONNECT TIME DHSS:  0:04:15 HH:MM:SS 0.071 DEC HRS.
   SESSION 249*
*SIGN-OFF  12.00.18          01.12.88
CLR PAD (00) 00:00:04:30  122  27
```

After disconnection from the computer, a message from the network shows how long the network was used (4 mins. 30 secs.) and how many 'segments' of data were received (122) and how many were sent (27). A 'segment' holds up to 64 characters, half a 'packet'.

UNIT TWO

2.1 Operations: displaying the index file; using both controlled and natural language terms; searching specific fields

Commands and features introduced: ROOT; searching for author with prefix AU=; limiting search statements to specific fields, e.g. .DE., .TI.

The ability to display terms from the index file, where all directly searchable terms are listed, is useful for finding out the occurrence of both controlled and natural language terms; and also for finding out the precise format of a term – for example, that of an author's name. For this operation the ROOT command is used. The ROOT command defaults to the whole index.

EXAMPLE: Psycinfo

```
4_: root self-inflict$                   ←┘
```

The searcher precedes the term SELF-INFLICT by the ROOT command. ($ = truncation symbol – see 2.2.) The system can display up to 100 terms beginning with the

```
                      SELF-INFLICT$
R1   164 DOCS         SELF-INFLICTED WOUNDS
```

word stem input, and gives each term a reference letter, the number of DOCS (records) containing that term, and the term itself. On Data-Star, phrases and authors' names and initials which are directly searchable are bound together using hyphens. The ROOT SELF-M command shows authors displayed (e.g. SELF-M-N), as well as search terms. It is always advisable to ROOT an author's name, to obtain the correct format for the initials.

```
D-S - SEARCH MODE - ENTER QUERY
  4_: r1                          ↵

  RESULT            164

  5_: root self-m                 ↵

                      SELF-M
R1         1 DOC    SELF-M-N
R2       200 DOCS   SELF-MANAGEMENT
R3       406 DOCS   SELF-MONITORING
R4        76 DOCS   SELF-MONITORING-PERSONALITY
R5       326 DOCS   SELF-MUTILATION

D-S - SEARCH MODE - ENTER QUERY

  5_: r5                          ↵

  RESULT            326

  6_: 4 or 5                      ↵

  RESULT            438

  7_:
```

The stem input by the searcher is repeated at the top of the display.

The searcher can choose a term or terms directly from the list by using the reference letters, as in the example; a range of letters can be chosen, e.g. R1 R4-R5; a set will then be established, as in the example.

The great majority of bibliographic databases use a controlled language for indexing records and these terms are held in one field in the record; on Data-Star they are called 'descriptors', and are directly searchable. In addition, most words taken from other fields within the record, e.g. title, abstract, are also directly searchable as natural language terms. The searcher will normally find appropriate terms when planning the search either from manual sources or from ROOTing terms online, as in the above example.

EXAMPLE: DHSS

```
1_: health-service-economics        ←┘

RESULT     644

2_: health-services and financing.de.  ←┘

RESULT     987

3_: europe.ti,de. or international.ti,de. ←┘

RESULT     2741

4_: 3 and (2 or 1)                  ←┘

RESULT     109

5_: ..p de/1-4                      ←┘
    1
DE Health-Services; Financing; Expenditure; Organisation-for-Economic-
   Cooperation-and-Development; International-comparisons; United-
   Kingdom; Europe; YYH

    2
DE Health-service-management; Planning; United-Kingdom; France;
   United-States-of-America; YYH

    3
DE Old-people; Geriatric-health-services; Canada; United-States-of-
   America; International-comparisons; YYH

    4
DE Health-service-economics; YYH; United-Kingdom; Europe; Scan-
   dinavia; United-States-of-America; New Zealand; Japan; YYH

          END OF DOCUMENTS

_:
```

HEALTH-SERVICE-ECONOMICS is a controlled language term on the DHSS database, and it is entered with hyphens. The searcher widens this concept by asking for HEALTH-SERVICES (another controlled language term) to occur with FINANCING as a term in the descriptor field only; EUROPE or INTERNATIONAL are required to occur in title or descriptor fields.

The searcher asks for just the descriptor field to be displayed; this is helpful in developing the search, as it may be possible to input other relevant terms which were not included in the initial search statements (e.g. searcher may wish to widen the geographical concept by including names of individual countries).

Although searches are generally well planned in advance, allowance is always made for modifying the search as a result of records retrieved – this is one great advantage of using an 'interactive' system. One common way of developing a search is to display the controlled language terms of relevant records retrieved, and then to input any of these which were overlooked or unknown previously.

2.2 Operations: proximity searching (full-text searching); (stringsearching not available on Data-Star); truncation

Commands and features introduced: WITH; SAME; ADJ; truncation symbol ($)

It is useful to be able to search for a term in a particular field, as we have seen, but the ability to search for terms in a particular proximity to each other enhances searching considerably. On Data-Star, if two or more words are required to occur together in a record, e.g. Urban Planning, by inputting the abbreviation ADJ (for ADJACENT), the searcher can retrieve records containing those terms together, in that order. If the requirement is to find two terms within the same sentence, but in any order, the word WITH is used; and to search for terms within the same field, the word SAME is used.

EXAMPLE: Psycinfo

```
4_: self adj inflicted adj wounds or self adj mutilation ↵
RESULT      526
5_: depression same children or depression same adolescents ↵
RESULT      1747
6_: 4 and 5            ↵
RESULT       15
7_: ..p ti/1-10        ↵
...etc...
```

A feature which is very important, particularly when searching natural language terms and phrases, is truncation – the ability to input the stem of a word, followed by the truncation symbol; the system will retrieve records where any term beginning with the word stem appears; e.g. INTEREST$ will retrieve INTEREST, INTERESTED, INTERESTS etc. On Data-Star, the truncation symbol is the dollar sign ($).

EXAMPLE: DHSS

```
1__: health with service$1      ←┘
RESULT    7836
2__: resourc$ or finan$         ←┘
RESULT    3814
3__: 1 and 2                    ←┘
RESULT    725
4__:
```

If a dollar sign is used on its own at the end of a word stem, any term with that word stem is retrieved; e.g. FINAN$ will retrieve FINANCE, FINANCIAL, FINANCING etc.; if only a certain number of further characters is required, e.g. just the plural of a word, that number of characters can be added after the ($) sign; e.g. SERVICE$1, will retrieve SERVICE or SERVICES, but not SERVICING.

2.3 Operations: searching using classification codes, subfiles etc.; (analysing search results not available on Data-Star)

When discussing the search in Chapter 6, reference was made to the fact that most databases have a feature whereby it is possible to search a subject area wider than that described by one term, or a few terms, by using a classification code, subfile, or other system or database feature.

EXAMPLE: Food Science and Technology Abstracts

```
1__: s.sc.                      ←┘
RESULT    39017
2__: collagen and ph.de.        ←┘
RESULT       125
3__: 1 and 2                    ←┘
RESULT        14
4__: ..p ti/1-3                 ←┘
...etc...
```

This database uses broad classification codes; for meat, this is 'S: Meat, Poultry and Game'. The searcher creates a set covering all aspects of meat, and then further refines the search.

UNIT THREE

3.1 Operations: limiting a retrieved set of records by some criteria, e.g. language, date of publication; ranging

Commands and features introduced: . . LIMIT (. . L)

Data-Star uses two methods for limiting by criteria such as language, type of publication, date of publication etc., namely the . . LIMIT (. . L) command and direct searching.

EXAMPLE: MEDLINE

```
  1_: root coccygodynia$                ←┘

      ROOT COCCYGODYNIA$
R1        13 DOCS           COCCYGODYNIA
R2         1 DOC            COCCYGODYNIAS
END OF ROOT

D-S - SEARCH MODE - ENTER QUERY
  1_: r1 r2                             ←┘

  RESULT          13

  2_: . . l/1 lg=en                     ←┘

  RESULT           7

D-S - SEARCH MODE - ENTER QUERY
  3_: . . l/2 yr gt 85                  ←┘

  RESULT           4

D-S - SEARCH MODE - ENTER QUERY

  4_:
```

A set of records can be limited by language directly – e.g. 3 AND EN.LG., but it is generally quicker to use the . . LIMIT (. . L) command where available. In this example, the retrieved set of records is limited to English language papers only. The form the . . LIMIT command takes is: the command/set number/the field (in this case LANGUAGE (LG)), and the particular two-letter abbreviation required within that field. The Data-Star manual gives details of the fields which can be limited on different databases.

Some numerical fields, such as year of publication, can be 'ranged' within the . . LIMIT command. In this example, the set of records is LIMITed to those papers published after 1985 (GT = greater than). Records can be 'ranged' using LT (less than) also.

3.2 Operations: saving a search on one database, changing to another database and conducting the same search on the new database; (searching a number of databases at once ('multifile' searching) not available on Data-Star); (searching elements of records across databases not available on Data-Star)

Commands and features introduced: ..SAVE (..SV); ..EXECUTE (..E); ..SAVE PS (..SV PS)

An online enquiry is often not satisfied by searching just one database. On Data-Star it is possible to conduct a search on one database, save the search, change to another database and conduct the same search on the new database; this avoids the necessity of typing in or uploading the search more than once while online.

On Data-Star, the ..SAVE (..SV) command is used to save the initial search temporarily for the day; use ..SV PS for saving the search permanently. The SAVEd search can be recalled on the same or another database later by using the ..EXECUTE (..E or ..EXEC) command, followed by the four-letter name given to the SAVEd search by the searcher.

EXAMPLE: MEDLINE (Current) / MEDLINE 1977–82

```
  10_: ..save cocc                    ↵
I1008 QUERIES HAVE BEEN SAVED
D-S - SEARCH MODE - ENTER QUERY
  10_: ..c me82                       ↵
```

The searcher wishes to SAVE a search temporarily, and therefore uses the ..SAVE command; this must be followed by a four-letter name for the SAVEd search.

The searcher changes to the earlier MEDLINE database.

```
*CONNECT TIME MEDL: 0:08:30 HH:MM:SS 0.142 DEC HRS.
    SESSION  287*
D-S/ME82/MEDLINE 1977 – 1982      SESSION 288
COPYRIGHT BY NATIONAL LIBRARY OF MEDICINE

D-S - SEARCH MODE - ENTER QUERY
  1_: ..exec cocc                     ↵
```

To recall and process the SAVEd search on the new database, the searcher uses the ..EXECUTE (..E or ..EXEC) command.

```
D-S SEARCH MODE
00001 COCCYGODYNIA COCCYGODYNIAS
                    COCCYGODYNIAS
                         KEYWORD NOT IN DICTIONARY
```

```
  RESULT        14
00002  1  LG = EN
  RESULT         9
00003  2  YR GT 85
  RESULT         0
I1326 NO MORE QUERIES - EXECUTION ENDED.

D-S - SEARCH MODE - ENTER QUERY
  4_:
```

(Obviously the GREATER THAN 85 (GT 85) will retrieve no records, as the database covers the years 1977–82.)

3.3 Operations: printing 'offline'; sorting records; downloading records; transferring records to an electronic mail facility

Commands and features introduced: ..PRINTOFF (..PO); ..PURGE (..PG)

After a set of relevant records has been retrieved, it can often be more economical, particularly if large numbers of records are required, to have them printed 'offline' by the online host and mailed to the searcher or end-user. The high-speed printing of search results generally takes place the evening of the day of the search, and mailing follows immediately. The longest wait, even across continents, is about six days, but it is often quicker than this; inland this can be as little as one or two days. Another alternative to printing online, as well as printing offline, is downloading into a local microcomputer or mainframe, or transferring records to Data-Star's electronic mail facility – Data-Mail. The searcher decides which method is preferable, depending on a number of variables, the principal ones being the speed of the terminal and printing equipment, how urgently the records are required, how many records there are, what format is required, and what the financial implications of the different methods are.

If it is decided to print offline, the command ..PRINTOFF (..PO) is used.

EXAMPLE: MEDLINE

```
  RESULT        50

D-S - SEARCH MODE - ENTER QUERY
  9_: ..po 8/all/doc = all/id = Smith
```

The searcher enters the offline print command, which includes the command (..PO), the set number,

```
PRINTOFF 8/ALL/DOC = ALL/ID = SMITH
I4632 TOTAL DOCUMENTS FOR OFFLINE PRINT: 50
I4607 PRINTOFF SAVED AS QUERY Q0002
```

D-S - SEARCH MODE - ENTER QUERY
9_:

the format, the number of records (DOC=ALL), and an identifier for the end-user. An offline print can be cancelled by using the ..PURGE (..PG) command, e.g. ..PG Q0002.

Records can be sorted by including the SORT command in the offline print command, e.g. ..PO 8/ALL/DOC=ALL/ID=SMITH/SORT=AU.

There are no specific commands for downloading records.

Offline prints can be transferred to Data-Star's electronic mail facility Data-Mail, by including MB=Y in the offline print command; records would be available for printing at 10.00 a.m. the following morning.

References

Chapter 1

1 Houghton, B., *Scientific periodicals*, London, Bingley, 1975.

2 De Solla Price, D. K., *Little science, big science*, New York, Columbia University Press, 1963, Ch. 1.

3 Hall, J. L., *On-line information retrieval sourcebook*, London, Aslib, 1977, Ch. 1.

4 Becker, J., 'A brief history of on-line bibliographic systems', in *Information systems and networks; 11th Annual Symposium, March 1974*, ed. J. Sherrod, Westport, Greenwood Press, 1975, 3–13.

5 Meadow, C. T., 'Back to the future: making and interpreting the database industry timeline', *Database*, **11**, (5), Oct. 1988, 14–22.

6 Meadow, C. T., 'Online database industry timeline', *Database*, **11**, (5), Oct. 1988, 23–31.

Chapter 2

1 *Directory of online databases*, Amsterdam, Cuadra/Elsevier, annual with quarterly updates.

2 'Subject index to databases', Lancashire Library (unpublished).

3 *The use of information technology by information services*, London, Aslib, 1987.

4 Deunette, J. and Hall, S., *1982 survey of UK online users – a report on current online usage*, London, Online Information Centre, 1983.

5 O'Leary, M., 'Surveying the numeric databanks', *Database*, **10**, (5), Oct. 1987, 65–8.

6 Wisdom, J. C. and Houghton, B., *An introduction to the use of selected on-line non-bibliographic database services*, London, British Library, 1982, BLRD Report No. 5721.

7 Houghton, B. and Wisdom, J. C., *Non-bibliographic online databases: an investigation into their uses within the fields of economics*

and business studies, London, British Library, 1981, BLRD Report No. 5620.
8 Suozzi, P., 'By the numbers: an introduction to numeric databases', *Database*, **10**, (1), Feb. 1987, 15–22.
9 Woggon, M., 'Economic statistical data online: a primer', *Database*, **10**, (5), Oct. 1987, 70–4.
10 Heller, S. R., 'Factual databases in chemistry: an introductory overview', in *Proceedings of the 10th International Online Meeting, London, Dec. 1986*, Oxford, Learned Information, 1986, 39–42.
11 Jochum, C., *et al.*, 'Search possibilities depend on the data structure: the Beilstein facts', *ibid.*, 43–52.
12 Macintyre, J., 'The Heilbron database: selected data and references for chemical substances', *ibid.*, 53–61.
13 News section, *Electronic library*, **6**, (3), June 1988, 204.

Chapter 3

1 'Big-money news gathers: behind the scenes look at the production of the ICIS-LOR database on DataStar', *Information world review*, Oct. 1987, 4.
2 'CAB – company profile', *Information world review*, Sep. 1987, 12–13.
3 'Context: new gateways to make legal information easy to access', *Information world review*, Sep. 1988, 12.
4 *Directory of online databases*, Amsterdam, Cuadra/Elsevier, annual with quarterly updates.
5 Pemberton, J. K., Editorial, *Online*, **12**, (4), July 1988, 6–8.
6 Conger, L., 'Online reaches a plateau', *Database*, **10**, (3), June 1987, 57–62.
7 Feldman, R. C., 'Managing a large-scale online information facility', in *Proceedings of the 10th International Online Meeting, London, Dec. 1986*, Oxford, Learned Information, 1986, 221–9.
8 O'Leary, Mike, 'DIALOG's new era', *Online*, **12**, (6), Nov. 1988, 15–21.
9 News section, *Online*, **11**, (4), July 1987, 90.
10 Davenport, L. and Cronin, B., 'Marketing electronic information', *Online review*, **11**, (1), Feb. 1987, 39–47.
11 *Online business sourcebook*, ed. Foster, P. and Foster, A., Hartlepool, Headland Press (2 per year).
12 News section, *Online*, **11**, (4), July 1987, 90.

13 *Brit-line: Directory of British databases*, Horley, EDI Ltd (Publishing) (2 per year).
14 'Ten years of BLAISE Online Services', *British Library Bibliographic Services newsletter*, 43, June 1987, 1–3.
15 '*Online* interviews Jim Terragno', *Online*, **11**, (6), Nov. 1987, 15–22.
16 *Online review*, **10**, (6), Dec. 1986, 323.
17 Deunette, J., 'European online activity', *Online*, **12**, (4), July 1988, 100.
18 *Online notes*, Nov. 1987, 6–7.
19 'European notes', *Online*, **11**, (4), July 1987, 121–4.
20 'Dimdi', *Information world review*, Oct. 1987, 12–13.
21 *The use of information technology by information services*, London, Aslib, 1987.
22 Deunette, J. and Hall, S., *1982 survey of UK online users – a report on current online usage*, London, Online Information Centre, 1983.
23 Vickers, P., 'Information consultancy in the UK – a growing profession', *Online*, **12**, (4), July 1988, 42–6.
24 Wootliff, V., 'Information brokering in the UK – an untapped market', *ibid.*, 44–5.
25 Warren, Lois, 'Information brokering in Canada – small firms prevail', *ibid.*, 47–8.
26 Rodwell, D., 'Information brokers – a future in the information market place?', *Information and library manager*, **6**, (4), Mar. 1987, 87–107.
27 O'Leary, M., 'The information broker – a modern profile', *Online*, **11**, (6), Nov. 1987, 15–22.
28 'Information broking – respectable at last?', *Information world review*, Oct. 1987, 16.
29 'Will businessmen use online brokers?', *Aslib information*, Nov./Dec. 1987, 283–4.
30 O'Leary, M., 'DIALOG Business Connection: DIALOG for the end-user', *Online*, **10**, (5), Sep. 1986, 15–24.
31 'Introduction of menus and end-user searching – DIALOG Medical Connection, BIOSIS Connection', *Online notes*, May 1987, 1, 8–9.
32 O'Leary, M., 'GENIE and BIX in the online vanguard', *Online*, **11**, (4), July 1987, 76–8.
33 Arnold, S., 'End-users: dreams or dollars?', *Online*, **11**, (1), Jan. 1987, 71–81.
34 Cotton, P., 'The evolving user', in *Proceedings of the 10th*

International Online Meeting, London, Dec. 1986, Oxford, Learned Information, 1986, 169–74.

35 Nicholas, D. *et al.*, 'End-users: threat, challenge or myth?', *Aslib proceedings*, **39**, (11/12), Nov./Dec. 1987, 337–44.

36 Dutton, B., 'End-user online search', *Aslib information*, Nov./Dec. 1987, 284–5.

37 *Information market*, no. 54, Sep.–Nov. 1988, 3.

38 'Searching BLAISE-LINE via JANET', *BLAISE newsletter*, no. 87, July/Aug. 1987, 3.

39 Buxton, Andrew, 'JANET and the librarian', *Electronic library*, **6**, (4), Aug. 1988, 250–63.

40 Longley, Dennis, *Macmillan dictionary of information technology*, 2nd ed, Basingstoke, Macmillan, 1985.

41 Zuther, H., 'Public data networks – can we improve the quality of service?', in *Proceedings of the 10th International Online Meeting, London, Dec. 1986*, Oxford, Learned Information, 1986, 151–9.

42 *Information world review*, Jul./Aug. 1987.

43 'Europe's data dial-up problems continue', *Information world review*, Sep. 1988, 1.

44 'Summary of EUSIDIC Report on European telecommunications', *Information world review*, Oct. 1987, 1, 6, 24.

45 Tucker, S., 'Electronic mail connections', *Online*, **11**, (4), July 1987, 55–62.

46 Conger, L., 'Gateways: an introduction', *Database*, June 1987, 114–15.

47 'The Toxnet gateway', *BLAISE newsletter*, no. 87, July/Aug. 1987, 10.

48 'Gateways', *Information world review*, Sep. 1987, 2.

49 'DIALOG via OCLC and RLIN', *Online review*, **11**, (3), June 1987, 131–2.

50 'Gateways', *Database*, **10**, (2), Apr. 1987, 11–12.

51 'Gateway: Dow Jones via ALANET', *Database*, **10**, (3), June 1987, 77–8.

52 'Searchlink', *Database*, **10**, (2), Apr. 1987, 92–3.

53 McCarthy, M., 'Infomaster', *Online*, **10**, (6), Nov. 1986, 52–3, 58.

54 Larsen, G. *et al.*, 'Intelligent gateways: evaluation of Easynet – an end-user test', in *Proceedings of the 10th International Online Meeting, London, Dec. 1986*, Oxford, Learned Information, 1986, 131–5.

55 *Online notes*, Apr. 1988, 1.

56 *Library and information news*, May 1988, 16.

57 Hawkins, D., 'The commodity nature of information', *Online*, **11**, (1), Jan. 1987, 67–70.
58 *Online*, **12**, (4), Jul. 1988, 11.
59 *Online databases*, London, Keynote Publications, 1987.
60 *Information market*, (54), Sep.–Nov. 1988, 1–2.
61 Holmes, P., *The UK information industry: a financial survey*, London, Jordan & Sons, 1987.
62 Deunette, J. and Anthony, L., 'Online services, information technology . . .', *Online*, **11**, (3), May 1987, 140–4.
63 Jewitt, C., 'Quality control in the information dissemination cycle', in *Proceedings of the 10th International Online Meeting, London, Dec. 1986*, Oxford, Learned Information, 1986, 209–20.
64 Arnold, S., 'Private or independent databases: a new trend?', *Database*, **10**, (5), Oct. 1987, 6–9.

Chapter 4

1 *The use of information technology by information services*, London, Aslib, 1987.
2 Deunette, J. and Hall, S., *1982 survey of UK online users – a report on current online usage*, London, Online Information Centre, 1983.
3 *Dictionary of computing*, Oxford, Oxford University Press, 1983.
4 Harris, R., 'The database industry: looking into the future', *Database*, **11**, (5), Oct. 1988, 42–6.
5 Stobie, Ian, 'Spotting the breakthroughs', *Practical computing*, **11**, (8), Aug. 1988, 68–9.
6 Ramsden, Ann, 'The micro as an online terminal' (unpublished talk given at Sheffield Library Technology Fair Conference, June 1988).
7 O'Leary, M., 'DIALOG Business Connection: DIALOG for the end-user', *Online*, **10**, (5), Sep. 1986, 15–24.
8 Niewwenhuysen, P., 'Microcomputer software for information and documentation work: a critical overview', in *Proceedings of the 10th International Online Meeting, London, Dec. 1986*, Oxford, Learned Information, 1986, 317–22.

Chapter 5

1 Dubois, C., 'Free text vs controlled vocabulary', *Online review*, **11**, (4), Aug. 1987, 243–53.
2 *Dictionary of scientific biography*, New York, Charles Scribner's Sons, 1970.
3 Negus, A. E., *Study to determine the feasibility of a standardized*

command set for EURONET, London, INSPEC, 1976.
4 *Online international command chart*, Weston CT, Online Inc., 1989.
5 *Quick guide to online commands*, London, UK Online User Group, 2nd ed. 1989.
6 Conger, L., 'Online reaches a plateau', *Database*, **10**, (3), June 1987, 57–62.

Chapter 6

1 Lancaster, F. W., 'Interaction between requesters and a large mechanized information retrieval system', *Information storage and retrieval*, 4, June 1968, 239–52.
2 Knapp, S. D., 'The reference interview in the computer-based setting', *RQ*, **17**, (4), Summer 1978, 320–4.
3 Somerville, A. N., 'The pre-search reference interview – step by step guide', *Database*, **5**, (1), Feb. 1982, 32–8.
4 Houghton, B. *et al.*, *Evaluation of a programme designed for teaching on-line information retrieval techniques*, London, British Library, 1978 (BLRD Report No. 5418).
5 Lancaster, F. W. and Fayern, E. G., *Information retrieval online*, Los Angeles, Melville, 1973.
6 Ojala, M., 'Finding timely business information', *Online*, **11**, (6), Nov. 1987, 74–7.
7 Profile – the *'Excerpta medica' newsletter*, **6**, (3), 1988, 3.
8 *Clover comparative cost chart for online files*, Biggleswade, Clover Publications (quarterly).
9 'DIALOG OneSearch', *Database*, **10**, (6), Dec. 1987, 13–14.
10 *Directory of online databases*, Amsterdam, Cuadra/Elsevier, annual with quarterly updates.
11 Snow, B., 'MAP command', *Database*, **10**, (3), June 1987, 100–9.
12 Kaback, S., 'Crossfile patent searching: a dream coming true', *Database*, **10**, (5), Oct. 1987, 17–30.
13 Ojala, M., 'Cost-effective business searching', *Online*, **11**, (5), Sep. 1987, 117–21.
14 Bawden, D., 'Ten years of online information for pharmaceutical research', in *Proceedings of the 10th International Online Meeting, London, Dec. 1986*, Oxford, Learned Information, 1986, 63–7.
15 Bates, M., 'How to use information search tactics online', *Online*, **11**, (3), May 1987, 47–54.
16 Hawkins, D., 'Online bibliographic search strategy development', *Online*, **6**, (3), May 1982, 12–19.

17 *INSPEC Thesaurus*, Hitchin, INSPEC, 1989.
18 Medical Subject Headings – 'Annotated Alphabetical List' and 'Tree Structures', National Library of Medicine, annual.
19 *BLAISE newsletter*, no. 92, May/June 1988, 11–13.
20 Wagner, E., 'False drops: how they arise . . . how to avoid them', *Online*, **10**, (5), Sep. 1986, 93–6.
21 Williams, B., 'Online and offline printing – relative costs', *Database*, **10**, (1), Feb. 1987, 58–61.
22 Ertel, M., 'Electronic mail for the online professional: a review of Dialmail', *Online*, **11**, (2), Mar. 1987, 48–54.
23 *ORBIT searchlight*, **14**, (3), Sep./Oct. 1986, 2–3.
24 *The use of information technology by information services*, London, Aslib, 1987.
25 Nicholls, T., 'The regulation of unauthorised downloading by the criminal law', in *Proceedings of the 10th International Online Information Meeting, London, Dec. 1986*, Oxford, Learned Information, 1986, 371–80.
26 Glossbrenner, A., 'Attitude problem (downloading, abstracts and copyright)', *Database*, **10**, (1), Feb. 1987, 6–7.
27 Berring, R. C., 'Copyright: online abstracts raise new issue', *Database*, **11**, (3), June 1988, 6–9.
28 Davenport, L., 'Downloading – what every user wants?', in *Proceedings of the 10th International Online Information Meeting, London, Dec. 1986*, Oxford, Learned Information, 1986, 365–70.
29 Saksida, M. F., 'The pirates of online (the reality four years on)', in *ibid.*, 381–4.
30 Colbert, A., 'Document delivery: a ten-year perspective', *Online*, **11**, (1), Jan. 1987, 121–2.
31 Genuine Article (Advertisement), *Online*, **10**, (5), Sep. 1986, 97.
32 Stern, B., 'Adonis – publishing on CD-ROM in mixed mode', in *Proceedings of the 10th International Online Information Meeting, London, Dec. 1986*, Oxford, Learned Information, 1986, 23–31.
33 'A new era', *Document supply news*, no. 15, March 1988, 1.
34 *Online*, **3**, (2), Apr. 1979, front cover.
35 Tenopir, C., 'What makes a good online searcher?', *Library journal*, **112**, (5), 15 Mar. 1987, 62–3.

Chapter 7

1 *Clover comparative cost chart for online files*, Biggleswade, Clover Publications (quarterly).

2 *The use of information technology by information services*, London, Aslib, 1987.
3 Deunette, J. and Hall, S., *1982 survey of UK online users – a report on current online usage*, London, Online Information Centre, 1983.
4 Houghton, B. *et al.*, 'A comparison of Excerpta Medica and MEDLINE for the provision of drug information to health care professionals', in *Proceedings of the 6th International Online Information Meeting, London, Dec. 1982*, Oxford, Learned Information, 1982.
5 Oulton, A. J. *et al.*, *The online public library*, London, British Library, 1982 (LIR report no.1).

Chapter 8

1 Kollin, D., 'CDROM – déja vu?', *Database*, **10**, (3), June 1987, 6–7.
2 Schwerin, J. B., 'Optical publishing: products, pricing and performance', in *Proceedings of the 10th International Online Information Meeting, London, Dec. 1986*, Oxford, Learned Information, 1986, 33–7.
3 Bleeker, A., 'MEDLINE on CD-ROM: an evaluation after six months' use', *Online review*, **12**, (4), Aug. 1988, 197–204.
4 Anders, V., 'Online vs CD-ROM – the impact of CD-ROM databases upon a large online searching program', *Online*, **12**, (6), Nov. 1988, 24–32.
5 'CD-ROM', *Library & information briefings*, No. 3, BLRDD and LITC, April 1988.
6 Lord, P. W., 'Progress with CD-ROM standardisation', in *Proceedings of the 10th International Online Information Meeting, London, Dec. 1986*, Oxford, Learned Information, 1986, 255–61.
7 Conger, L., 'Online reaches a plateau', *Database*, **10**, (3), June 1987, 57–62.
8 Arnold, S. E., 'A baker's dozen of CD-ROM myths', in *Proceedings of the 10th International Online Information Meeting, London, Dec. 1986*, Oxford, Learned Information, 1986, 11–21.
9 Herther, N. K., 'Microsoft's Third CD-ROM Conference: the industry is emerging', *Online*, **12**, (4), July 1988, 96.
10 Stern, B., 'Adonis – publishing on CD-ROM in mixed mode', in *Proceedings of the 10th International Online Information Meeting, London, Dec. 1986*, Oxford, Learned Information, 1986, 23–31.
11 'Market projections for CD-ROM', *Database*, **10**, (4), Aug. 1986, 114–18.

12 White, M. S., 'The market for CD-ROM and CD-I products and services in the USA and Europe', in *Proceedings of the 10th International Online Information Meeting, London, Dec. 1986*, Oxford, Learned Information, 1986, 263–9.
13 *Optical data systems*, **3**, (11), Nov. 1988, 3–4.
14 'European market slow on CD-ROM', *Information market*, no. 55, Dec. 1988/Jan. 1989, 8.
15 'DAT (Digital Audio Tape)', *Database*, **10**, (3), June 1987, 116–21.
16 *Online*, **10**, (5), Sep. 1986, 132–6.
17 Miller, D., 'Evaluating CD-ROMs: to buy or what to buy?', *Database*, **10**, (3), June 1987, 36–42.

Chapter 9

1 Wagner, J. *et al.*, *On-line impact study: survey report of on-line users*, Santa Monica, CA, System Development Corporation, 1975.
2 'British Library report claims online searches ineffective', *Online review*, **12**, (4), Aug. 1988, 234–5.

Chapter 10

1 Lewis, D., 'The next decade . . .', *Online*, **11**, (1), Jan. 1987, 56–7.
2 Jewitt, C., 'Quality control in the information dissemination cycle', in *Proceedings of the 10th International Online Information Meeting, London, Dec. 1986*, Oxford, Learned Information, 1986, 209–20.
3 Henderson, H. and Leamy, C., 'The future of online in Europe', *Online*, **11**, (1), Jan. 1987, 51–2.
4 Pemberton, J., 'The future of online services . . .', *Database*, **9**, (6), Dec. 1986, 6–7.
5 Holmes, P., 'Is there life beyond online?', in *Proceedings of the 10th International Online Information Meeting, London, Dec. 1986*, Oxford, Learned Information, 1986, 385–93.
6 Cuadra, C., 'History offers clues to the future: user control returns', *Online*, **11**, (1), Jan. 1987, 46–8.
7 Summit, R., 'Online information: a ten-year perspective and outlook', *Online*, **11**, (1), Jan. 1987, 61–4.
8 Conger, L., 'Predictions', *Online*, **11**, (1), Jan. 1987, 44–5.
9 Harris, R., 'The database industry: looking into the future', *Database*, **11**, (5), Oct. 1988, 42–6.

Appendix 1

Some useful sources of information

Online hosts

The contacts for the seven online hosts featured in Part Two are as follows:

1 DIALOG Information Services, Inc.
3460 Hillview Ave, Palo Alto, CA 94304. Tel: 800-3-DIALOG
UK: PO Box 188, Oxford OX1 5AX. Tel: (0865) 730275
Manuals: *Searching DIALOG: the complete guide*
DIALOG databases (2 vols.)
Newsletter:*DIALOG chronolog* (M)

2 European Space Agency Information Retrieval Service (ESA-IRS)
ESRIN, Via Galileo Galilei, 00044 Frascati (Rome), Italy. Tel: (06) 941801
UK: IRS-Dialtech, Dept of Trade and Industry, Room 392, Ashdown House, 123 Victoria Street, London SW1E 6RB Tel: 01-215 6582
Manuals: *Quest user manual – online commands*
Quest user manual – databases (2 vols.)
Newsletters: *Dialtech newsletter* (Irr.); *News and views* (M)

3 BLAISE-LINE
BLAISE, The British Library, Bibliographic Services,
2 Sheraton Street, London W1V 4BH. Tel: 01-323 7077
Manuals: *BLAISE-LINE user manual*
BLAISE-LINE mini manual
Newsletter: *BLAISE newsletter* (M)

4 National Library of Medicine (BLAISE-LINK)
National Library of Medicine, Bethesda, MD 20894. Tel: (301) 496-6095
UK: BLAISE (as above)

Manuals: *BLAISE-LINK user manual*
BLAISE-LINK mini manual
Newsletter: *BLAISE newsletter* (M)

5 ORBIT Search Service
8000 Westpark Drive, McLean, VA 22102. Tel: (703) 442-0900
UK: Achilles House, Western Ave, London W3 0UA
Tel: 01-992 3456
Manuals: *Quick reference guide*
Newsletter: *ORBIT searchlight* (M)

6 Pergamon Financial Data Services
Achilles House (as above)
Manuals: *User guide*
Newsletter: *Update*

7 Data-Star
Plaza Suite, 114 Jermyn Street, London SW1Y 6HJ
Tel: 01-930 5503
Manuals: *Data-Star system reference manual*
Newsletter: *Data-Star news*

Fuller lists of online hosts can be obtained from publications such as: *Online bibliographic databases*, *Directory of online databases* (see below under 'Databases').

Getting started

Turpie, G., *Going online 1988*, London, Aslib.

Aslib also publishes several other titles relating to online.

Online terminal/microcomputer guide and directory, Online Inc., Westport, CT.

Bibliographies

Bibliographies appear regularly in *Online review* and *Electronic library* (see below).

Hall, James L. (ed.), *Online information retrieval 1965–1976: a bibliography with a guide to on-line data bases and systems*, London, Aslib, 1977.

Hall, James L. and Dewe, A. (eds.), *Online information retrieval 1976–1979: an international bibliography*, London, Aslib, 1980.

Hawkins, D. (ed.), *Online information retrieval bibliography 1983–1986*, Oxford, Learned Information, 1987.

Aslib information, London, Aslib.

Library and information science abstracts (LISA), London, LA Publishing (M).

Some online databases covering the subject of online information retrieval include: LISA, INSPEC, ERIC and Information Science Abstracts.

Journals

Some of the specialist journals for online information retrieval are:

Online, Online Inc., Weston, CT, bi-monthly.

Online notes, Aslib, London, monthly.

Online review, Learned Information, Oxford, bi-monthly.

Database, Online Inc., Weston, CT, bi-monthly.

The electronic library, Learned Information, Oxford, bi-monthly.

Library micromation news, London, Library and Information Technology Centre, quarterly.

Laserdisk professional, Online Inc., Weston, CT, bi-monthly.

The following are some of the journals in which articles on online information retrieval appear regularly: *Journal of chemical information and computer science*; *Bulletin of the Medical Library Association*; *Aslib proceedings*; *Special libraries*; *Program.*

Databases

Hall, James L., *Online bibliographic databases*, 4th edn, London, Aslib, 1986.

Lists of databases appear regularly in *Online review* (above).

EUSIDIC database guide 1988, Oxford, Learned Information.

Directory of online databases, Los Angeles, Cuadra/Elsevier, annual with quarterly updates.

Database directory, New York, Knowledge Industry Publications.

Clover comparative cost chart for online files, Biggleswade, Clover Publications, quarterly.

Foster, P. and Foster, A. (eds.), *Online business sourcebook*, Headland Press (2 per year).

Brit-line: Directory of British databases, McGraw-Hill (2 per year).

The CD-ROM directory 1989, 3rd edn, London, TFPL Publishing.

CD-ROMs in print, Westport: London, Meckler.

For online databases giving database information, see Appendix 2 under 'Databases'.

Organizations

Aslib Information Resources Centre, Information House, 26–27 Boswell Street, London WC1N 3JZ. Tel: 01-430 2671.

Library and Information Technology Centre, Polytechnic of Central London, 235 High Holborn, London WC1V 7DN. Tel: 01-430 1561.

Command languages

Online international command chart, Weston, CT, Online Inc.

Quick guide to online commands, London, UK Online User Group.

Appendix 2

Databases offered by the seven online host systems featured in Part Two

(a) Alphabetical Subject Index

DI=DIALOG IR=ESA-IRS NL=NLM (BLAISE-LINK)
BL=BLAISE-LINE O=ORBIT P=Pergamon D=Data-Star

Subject database(s)	*Host(s)*
Accounting	
ACCOUNTANTS INDEX	O
Advertising	
ADTRACK	DI
PTS MARS	DI D
Aerospace	
AEROSPACE DAILY	IR
AEROSPACE DATABASE	DI
AEROSPACE GLOSSARY	IR
JANE'S DEFENSE & AERO NEWS/ANAL.	DI
Agriculture	
AGRIBUSINESS USA	DI
AGRICOLA	DI
AGRIS	DI IR
AGROCHEMICALS HANDBOOK	DI D
CAB ABSTRACTS	DI IR
EUROPEAN DIRECTORY OF AGROCHEM. PRODUCTS	DI D
USDA/CRIS	DI
Agriculture, tropical	
TROPAG	O
Aids	
AIDS	D
Aluminium	
WORLD ALUMINUM ABSTRACTS	DI IR
Architecture	
ARCHITECTURE DATABASE	DI
Art and design	
ART BIBLIOGRAPHIES MODERN	DI
ART LITERATURE INTERNATIONAL (RILA)	DI
ARTQUEST	P

Associations	
DIRECTORY OF AMER. RESEARCH & TECHNOLOGY	O
DIRLINE	NL
ENCYCLOPEDIA OF ASSOCIATIONS	DI
Banking	
AMERICAN BANKER	DI D
BANKNEWS	DI
FINIS	DI P
SOCIETE GENERALE DE BANQUE	D
Bible	
BIBLE (KING JAMES' VERSION)	DI
Biography	
AMERICAN MEN AND WOMEN OF SCIENCE	DI
BIOGRAPHY MASTER INDEX	DI
MARQUIS WHO'S WHO	DI
WHO'S WHO IN TECHNOLOGY	O
Biotechnology	
BIOBUSINESS	DI D IR
BIOCOMMERCE ABSTRACTS	DI D
BIOTECHNOLOGY	O DI
CURRENT BIOTECHNOLOGY ABSTRACTS	IR D O DI
SUPERTECH	DI IR
Book reviews	
BOOK REVIEW INDEX	DI
SOCIAL SCISEARCH	DI
Building	
ARCHITECTURE INDEX	DI
BRIX	IR
IBSEDEX	IR P
ICONDA	O
PICA	P
Business – general (see also News – business)	
ACADEMIC AMERICAN ENCYCLOPEDIA	DI D
BOOKS IN PRINT	DI
BRITISH BOOKS IN PRINT	DI BL
BUSINESS DATABASE	D
CONFERENCE PROCEEDINGS INDEX	BL
CURRENT RESEARCH IN BRITAIN	P
DIALOG BUSINESS CONNECTION	DI
DISSERTATION ABSTRACTS ONLINE	DI
DOCUMENT SUPPLY CENTRE MONOGRAPHS	BL
DPB CATALOGUE	BL
EVERYMAN'S ENCYCLOPEDIA	DI
FACTS ON FILE	DI
FINANCIAL TIMES BUSINESS REPORTS	D
FOREIGN TRADE AND ECON. ABSTRACTS	DI D
GERMAN BUSINESS PRESS ABSTRACTS	D

GERMAN BUYERS GUIDE	D
GPO MONTHLY CATALOG	DI
HARVARD BUSINESS REVIEW ONLINE	DI D
ICC INTERNATIONAL BUSINESS RESEARCH	DI
INDUSTRY DATA SOURCES	DI D
INFORM	DI O IR D
KEYNOTES	D
MANAGEMENT CONTENTS	DI O D
MARC	BL DI
MATERIALS BUSINESS FILE	O DI D IR
MIDDLE EAST: ABSTRACTS AND INDEX	DI
MIDEAST FILE	DI
PTS INDEXES TO BUSINESS ARTICLES	D
PUBLIC AFFAIRS INFORMATION SERVICE (PAIS)	DI D
REMARC	DI
RESEARCH INDEX	P
SIGLE	BL
SOCIAL SCISEARCH	DI
TRADE AND INDUSTRY ASAP	DI
TRADE AND INDUSTRY INDEX	DI
US CLASS	O
WHITAKER	BL
WILEY CATALOGUE/ONLINE	DI
Canada	
CANADIAN BUSINESS AND CURRENT AFFAIRS	DI
Cancer	
CANCERLIT	NL D DI
CANCERPROJ	NL
CHEMICAL CARCINOGENESIS RESEARCH (CCRIS)	NL
CLINPROT	NL
PHYSICIAN DATA QUERY	NL
Careers	
CAREER PLACEMENT REGISTRY	DI
Ceramics	
CERAMIC ABSTRACTS	O DI
GLASSFILE	IR
Chemical dictionaries	
BEILSTEIN	O
CHEMDEX	O
CHEMICAL NOMENCLATURE	D
CHEMLINE	NL
CHEMNAME	DI
CHEMSEARCH	DI
CHEMSIS	DI
CHEMZERO	DI
HEILBRON	DI
MERCK INDEX	DI

Chemical engineering	
CA SEARCH	DI O IR D
CHEMICAL ENGINEERING ABSTRACTS	D O IR DI
CHEMICAL PLANT DATABASE	D
KIRK-OTHMER ENCYCLOPEDIA	D DI
Chemical industry	
CHEMICAL AGE PROJECT FILE	P
CHEMICAL BUSINESS NEWSBASE	D P DI
CHEMICAL INDUSTRY NOTES	DI O D
CHEMICAL PLANT DATABASE	D
CHEMICAL REGULATIONS AND GUIDELINES	DI
CHEMICAL SAFETY NEWSBASE	D O
CHEM-INTELL	DI P
CHEMQUEST	O
EAST EUROPEAN CHEMICAL MONITOR	D
Chemistry	
ANALYTICAL ABSTRACTS	D O DI
CA SEARCH	DI O IR D
CASSI	O
CHEMICAL AGE PROJECT FILE	P
CHEMICAL ECONOMICS HANDBOOK	O
CHEMICAL PLANT DATABASE	D
CHEMICAL REACTIONS DOCUMENTATION SERVICE	O
CHEMQUEST	O
HAZARDOUS SUBSTANCES DATABANK	NL
KIRK-OTHMER ENCYCLOPEDIA	D DI
KOSMET	D
MASS SPECTROMETRY BULLETIN	IR
Child abuse	
CHILD ABUSE AND NEGLECT	DI
Coffee	
COFFEELINE	DI
Cold regions	
COLD REGIONS	O
Companies	
CORPORATE AFFILIATIONS	DI
D & B CANADIAN DUN'S MARKET IDENTIFIERS	DI
D & B DUN'S ELECTRONIC YELLOW PAGES	DI
D & B DUN'S MARKET IDENTIFIERS	DI
D & B INTERNATIONAL DUN'S MARKET IDENT.	DI
D & B KEY BRITISH ENTERPRISES	P
D & B MARKET IDENTIFIERS	P
D & B MILLION DOLLAR DIRECTORY	DI
DISCLOSURE FINANCIALS	DI
DISCLOSURE HISTORY DATABASE	DI
DISCLOSURE/SPECTRUM OWNERSHIP	DI

EUROPE'S LARGEST COMPANIES	P
FINANCIAL INSTITUTIONS DATABASE	P
FINANCIAL TIMES	D
FINANCIAL TIMES COMPANY ABSTRACTS	DI
FOREIGN TRADERS INDEX	DI
GERMAN COMPANIES	D
HOPPENSTEDT AUSTRIA	D
HOPPENSTEDT GERMANY	D DI P
HOPPENSTEDT NETHERLANDS	D
ICC BRITISH COMPANY DIRECTORY	DI D
ICC BRITISH COMPANY FINANCIAL DATASHEETS	DI D
ICC CANADIAN CORPORATION DATABASE	D
INDUSTRIAL MARKET LOCATIONS	P
INFOCHECK	P
IRISH COMPANY PROFILES	P
JORDANWATCH	P
KOMPASS EUROPE	DI
KOMPASS ONLINE	DI
MERGERS & ACQUISITIONS FILINGS	DI
MOODY'S CORPORATE NEWS – INTERNATIONAL	DI
MOODY'S CORPORATE NEWS – US	DI
MOODY'S CORPORATE PROFILES	DI
PTS ANNUAL REPORTS ABSTRACTS	DI D
PTS F & S INDEXES	DI D
PTS PROMT	DI D
REFERENCE BOOK OF CORPORATE MANAGEMENT	P
SAMI SHOPPING CENTRES	P
STANDARD & POOR'S CORPORATE DESCRIPTIONS	DI
STANDARD & POOR'S NEWS	DI
STANDARD & POOR'S REGISTER – BIOGRAPHICAL	DI
STANDARD & POOR'S REGISTER – CORPORATE	DI
THOMAS REGIONAL INDUSTRIAL SUPPLIERS	DI
THOMAS REGISTER ONLINE	DI
TRINET COMPANY DATABASE	DI
TRINET ESTABLISHMENT DATABASE	DI
WHO OWNS WHOM	P
Computers	
ARTIFICIAL INTELLIGENCE	IR
CAD/CAM	IR
COMPUTER ASAP	DI
COMPUTER DATABASE	DI D
ELCOM	IR
ELECTRONIC MATERIALS INFORMATION SERVICE	IR
ELECTRONIC PUBLISHING ABSTRACTS	O
INSPEC	DI D O IR
MERLIN-TECH	IR
MICROCOMPUTER INDEX	DI

MICROCOMPUTER SOFTWARE & HARDWARE GUIDE	DI
MICROSEARCH	O
NATIONAL COMPUTER INDEX	P
ROBOMATIX	IR
SUPERTECH	DI IR
TELECOMMUNICATIONS ABSTRACTS	IR
Contracts	
DMS CONTRACT AWARDS	DI
DMS CONTRACTORS	DI
DMS DEFENSE NEWSLETTERS	DI
EMITS	IR
JANE'S DEFENSE & AERO NEWS/ANAL.	DI
Cosmetics	
KOSMET	D
Courses	
GRADLINE	DI
Databases online	
CROS	D
CUADRA'S DIRECTORY OF ONLINE DATABASES	D O
DATABASE OF DATABASES	DI
DBI	O
DIALINDEX	DI
QUESTINDEX	IR
Drugs	
CA SEARCH	DI O IR D
CONSUMER DRUG INFORMATION FULLTEXT	DI
DE HAEN DRUG DATA	DI
DIOGENES	D DI
DRUG EFFECTS ON LABORATORY TESTS	D
IDIS DRUG FILE	D
INTERNATIONAL PHARMACEUTICAL ABSTRACTS	DI NL IR D
MARTINDALE ONLINE	D DI
MERCK INDEX	DI
PHARMACEUTICAL BUSINESS DATA	D
PHARMACEUTICAL INDUSTRY NEWS DATABASE	D
PHARMACEUTICAL NEWS INDEX	DI O
PHARMAPROJECTS	D
PHARMLINE	D
SEDBASE	D DI
STANDARD DRUG FILE	O
Earth sciences	
ASIAN TECHNOLOGY	IR
GEOARCHIVE	DI
GEOBASE	DI
GEOMECHANICS ABSTRACTS	O
GEOREF	DI O

METEOROLOGICAL & GEOASTROPHYSICAL ABS.	DI
METEOSAT	IR
MOLARS	IR
Economics	
BI/DATA FORECASTS	DI
ECONBASE	DI
ECONOMIC LITERATURE INDEX	DI
FINIS	DI P
FOREIGN TRADE AND ECON. ABSTRACTS	DI D
FROST & SULLIVAN POLITICAL RISK	D
IRS TAXINFO	DI
TAX NOTES TODAY	DI
Education	
BRITISH EDUCATION INDEX	DI
ELECTRONIC DIRECTORY OF EDUCATION	DI
ERIC	DI O
EUDISED	IR
PETERSON'S COLLEGE DATABASE	DI
Education – audio-visual	
A-V ONLINE	DI
AVMARC	BL
HELPIS	BL
Education – special	
EXCEPTIONAL CHILD EDUCATION RESOURCES	DI
Education – vocational	
AIM/ARM	DI
ERIC	DI O
Educational establishments	
PETERSON'S COLLEGE DATABASE	DI
Electrical engineering	
EDF-DOC	IR
ELECTRIC POWER DATABASE	DI
ELECTRIC POWER INDUSTRY ABSTRACTS	O
ELECTRO/ELECTRONIC BUYERS GUIDE	D
ENEL	IR
INSPEC	DI D O IR
MERLIN-TECH	IR
POWER	O
Electronic engineering	
ARTIFICIAL INTELLIGENCE	IR
CAD/CAM	IR
ELCOM	IR
ELECTRO/ELECTRONIC BUYERS GUIDE	D
ELECTRONIC MATERIALS INFORMATION SERVICE	IR
INSPEC	DI D O IR
MERLIN-TECH	IR
ROBOMATIX	IR

SUPERTECH	DI IR
TELECOMMUNICATIONS ABSTRACTS	IR
Energy	
DOE ENERGY	DI
ENEL	IR
ENERGY BIBLIOGRAPHY AND INDEX	O
ENERGYLINE	DI O IR
POWER	O
TULSA	O
Engineering	
CAD/CAM	IR
COMPENDEX	DI D IR O
EI ENGINEERING MEETINGS	DI O D
ENGINEERING & INDUSTRIAL SOFTWARE DIR.	D
ENGINEERING INFORMATION INC.	D
ENGINEERING MATERIALS ABSTRACTS	DI IR
INTIME	IR
MATERIALS BUSINESS FILE	O DI IR D
SUPERTECH	DI IR
Environment	
ENVIROLINE	DI O IR
ENVIRONMENTAL PERIODICALS BIBLIOGRAPHY	DI
UMWELTBUNDESAMT	D
Exhibitions	
FAIRBASE	D
Family	
FAMILY RESOURCES	DI
Films	
MAGILL'S SURVEY OF CINEMA	DI
Fluid engineering	
BHRA FLUID ENGINEERING	DI IR
DELFT HYDRO	IR
HEATFLO	IR
Food science and technology	
FOOD SCIENCE AND TECHNOLOGY ABSTRACTS	DI O IR D
FOOD SCIENCE (VITIS)	IR
FOODS ADLIBRA	DI
Forensic science	
FORS	D
Forestry	
FOREST	O
Forthcoming events	
FAIRBASE	D
WATCH	D
Glass	
GLASSFILE	IR

Subject / Database	
Government – UK	
BRITISH OFFICIAL PUBLICATIONS (NON-HMSO)	DI
DHSS	D
HMSO	BL
HSELINE	IR D O
Government – US	
CONGRESSIONAL INFORMATION SERVICE	DI
CONGRESSIONAL RECORD ABSTRACTS	DI O
FEDERAL INDEX	DI O
FEDERAL REGISTER ABSTRACTS	DI O
FEDERAL RESEARCH IN PROGRESS	DI
WASHINGTON PRESSTEXT	DI
Government, local – UK	
ACOMPLINE	IR
PLANEX	P
Grant-making organizations	
FOUNDATION DIRECTORY	DI
FOUNDATION GRANTS INDEX	DI
GRANTS	DI
NATIONAL FOUNDATIONS	DI
Health and safety	
CANCERLIT	NL DI D
CHEMICAL EXPOSURE	DI
CHEMICAL SAFETY NEWSBASE	D O
CISDOC	IR
HAZARDOUS SUBSTANCES DATABANK	NL
HSELINE	IR D O
LABORATORY HAZARDS BULLETIN	D IR
OCCUPATIONAL SAFETY AND HEALTH	DI O
SAFETY	O
TOXLINE	NL D
Health planning and administration	
HEALTH PLANNING AND ADMINISTRATION	DI NL
Heat	
HEATFLO	IR
History	
AMERICA: HISTORY AND LIFE	DI
HISTORICAL ABSTRACTS	DI
HISTORY OF MEDICINE	NL
SOCIAL SCISEARCH	DI
Industrial classification	
STANDARD INDUSTRIAL CLASSIFICATION (UK)	P
STANDARD INDUSTRIAL CLASSIFICATION (US)	P
Information science	
AMERICAN LIBRARY DIRECTORY	DI
ELECTRONIC MAGAZINE	IR
ERIC	DI O

INFORMATION SCIENCE ABSTRACTS	DI
INSPEC	DI O IR D
LIBRARY AND INFORMATION SCIENCE ABS.	DI O
Insurance	
INSURANCE ABSTRACTS	DI
Japan	
JAPAN ECONOMIC NEWSWIRE PLUS	DI
JAPIO	O
Labour	
LABORDOC	O IR
LABORLAW	DI
LABOUR INFORMATION	IR
Language	
LINGUISTICS AND LANGUAGE BEHAVIOR ABS.	DI
MODERN LANGUAGE ASSOCIATION BIBLIOGRAPHY	DI
Legal information	
CHEMICAL REGULATIONS AND GUIDELINES	DI
CONGRESSIONAL INFORMATION SERVICE	DI
CONGRESSIONAL RECORD ABSTRACTS	DI O
CRIMINAL JUSTICE PERIODICAL INDEX	DI
FEDERAL INDEX	DI O
FEDERAL REGISTER ABSTRACTS	DI O
LABORLAW	DI
LEGAL RESOURCE INDEX	DI
LITALERT	O
NCJRS	DI
Life sciences	
AFEE	IR
AQUACULTURE	DI
AQUATIC SCIENCES AND FISHERIES ABSTRACTS	DI IR
BIOSIS PREVIEWS	DI D IR
LIFE SCIENCES COLLECTION	DI
MERCK INDEX	DI
ZOOLOGICAL RECORD	DI
Management	
INFORM	DI O IR D
MANAGEMENT AND MARKETING ABSTRACTS	P
MANAGEMENT CONTENTS	DI O D
Maps	
MAPS	BL
Marketing/Market research	
ARTHUR D. LITTLE/ONLINE	DI
D & B MARKET IDENTIFIERS (UK)	P
DMS MARKET INTELLIGENCE REPORTS	DI
FINDEX	DI
FROST & SULLIVAN MARKET RESEARCH	D

INDUSTRIAL MARKET LOCATIONS	P
INVESTEXT	DI D
KEYNOTES	D
MANAGEMENT AND MARKETING ABSTRACTS	P
PTS F & S INDEXES	DI D
PTS MARS	DI D
PTS PROMT	DI D
SAMI SHOPPING CENTRES	P
Mathematics	
MATHFILE	DI IR
Mechanical engineering	
CETIM	IR
ISMEC	DI IR
Medicine	
AVLINE	NL
BRITISH MEDICAL ASSOC. PRESS CUTTINGS	D
CLINICAL ABSTRACTS	DI
CLINICAL NOTES ONLINE	D
DHSS	D
DIALOG MEDICAL CONNECTION	DI
DIRLINE	NL
EMBASE	DI D
EXPERTNET	DI
GENERAL PRACTITIONER	D
HEALTH DEVICES SOURCEBOOK	DI
IRCS MEDICAL SCIENCE DATABASE	D
MEDICAL/PSYCHOLOGICAL PREVIEWS	D
MEDICAL PUBLICATIONS LTD	D
MEDICAL RESEARCH DIRECTORY	D
MEDLINE	NL DI D
MESH VOCABULARY	NL D
NEW MESH VOCABULARY	NL
OLD MESH VOCABULARY	NL
PREMED	D
REPERTOIRE BIOMEDICAUX SUISSE	D
SWISS LIBRARIES BIOMEDICAL JOURNALS	D
Medicine – ethics	
BIOETHICSLINE	NL
Medicine – history	
HISTORY OF MEDICINE	NL
Mental health	
MENTAL HEALTH ABSTRACTS	DI
NATIONAL INSTITUTE OF MENTAL HEALTH	D
Metallurgy	
BIIPAM	IR
CORROSION	O
MATERIALS BUSINESS FILE	D DI IR O

METADEX	DI O IR D
METALS DATAFILE	O
Metals – non-ferrous	
BRITISH NON-FERROUS METALS	DI IR
Meteorology, astrophysics	
METEOROLOGICAL & GEOASTROPHYSICAL ABS.	DI
MOLARS	IR
OCEANIC ABSTRACTS	DI IR
Motor cars	
AUTOMOTIVE NEWS SERVICE	P
DOKUMENTATION KRAFTSFAHRWESEN	D
SAE ABSTRACTS	O IR
VOLKSWAGENWERK	D
Music	
BRITISH CATALOGUE OF MUSIC	BL
RILM ABSTRACTS	DI
News – business	
AEROSPACE DAILY	IR
AGRIBUSINESS USA	DI
AMERICAN BANKER	DI D
AP NEWS	DI
AUTOMOTIVE NEWS SERVICE	P
BANKNEWS	DI
BUSINESS AND INDUSTRY NEWS	DI
BUSINESS DATABASE	D
BUSINESS DATELINE	DI
BUSINESSWIRE	DI
CHEMICAL BUSINESS NEWSBASE	D DI P
CHEMICAL INDUSTRY NOTES	DI O D
CHEMICAL SAFETY NEWSBASE	D O
CHICAGO TRIBUNE	DI
DEUTSCHE PRESSE-AGENTUR	D
DOW JONES NEWS SERVICE	D
EAST EUROPEAN CHEMICAL MONITOR	D
EUROPEAN CHEMICAL NEWS	D
FACTS ON FILE	DI
FAIRBASE	D
FINANCIAL TIMES	D
FINANCIAL TIMES BUSINESS REPORTS	D
FINANCIAL TIMES FULLTEXT	DI
GERMAN BUSINESS PRESS ABSTRACTS	D
FROST & SULLIVAN MARKET RESEARCH	D
INFOMAT INTERNATIONAL BUSINESS	P DI D
INSIDER TRADING MONITOR	DI
JANE'S DEFENSE & AERO NEWS/ANAL.	DI
JAPAN ECONOMIC NEWSWIRE PLUS	DI
KYODO	D

MCGRAW-HILL PUBLICATIONS ONLINE	DI
MEDIA GENERAL PLUS	DI
MERGERS & ACQUISITIONS FILINGS	DI
MOODY'S CORPORATE NEWS – INTERNATIONAL	DI
MOODY'S CORPORATE NEWS – US	DI
NATIONAL NEWSPAPER INDEX	DI
NEWSEARCH	DI
NEWSPAPER ABSTRACTS	DI
NEWSWIRE ASAP	DI
P/E NEWS	O DI D
PHARMACEUTICAL BUSINESS DATA	D
PHARMACEUTICAL INDUSTRY NEWS DATABASE	D
PHARMACEUTICAL NEWS INDEX	DI O
PTS F & S INDEXES	DI D
PTS INDEXES TO BUSINESS ARTICLES	D
PTS PROMT	DI D
RESEARCH INDEX	P
STANDARD AND POOR'S NEWS	DI
SWISS NEWS AGENCY	D
UPI NEWS	DI
USA TODAY DECISIONLINE	DI
WASHINGTON POST ELECTRONIC EDITION	DI
WATCH	D
News – current affairs	
AP NEWS	DI
CURRENT DIGEST OF THE SOVIET PRESS	DI
CHICAGO TRIBUNE	DI
DEUTSCHE PRESSE-AGENTUR	D
FACTS ON FILE	DI
LA SUISSE	D
MAGAZINE ASAP	DI
MAGAZINE INDEX	DI
NATIONAL NEWSPAPER INDEX	DI
NEWSEARCH	DI
NEWSPAPER ABSTRACTS	DI
NEWSWIRE ASAP	DI
SWISS NEWS AGENCY	D
UPI NEWS	DI
USA TODAY DECISIONLINE	DI
WASHINGTON POST ELECTRONIC EDITION	DI
WORLD AFFAIRS REPORT	DI
News – French	
FRANCE ACTUALITE	IR
Nuclear science	
INIS	IR
NUCLEAR SCIENCE ABSTRACTS	DI

Nursing	
NURSING AND ALLIED HEALTH	DI D
Oceanic engineering	
OCEANIC ABSTRACTS	DI IR
Oil	
APILIT	O
APIPAT	O
ICIS/LOR	D
INTERNATIONAL PETROLEUM ABSTRACTS	O
P/E NEWS	O DI D
TULSA	O
Packaging industry	
PACKAGING SCIENCE AND TECHNOLOGY ABS.	DI IR
PIRA ABSTRACTS	O
Paints/surface coatings	
RAPRA ABSTRACTS	O
WORLD SURFACE COATINGS ABSTRACTS	O
Paper and pulp industry	
PAPERCHEM	DI
PIRA ABSTRACTS	O
Patents	
CHINAPAT	O DI
CLAIMS/CITATION	DI
CLAIMS/COMPOUND REGISTRY	DI O
CLAIMS/COMPREHENSIVE DATABASE	DI
CLAIMS/REASSIGNMENT AND REEXAMINATION	DI O
CLAIMS/REFERENCE	DI O
CLAIMS/US PATENTS	DI O
INPADOC	O
INPADOC/FAMILY AND LEGAL STATUS	DI O
JAPIO	O
PATENT DATA	D
PATO	D
SPACE PATENTS	IR
US CLASS	O
USPA/USP77/USP70	O
WORLD PATENT INDEX	O DI
Periodicals	
SERLINE	NL
SWISS LIBRARIES BIOMEDICAL JOURNALS	D
ULRICH'S INTERNATIONAL PERIODICALS DIR.	DI IR
Pesticides	
PESTICIDES DATABANK	O
Philosophy	
PHILOSOPHERS INDEX	DI
Photography	
IMAGING ABSTRACTS	O

Physics	
INSPEC	D IR DI O
SEARCHABLE PHYSICS INFORMATION NOTICES	DI
Plastics	
RAPRA ABSTRACTS	O
Politics	
SOCIAL SCISEARCH	DI
FROST & SULLIVAN POLITICAL RISK	D
US POLITICAL SCIENCE DOCUMENTS	DI
Pollution	
ACID RAIN	IR
APTIC	DI
ENVIROLINE	DI O IR
ENVIRONMENTAL PERIODICALS BIBLIOGRAPHY	DI
NTIS	D O IR DI
POLLUTION	D DI IR
Population	
CENDATA	DI
D & B DONNELLEY DEMOGRAPHICS	DI
POPLINE	NL
POPULATION BIBLIOGRAPHY	DI
Prices	
PRICE DATA	IR
Printing	
PAPERCHEM	DI
PIRA ABSTRACTS	O
Products – news	
FINANCIAL TIMES	D
PTS F & S INDEXES	DI D
PTS NEW PRODUCT ANNOUNCEMENTS	DI D
PTS PROMT	D DI
THOMAS NEW INDUSTRIAL PRODUCTS	DI
THOMAS REGIONAL INDUSTRIAL SUPPLIERS	DI
Psychology	
MEDICAL/PSYCHOLOGICAL PREVIEWS	D
PSYCALERT	DI
PSYCINFO	DI D
Publishing	
ELECTRONIC PUBLISHING ABSTRACTS	D
PUBLISHERS, DISTRIBUTORS AND WHOLESALERS	DI
Religion	
BIBLE (KING JAMES' VERSION)	DI
RELIGION INDEX	DI
Robotics	
ARTIFICIAL INTELLIGENCE	IR
INSPEC	O DI D IR
ROBOMATIX	IR

SUPERTECH	DI IR
Rubber	
RAPRA ABSTRACTS	O
RAPRA TRADE NAMES	O
Science – general	
ACADEMIC AMERICAN ENCYCLOPEDIA	DI D
BOOKS IN PRINT	DI
BRITISH BOOKS IN PRINT	DI BL
CONFERENCE PAPERS INDEX	DI IR
CONFERENCE PROCEEDINGS INDEX	BL
CURRENT RESEARCH IN BRITAIN	P
DISSERTATION ABSTRACTS ONLINE	DI
DOCUMENT SUPPLY CENTRE MONOGRAPHS	BL
EVERYMAN'S ENCYCLOPEDIA	DI
FEDERAL RESEARCH IN PROGRESS	DI
GPO MONTHLY CATALOG	DI
GPO PUBLICATIONS REFERENCE FILE	DI
INDEX TO SCIENTIFIC & TECHNICAL PROC.	O
MARC	BL DI
NATO-PCO	IR
NTIS	D O DI IR
NUC/CODES	O
PASCAL	IR DI
REMARC	DI
SCIENTIFIC INFORMATION	D
SCISEARCH	DI D
SIGLE	BL
SOVIET SCIENCE AND TECHNOLOGY	DI
SRIS CATALOGUE	BL
SSIE CURRENT RESEARCH	DI
WHITAKER	BL
WILEY CATALOGUE/ONLINE	DI
Smoking	
SMOKING AND HEALTH	DI
Social sciences/humanities – general	
ACADEMIC AMERICAN ENCYCLOPEDIA	DI D
ARTS AND HUMANITIES SEARCH	DI
BOOKS IN PRINT	DI
BRITISH BOOKS IN PRINT	BL DI
CONFERENCE PROCEEDINGS INDEX	BL
DISSERTATION ABSTRACTS ONLINE	DI
DOCUMENT SUPPLY CENTRE MONOGRAPHS	BL
EIGHTEENTH CENTURY SHORT TITLE CATALOGUE	BL
EVERYMAN'S ENCYCLOPEDIA	DI
FACTS ON FILE	DI
GPO MONTHLY CATALOG	DI
GPO PUBLICATIONS REFERENCE FILE	DI

HUMANITIES AND SOCIAL SCIENCE CATALOGUE	BL
INCUNABLE SHORT TITLE CATALOG	BL
MARC	BL DI
PLANEX	P
PUBLIC AFFAIRS INFORMATION SERVICE	DI D
REMARC	DI
SIGLE	BL
SOCIAL SCISEARCH	DI
WHITAKER	BL
WILEY CATALOGUE/ONLINE	DI
Sociology	
DHSS	D
SOCIAL SCISEARCH	DI
SOCIOLOGICAL ABSTRACTS	D DI
Software	
ABI/SOFT	IR
BUSINESS/PROFESSIONAL SOFTWARE	D
BUSINESS SOFTWARE DATABASE	DI IR
ENGINEERING AND INDUSTRIAL SOFTWARE DIR.	D
ISIS SOFTWARE	D
MENU – INTERNATIONAL SOFTWARE DATABASE	DI
MICROCOMPUTER SOFTWARE & HARDWARE GUIDE	DI
SPACESOFT	IR
Space	
SATELDATA	IR
SPACECOMPS	IR
SPACE GLOSSARY	IR
SPACE PATENTS	IR
SPACESOFT	IR
Sports and recreation	
SPORTS AND RECREATION	DI
Sports – medical aspects	
SPORTS AND RECREATION	DI
Standards	
BSI STANDARDLINE	P
DIN – GERMAN STANDARDS	P
IHS INTERNATIONAL STANDARDS & SPECS.	DI
STANDARDS AND SPECIFICATIONS	DI IR
STANDARDS SEARCH	O
Statistics	
AMERICAN STATISTICS INDEX	DI
BI/DATA FORECASTS	DI
BI/DATA TIME SERIES	DI
PRICE DATA	IR
PTS FORECASTS	DI D
PTS TIME SERIES	DI D

Stocks and shares	
BONDBUYER	DI
ICC STOCKBROKER RESEARCH	D
INSIDER TRADING MONITOR	DI
JORDANS SHAREHOLDER SERVICE	P
MERGERS AND ACQUISITIONS FILINGS	DI
QUOTES	DI
Technology – general	
ACADEMIC AMERICAN ENCYCLOPEDIA	DI D
BOOKS IN PRINT	DI
BRITISH BOOKS IN PRINT	DI BL
BSI STANDARDLINE	P
CHINAPAT	O DI
CLAIMS/CITATION	DI
CLAIMS/COMPOUND REGISTRY	DI O
CLAIMS/COMPREHENSIVE DATABASE	DI
CLAIMS/REASSIGNMENT AND REEXAMINATION	DI O
CLAIMS/REFERENCE	DI O
CLAIMS/US PATENTS	DI O
CONFERENCE PAPERS INDEX	DI IR
CONFERENCE PROCEEDINGS INDEX	BL
CURRENT RESEARCH IN BRITAIN	P
DIRECTORY OF AMERICAN RESEARCH & TECH.	O
DISSERTATION ABSTRACTS ONLINE	DI
DOCUMENT SUPPLY CENTRE MONOGRAPHS	BL
EVERYMAN'S ENCYCLOPEDIA	DI
FEDERAL RESEARCH IN PROGRESS	DI
GPO MONTHLY CATALOG	DI
GPO PUBLICATIONS REFERENCE FILE	DI
INDEX TO SCIENTIFIC & TECHNICAL PROC.	O
INPADOC	O
INPADOC/FAMILY & LEGAL STATUS	DI O
JAPAN TECHNOLOGY	DI
JAPIO	O
LITALERT	O
MARC	BL DI
NATO-PCO	IR
NTIS	D O DI IR
PASCAL	IR DI
PATENT DATA	D
PATO	D
PTS AEROSPACE/DEFENCE MARKET & TECHNOL.	DI D
REMARC	DI
SCISEARCH	DI D
SIGLE	BL
SOVIET SCIENCE AND TECHNOLOGY	DI
SPACE PATENTS	IR

SRIS CATALOGUE	BL
SSIE CURRENT RESEARCH	DI
STANDARDS AND SPECIFICATIONS	DI IR
STANDARDS SEARCH	O
SUPERTECH	DI IR
US CLASS	O
USPA/USP77/USP70	O
WHITAKER	BL
WHO'S WHO IN TECHNOLOGY	O
WILEY CATALOGUE/ONLINE	DI
WORLD PATENT INDEX	O DI
Textiles	
TEXTILE TECHNOLOGY DIGEST	DI
WORLD TEXTILES	DI O
Tourism, leisure	
CAB ABSTRACTS	DI IR
SPORTS AND RECREATION	DI
Toxicology	
RTECS	NL
TOXLINE	NL D
TOXLIT	NL
TSCA CHEMICAL SUBSTANCES	DI
Trademarks	
TRADEMARKSCAN	DI
UK TRADE MARKS	P
Translations	
WORLD TRANSINDEX	IR
Transport	
INTERNATIONAL ROAD RESEARCH DOCUMENTATION	IR
SAE ABSTRACTS	O IR
TRIS	DI
Veterinary medicine	
CAB ABSTRACTS	DI IR
Water resources	
AQUALINE	O
BHRA FLUID ENGINEERING	DI IR
DELFT HYDRO	IR
WATERNET	DI
WATER RESOURCES ABSTRACTS	DI
Welding	
WELDASEARCH	DI
Zoology	
ZOOLOGICAL RECORD	DI

(b) Subject headings arranged hierarchically in broad subject areas (see under the subject headings in (a) above for databases)

1 Science – general

- Agriculture
  - Forestry
  - Food science and technology
    - Coffee
  - Agriculture, tropical
- Life sciences
  - Biotechnology
  - Zoology
    - Veterinary medicine
- Medicine
  - Cancer
  - Aids
  - Drugs
    - Alcohol
    - Smoking
  - Medicine, ethics
  - Health planning and administration
  - Medicine, history
  - Sports, medical aspects
  - Toxicology
  - Mental health
  - Nursing
- Chemistry
  - Chemical dictionaries
  - Chemical industry
  - Ceramics
  - Pesticides
  - Cosmetics
- Earth sciences
  - Cold regions
- Physics
- Mathematics

2 Technology – general

- Standards
- Patents
- Engineering
  - Motor cars
  - Fluid engineering
  - Chemical engineering
    - Glass
  - Electrical engineering
  - Electronic engineering
  - Mechanical engineering
  - Oceanic engineering
  - Textiles
  - Biotechnology
  - Water resources
  - Welding
- Building
- Metallurgy
  - Aluminium
  - Metals, non-ferrous
- Aerospace
  - Space
- Computers
  - Software
  - Robotics
- Energy
  - Heat
- Nuclear science
- Oil
- Environment
  - Pollution
- Meteorology, astrophysics
- Oceanography
- Paper and pulp industry
- Printing
- Packaging industry
- Rubber
- Plastics
- Paints/surface coatings
- Photography

3 Business – general

- Accounting
- Banking
- Stocks and shares
- Companies
- Economics
- Labour
- Management
- Marketing
- News – business
- Canada – business
- Japan

Products – news
Statistics
Contracts
Advertising
Publishing
Insurance
Prices
Trademarks
Transport
Tourism, leisure

4 Social sciences/humanities – general

Art and design
Architecture
Education
  Education – special
  Child abuse
  Education – audio-visual
  Education – vocational
Government – US
Government – UK
Government, local – UK
History
Labour
Language
Legal information
Forensic science
Information science
Music
News – current affairs
  News – French
Philosophy
Politics
Population
Psychology
Sociology
Sports and recreation
Family
Films
Religion
  Bible

5 Miscellaneous

Associations
Grant-making organizations
Courses
Educational establishments
Biography
Translations
Book reviews
Careers
Databases online
Periodicals
Maps
Industrial classification
Forthcoming events
Exhibitions

Index